Diplomatic Bag

An Anthology of
Diplomatic Incidents
and Anecdotes from the
Renaissance to the Gulf War

Edited by
JOHN URE

JOHN MURRAY

© John Ure 1994

First published in 1994
by John Murray (Publishers) Ltd,
50 Albemarle Street, London W1X 4BD

The moral right of the author has been asserted

A catalogue record for this book is available from the British Library

ISBN 0-7195-4826 8

Typeset in 11.5/13pt Baskerville by Colset (Private) Ltd, Singapore
Printed and bound in Great Britain by
Cambridge University Press, Cambridge

Contents

v

Acknowledgements

The many people to whom I am endebted for their help in the compilation of this anthology divide themselves broadly into three groups.

First chronologically come those who have pointed me towards promising source material or who have shared with me their own reminiscences of diplomatic life. Notable among these are Dr Rohan Butler, former historical adviser to successive Foreign Secretaries; Sir Patrick Reilly, my first chief when he was ambassador in Moscow; Ambassador Harry Shlaudeman, my American colleague in Brazil; Sir Richard Parsons, my predecessor as ambassador in Sweden; Sir Hugh Cortazzi, a former ambassador to Japan; Mr Richard Bone, head of the Foreign and Commonwealth Office Library and Records Department, and Dr Keith Hamilton of the Historical Branch; and Mr Douglas Matthews and the staff of the London Library.

Next come those friends and others who have most generously allowed me to quote without charge from their own writings, or from those of parents for whom they are the literary executors: The Rt. Hon. Lord Carrington, KG, The Rt. Hon. Paul Channon, MP (the Chips Channon quotation), Sir Hugh Cortazzi, GCMG, Mr Nicholas Fleming, The Lord Gladwyn, GCMG, Sir Nicholas Henderson, GCMG, Mr Peter Hopkirk, The Hon. Miles Jebb (the Cynthia Gladwyn passages), Mr Simon Jenkins, Dr Raymond Jones, Sir Fitzroy Maclean, Mr Nigel

Nicolson (the Harold Nicolson passages), The Viscount Norwich (the Duff Cooper passages), Mr Jasper Ridley, Mr Kenneth Rose, Sir Steven Runciman, Sir Brian Urquart, Mr Philip Ziegler.

I am also grateful for the gracious permission of Her Majesty The Queen to reproduce a passage from the Royal Archives at Windsor; and for the permission of Lady Gore-Booth, Dr Eva Taylor and Mrs Michael Lowery to quote passages from the works of their late husbands.

I am grateful to the following publishers and literary agents for permission to quote the extracts which are attributed in the text to them and to their respective authors or editors: Cambridge University Press; Constable and Company; Curtis Brown; HarperCollins UK; HarperCollins USA; Little, Brown and Company; London Independent Books; Methuen; W.W. Norton & Company, Inc.; The Penguin Group; Penguin USA; Peters Fraser & Dunlop; Random House; R.I.B. Library; University of South Carolina Press; Weidenfeld & Nicolson.

I believe that wherever the sources quoted are still in copyright the necessary permissions have been sought, but if inadvertently I have overlooked anyone, I can only hope that I shall be forgiven for this unintended failure.

Finally, I am indebted to Grant McIntyre, editorial director of John Murray, who has patiently and skilfully steered me away from at least some of the pitfalls of editing an anthology. I am painfully aware that any such selection is an extremely personal and often arbitrary one; I alone stand responsible for this one.

Dedicated with gratitude to
MAGDALENE COLLEGE
CAMBRIDGE
who have produced
Foreign Secretaries
as well as diplomats

Introduction

'Diplomacy is to do and say
The nastiest thing in the nicest way.'

To THE OXFORD dictionary, diplomacy is the management of international relations. To others it is confused with foreign policy. To all too many the word is synonymous with tactfulness. But this anthology is not concerned with definitions: it is concerned with examples – examples of diplomatic coups and diplomatic cock-ups, of courtiers elaborating the rules and of spies breaking them, of envoys in danger of losing their lives and of hostesses in danger of losing their reputations.

To achieve this a broad canvas is necessary. Examples are here presented of diplomacy in action over the centuries, ranging from the early heralds who bore messages from one sovereign to another, to contemporary envoys who are sometimes accredited not to a sovereign or a country but to an international organization such as the United Nations. I have included the activities of Foreign Ministers, consuls, intelligence agents and others who may not strictly be diplomats, though engaged in the practice of diplomacy in a wider sense. But I have excluded fiction – rich though that vein is – except where a dramatized account is of an historical incident. The incidents and anecdotes are grouped broadly under themes, and within each theme the entries are generally in chronological order. Where the incident has no attribution at the end, this is because I have written it from my own printed or private sources. I have provided explanatory headings to each entry, trying to put them in the context of their place and time. I have also provided short introductions to each section or chapter, drawing together some of the threads of the theme concerned, and on occasion interpreting events. But some more general background may also help the reader to savour the events described.

The heralds who were the precursors of ambassadors had two main functions: to act as spokesmen for their sovereigns and to report back on the reception they received. Initially, they were often little more than the bearers of messages of truce in war or of ultimata before a war; but even for this limited function they required – and usually received – some measure of personal immunity. The messenger had to be returned intact if his usefulness was not to be sacrificed.

By the time of the Renaissance, it was found that occasional visits by heralds or other envoys on special missions were not sufficient to deal with the ongoing communication between states; in particular, the Italian city states of the fourteenth and fifteenth centuries felt the need for a more permanent dialogue with each other: Dante, Petrarch, Boccaccio and Machiavelli were all sent out at different times by the rulers of Florence to represent them elsewhere in Italy. By the sixteenth century, the practice of sending and receiving resident ambassadors was well developed in Europe: Anne Boleyn's father had been ambassador in Paris, and the Spanish and French ambassadors were continual focuses for intrigue at the court of Elizabeth I of England.

But the formal recognition of diplomacy as a profession distinct from politics and statecraft, as well as the regulation of that profession, had to await the Congress of Vienna in 1815. And for long after that, ambassadors were a relative rarity: as late as the beginning of Queen Victoria's reign, there were only three British ambassadors anywhere in the world – in Paris, Constantinople and St Petersburg, to be followed in due course by those in Vienna (1860), Berlin (1862), Rome (1876), Madrid (1887) and Washington (1893). Elsewhere there were legations rather than embassies, and ministers rather than ambassadors.

The functions of these resident embassies or legations remained essentially those of the original heralds: they spoke for their own governments to the regime to which they were accredited, and they reported on the local scene to the government which had sent them. These continue to be the main activities of diplomats. The difference between the reports of a diplomat and those of a foreign correspondent (of a newspaper, news agency or television station) is that the former only reports what may affect the actions and interests of his government and countrymen (frequently these days the commercial interests), while the correspondent will report whatever seems likely to entertain or inform his readers or viewers. Despite this, they often have much to learn from each other.

Among the earlier exponents of the practice of diplomacy was the Papacy. Pope Pius II (Aeneas Silvius Piccolomini) had himself been a Renaissance envoy to numerous courts including that of King James I of Scotland, and the Vatican early established a network of efficient papal nuncios and legates who kept the Holy See accurately informed of political and religious developments throughout Christendom and beyond. The task has become more complicated with the passing centuries, not least because the Catholic Church frequently finds itself pulled in different directions – for instance in Latin America – by the conflicting claims of traditional supporters of the Establishment on the one hand and of Liberation Theology on the other. And after the Second World War, the Vatican was criticized for not making more use of the information it had about the fate of the Jews in Nazi-occupied Europe. As well as reporting diplomatic developments, papal nuncios also often act as talent spotters for the Vatican in the countries to which they are accredited. Nor was Pius II unique among Popes in being a diplomat: in the present century Pope John XXIII had been nuncio in Paris before ascending the throne of St Peter.

In the section of this book dealing with the characteristics and qualities of a diplomat I shall have something to say about the requirements for the profession as it has developed over the centuries. But it is worth stating at the outset that, despite the cynical conclusions of Machiavelli, it is generally recognized that dishonesty, or even disingenuousness, is not the key to diplomatic success; credibility is all-important and is bred from integrity rather than from duplicity. As Ambassador Jules Cambon of France said early in this century: 'The most persuasive method at the disposal of a government is the word of an honest man.'

Even among those who acknowledge that diplomacy should not be duplicitous, there is a strong feeling that it must be secretive. Diplomatic communications have traditionally been in cipher or code, and diplomatic bags have enjoyed greater protection against interception than the ordinary mail (although, as this book shows, they have not always been inviolate). Discussions of important issues, and the drafting of treaties between nations, have generally been conducted behind closed and guarded doors. As public opinion became more vocal in democratic states, so there was a demand for less secrecy about issues – often war and peace issues – which affected the safety and prosperity of the man in the street. This demand reached its apogee with the call by President Wilson of the United States in 1918 for 'open covenants of peace openly arrived at'. Nobody objected to open covenants, but all sensible diplomats realized that it was not possible for these to be openly arrived at; even Wilson himself retreated at the Paris peace conference into private huddles with Lloyd George and Clemenceau. To have tried to work everything out in public would have meant that no one could put forward any tentative idea: once a proposition is on the open debating table, it cannot be withdrawn. Diplomatic negotiation had to remain – and has remained – largely a private art. 'Megaphone diplomacy' is often a contradiction in terms.

There have been other pressures for change. The reader may be struck in leafing through this anthology by how many of the protagonists are titled aristocrats. This reflects the fact that until the present century the diplomatic profession was sometimes described as 'outdoor relief for the upper classes'; it was certainly the case that in all European countries, diplomatic services tended to be the preserve of the wealthy and patrician; consequently there was an international freemasonry of aristocratic diplomats who often had more in common with their opposite numbers in other countries than they did with their compatriots. This fact naturally and properly worried the elected rulers of modern democracies. Strenuous steps have been taken in Britain and elsewhere to try to recruit from a wider social spectrum, and the pursuit of academic excellence has replaced – in reality if not always in image – the old élitist Diplomatic Corps of the world. There are fewer quotations from dukes and counts in the later entries than in the earlier ones.

Nor is the world of diplomacy any longer the male preserve that it was for over five centuries. In a period when women Foreign Ministers and even women Prime Ministers have become familiar, it is hardly surprising to find women ambassadors. For every woman diplomat there is one potential problem: her husband. Few men are willing or able to follow a wife's career round the world, and not all have the advantage of Mrs Clare Boothe Luce at the US Embassy in Rome, whose millionaire-publisher husband could afford to come and go at will and maintain his own independent prestige. One contemporary British lady-diplomat has solved the problem by having as a husband a highly distinguished retired British ambassador, who now travels the world as a First Secretary's spouse, only occasionally grumbling about still being locked into the diplomatic cocktail-party circuit. (Another changing factor – which I mention elsewhere – is that the wives of male diplomats now frequently have careers every bit as significant as their husbands', and they no longer 'follow the colours' as meekly as before.)

But the element of change most frequently brought up by those who wish to denigrate modern diplomats is that of communications. What influence or job satisfaction can an ambassador have, the argument runs, when the Foreign Secretary can telegraph or telephone instructions on every issue of any significance? Those who ask this question often forget that communication is a two-way process; the ambassador can inject his advice and views just as quickly and on just as many subjects as the Foreign Secretary can send instructions. So although a modern ambassador may not be plenipotentiary in the way that – say – Stratford Canning was at the Sublime Porte at the time of the Crimean War, he probably has much more influence on policy (and hence on his own instructions) than Stratford Canning could ever have had. As for Foreign Ministers talking to each other on the telephone, and thus short-circuiting ambassadors, this sometimes happens, but language difficulties usually intervene.

One of the great watersheds of diplomatic practice – more significant perhaps than even the invention of the electric telegraph – was the shift in power during the nineteenth century from autocracies to public opinion. In the world where Metternich and Castlereagh practised their craft, policies were still made by kings and emperors, or at least by their artistocratic advisers; but in the era initiated by George Canning – even before the death of Metternich – public opinion was being invoked as 'a power more tremendous than was perhaps ever yet brought into action in the history of mankind'. Policies had to take account more frequently of popular sentiment; there was no longer the possibility of a 'Holy Alliance' between monarchs to protect each other from the effects of revolution at home. The public could, at times, even dictate foreign and defence policy at the expense of its democratically elected representatives: successive British governments – for example – had declined to spend anything on defending the Falkland Islands, but when the Argentine invasion of 1982 occurred, public opinion (rightly sensed by Mrs Thatcher) demanded a massive outlay of diplomatic and military resources to reverse the situation. But observance of public opinion in foreign policy gives a tactical advantage to the remaining dictatorships; where public opinion either motivates policy or has to be carried along with policy, it is no longer possible to spring sudden surprises: George Bush was less flexible than Saddam Hussein.

Despite all the changes over the centuries, the image of the smooth diplomat – the 'cookie-pusher' of American imagination – dies hard. As Harold Nicolson (who has written so much good sense about diplomacy) puts it: 'the professional diplomatist does, it must be admitted, acquire a habit of conventional suavity which is sometimes irritating'. Many people would say *usually* irritating. There are plenty of instances of it in this book; but I trust there are far more instances of imagination, ingenuity, integrity and intelligence – qualities less popularly associated with diplomacy, but much more important than suavity or even politeness. Indeed, too many people – including some diplomats – exaggerate the importance of being polite, or 'diplomatic' as it is frequently termed. It is nice for diplomats to be liked; it facilitates their work; they get better access to VIPs in the countries where they are accredited, and this redounds to their reputation at home. But the important thing is to be believed, rather than to be liked. Good relations are a means to an end in diplomacy. It is said that when, during the Second World War, Winston Churchill wanted Sir Samuel Hoare (then ambassador in Spain) to press Franco to release interned British pilots who had escaped across France to Spain, Hoare protested that to do so would ruin his relations with Franco. 'Stuff your relations with Franco,' Churchill is said to have replied; 'what do you think they're for!'

If this anthology gives some entertainment, it will have achieved its purpose; if it also broadens the reader's view of diplomacy, it will have more than achieved that purpose.

1

Diplomatic Coups and Disasters

MILITARY MEN TEND to relive and recount endlessly their triumphs: the first Duke of Wellington got so tired of hearing other people tell how they had been responsible for winning the battle of Waterloo that he remarked, 'I sometimes wonder if I was there myself!' But diplomats – or at least good diplomats – are more coy, if not more modest, because a diplomatic victory that is blazoned abroad as such, usually loses its value. The best diplomatic victories are those when everyone goes away thinking they have won.

Count Gondomar, the Spanish Ambassador to King James I of England whose early demonstration of arrogance opens this section, over-reached himself later when he demanded that Sir Walter Raleigh (after the latter's last and fatal clashes with Spanish colonizers in the New World) should be handed over to him for public execution in Spain; the English repugnance towards his demands did not save Raleigh from execution at home, but did move court and public opinion in England away from Spain.

Similarly, Bismarck's blatant manipulation of the German monarchy and of international events led ultimately to his own undoing and his dismissal by the Kaiser, and to the famous *Punch* cartoon, 'Dropping the pilot'.

Often the most telling diplomatic coups and triumphs result from one side overplaying its hand to the advantage of the other side. Khrushchev misjudged the mood of the United Nations badly when he launched into a vitriolic attack on Hammarskjöld's methods, and so left it open for Hammarskjöld to win international support in his defence and for his policy of intervening with UN troops in the Congo – a radical move with far-reaching consequences. Similarly, Mrs Kirkpatrick's action in attending an Argentine embassy dinner on the night of their invasion of the Falklands, and the adverse reaction this generated in many quarters, may have made it easier for the British Ambassadors in Washington and at the UN eventually to get a more friendly attitude adopted by the US government.

Many diplomatic gaffes and disasters are connected with breaches of confidence. President de Gaulle, for instance, was deeply offended when he thought Sir Christopher Soames had leaked a distorted account of a confidential conversation between the two of them. Dr Kissinger, knowing how a premature leak of his intention to visit Communist China would have risked aborting the whole process of an American–Chinese *rapprochement*, went to immense lengths to throw the press and others off the scent by feigning a retreat to a hill-station in Pakistan, when in fact he was making a secret flight from Islamabad to Peking with the amused connivance of the rulers of Pakistan.

No one knew better than Talleyrand how to establish mastery over his interlocutors by nimble manoeuvring of the sort which he demonstrated at the Congress of Vienna, but this never blinded him to the fact that more diplomatic disasters are caused by overactivity than by under-activity: hence his famous dictum, 'Surtout, pas trop de zèle'.

COUNT GONDOMAR, the 'meagre, thin-haired, tight-lipped' Spanish Ambassador to the court of King James I of England, establishes an early ascendancy over the King, at a time when – only two decades after the Spanish Armada – Spain was viewed with open hostility by most Englishmen.

The first incident of his embassy, before he had seen James or estimated what his own position might be, showed how he was determined to play that part of his game. When the two galleons which brought him to England made Portsmouth harbour, they found there the flagship of the Channel fleet and exchanged with her equal courtesies. It was not until Gondomar had gone ashore to be welcomed by the city fathers that the English captain (the vice-admiral was not aboard) sent word that he was sure the Spaniards would now pay the customary honours which they must have omitted through inadvertence. In any harbour of the Narrow Seas, all ships were required to strike their flags and keep them lowered as long as one of His Majesty's ships was in port, just as, at sea, they must dip their flags three times, strike their topsails, and pass to leeward in token of the king of England's sovereignty of the seas. The Spanish commander forwarded the demand to Gondomar, and Gondomar, speaking as the direct representative of the king of Spain, ordered him not to strike his colours.

Now, no point of naval etiquette was dearer to the English than this. There was a firm tradition (perhaps a truthful one) that Philip II on his way to marry Mary had been obliged to strike to the English admiral. Certainly the king of Denmark's ship had done so recently; so had the Spanish squadron which brought the duke of Frias as special ambassador in 1604. And in the presence of the duke of Sully, special ambassador of Henry IV, the vice-admiral of England had fired into the flagship of the vice-admiral of France and compelled him to lower his flag in Calais harbour itself. No wonder that on Gondomar's refusal the English captain threatened to blow the Spaniards out of the water. Gondomar replied that he hoped the impending battle could be delayed until he had time to send a message. To James he wrote a bald narrative of the imbroglio, merely adding that he begged, if circumstances were to prevent his fulfilling his mission in England, to be allowed to return aboard the Spanish flagship, since if it were sunk, he was determined to go down with it.

Probably James fumed and fretted; of course he knuckled under. James's weakness (though Gondomar could not have known it) was that he was too civilized a man to risk killing an ambassador and starting a war over an empty salute. The result was a notable victory for Spanish prestige. It may have been also the first step towards the ascendancy which the ambassador established over the spirit of the king.

From Renaissance Diplomacy *by Garrett Mattingly (Jonathan Cape, London, 1955).*

PRINCE TALLEYRAND, as the Foreign Minister of a defeated France at the conclusion of the Napoleonic wars, attended the Congress of Vienna to settle the future of Europe with the representatives of the victorious Allies; but far from being apologetic about his previous service to Napoleon, he managed by his adroitness and personality to impose his will – as the representative of the reinstated Louis XVIII – on his former conquerors.

A conference paper was handed to Talleyrand [by Castlereagh and Metternich] who, casting one glance at it, immediately pounced upon the word 'allies'. It compelled him to ask, he said, . . . had not peace been made? If they were still at war, whom was it against? Not Napoleon, he was at Elba; surely not against the King of France – he was the guarantee of the duration of peace. 'Let us speak frankly, gentlemen; if there are still any "allied powers" this is no place for me.'

The other Ministers found little to say in reply. They disclaimed any sinister motive in making use of the peccant word which they had employed only for convenience and brevity. 'Brevity,' retorted Talleyrand, 'should not be purchased at the price of accuracy,' and returned once more to the study of the protocol. Presently he laid it down with the words: 'I don't understand,' and then picking it up again pretended to be making a great effort to follow the sense of it. 'I still don't understand,' he finally exclaimed [picking up a

11

reference to arrangements that had been made between the Allies in advance of the conference]: 'for me there are two dates and between them there is nothing – the 30th of May when it was agreed to hold the Congress, and the 1st of October when the Congress is to open. Nothing that has taken place in the interval exists so far I am concerned.'

Once more the other Ministers accepted defeat. They attached, they said, little importance to this document and were prepared to withdraw it. It was accordingly withdrawn and no more was heard of it.

Somebody mentioned the King of Naples, meaning Murat [the Marshal placed by Napoleon on the throne of Naples]. 'Of what King of Naples are you speaking?' Talleyrand coolly inquired, and added, 'We do not know the man in question.' The effrontery of such a question and such a statement coming from one who had been for years in the service of Napoleon must have staggered even the trained diplomatists gathered round that table. Yet it was part of the supreme irony of the situation that there was not one of them except the representative of England who was in a position to remind Talleyrand of his past. The Prussian could not forget that his master had once humbly thanked Napoleon for leaving him a fragment of his kingdom, the Russian had been a witness of the adulation with which his master had overwhelmed Napoleon at Tilsit, the Austrian had been proud to conduct his master's daughter to Napoleon's bed. Who were they to question the orthodoxy of one who represented His Most Christian Majesty, who alone of all the monarchs had never even treated with the usurper? On another occasion when the Emperor Alexander, referring to the King of Saxony, spoke bitterly of 'those who have betrayed the cause of Europe', Talleyrand replied with justice, 'that, Sire, is a question of dates'.

From Talleyrand *by Duff Cooper (Jonathan Cape, London, 1932).*

BISMARCK, the creator of a united Germany, said towards the end of his life: 'We could not have set up the German Reich in the middle of Europe without having defeated France . . . the war with France [of 1870] was a necessary conclusion.' With this objective in mind, Bismarck edited William I of Prussia's telegram from Ems to the Emperor Napoleon III in such a way as to make war inevitable.

While Bismarck sat in Berlin intriguing against the king, Napoleon III and Gramont fired a new shot from Paris. They made further, more extreme demands – demands which would either display the humiliation of Prussia or force war upon her. William must endorse Leopold's withdrawal; he must apologize for the candidature and promise that it should never be renewed. If not, war would follow. These demands were presented to William I at Ems on 13 July. He still did not understand what was at stake. Though he rejected the new French demands, he repeated the announcement of Leopold's withdrawal [as a candidate for the Spanish throne] and supposed that he had made a fine stroke for peace.

When William's report of these doings reached Berlin, Bismarck saw his chance at last. He cut out William's conciliatory phrases and emphasized the real issue. The French had made certain demands under threat of war; and William had refused them. This was not forgery; it was a clear statement of the facts. There is curious evidence of this, which is often overlooked. After Bismarck had issued his edited version of 'the Ems telegram', a second message from William reached Berlin. He had refused to see the French representative and had said: 'If what you have to say concerns the Spanish candidature, I have nothing to add.' Bismarck did not forge the king's message; he anticipated it. But, just as he had intended to blame William for any failure, now he would not allow him credit for any success. The edited 'Ems telegram' was to be presented henceforth as the cause of the war. What is more, Bismarck was now eager to snatch the initiative from the French. This is the key to all his subsequent explanations. He had neither planned the war nor even foreseen it. But he claimed it as his own once it became inevitable. He wished to present himself as the creator of Germany, not as a man who had been mastered by events.

From Bismarck *by A.J.P. Taylor (Hamish Hamilton, London, 1955).*

MRS CLARE BOOTHE LUCE, as American Ambassador to Italy in the 1950s, sets up a secret exchange with Marshal Tito of Yugoslavia that secures the peaceful settlement of the Trieste affair – which was in dispute between the governments of Italy and Yugoslavia (who claimed ownership) and the US and the UK (who were in occupation) after the Second World War.

In London the secret negotiations over Trieste made good progress during the spring and early summer. But in August they bogged down. The representative of the Yugoslav Government, Vladimir Velebit, began to insist on more concessions than the Italian, British and US representatives were prepared to grant.

In Rome Clare was almost [in despair about this matter] when an American, who refused to identify himself on the telephone, promised to give her some helpful information about Trieste if she would see him privately.

Clare realized the caller might be an impostor. She had learned that some people would go to any lengths to see the Ambassador. But there was an implication that her anonymous caller knew about the talks in London. If he did, he just might have information which would be helpful. She agreed to see him. They met at the Villa Taverna [the Ambassador's residence] late one afternoon.

The man's appearance was reassuring, and when they were alone in the Ambassador's study he came directly to the point. 'My name wouldn't mean anything to you and I don't want to be involved in this, but I have been doing some work for the CIA in Yugoslavia. Their man in London is giving our people trouble, and I know why.'

If the caller knew this much, it might be worthwhile to listen to him. 'Is there something you think I can do?'

'The problem, Mrs Luce, is the crop failure. Tito needs wheat. If he doesn't get it, there will be a famine next winter.'

'How does that relate to Trieste?'

'Surely, Mrs Luce, you know how the mind of a dictator works – create a crisis and divert the public attention, and I think that's what he intends to do.'

'If the United States gave him enough wheat to carry them through this winter, would that help?'

The man smiled. 'You have anticipated my suggestion, Mrs Luce. A half a million tons of wheat would relieve the present shortage and unfreeze the situation in London.'

There was a certain undeniable logic in the mysterious stranger's explanation of the sudden turnabout in London. Mrs Luce telephoned Joe Jacobs at the Embassy and asked him what he knew about the wheat crop in Yugoslavia. He confirmed what her caller had told her. Three days later she was on her way to Washington.

'Your informant may have given you the truth,' John Foster Dulles told Clare, 'but Tito could never afford to admit to us or anyone else that he would trade Trieste for a gift of wheat.'

The Secretary said the delicacy of the situation would demand an emissary who could deal with the Communist dictator in absolute secrecy, someone whom Tito would trust never to reveal the details of the arrangement.

'Let's not give up. There must be someone we can send.'

'Put yourself in the Marshal's place, Mrs Luce. The rulers of a totalitarian country are just as sensitive to public opinion as we are in a democracy. Tito has domestic enemies and opposition at home. He would be destroyed if the news ever got out that he had traded Trieste for a gift of grain to cover up the failures of his own farm program.'

'Believe me, Clare, it won't work unless we can find the right man.'

Two nights later, at a dinner party hosted by correspondent Arthur Krock, Mrs Luce found herself seated next to Bob Murphy, the veteran trouble shooter of the State Department who had carried on the secret negotiations between the US Government and the Yugoslav patriots during World War II. The conversation turned to the problem of Trieste. Murphy casually mentioned his long-established, friendly relations with Tito.

'You're just the man we've been looking for,' Clare said. 'I have an appointment with President Eisenhower in the morning. We need someone who can carry out a very difficult confidential mission to Tito. Would you go?'

'I'll go anywhere the President wants to send me,' Murphy replied.

Twelve hours later Secretary Murphy was on his way to the island of Brioni, off the Dalmatian coast, where Tito had constructed a sumptuous summer palace. Murphy carried a personal letter from President Eisenhower to the Yugoslav dictator.

The Trieste affair was settled in London on October 5. Zone A, including the city of Trieste, with an area of 85 square miles and a population of 300,000, was returned to Italy. Zone B, with some addition from Zone A, comprising a total of 200 square miles and a population of 74,000, was annexed to Yugoslavia. Twenty days later the military forces of the United States and Great Britain, which had occupied the contested territories since the end of World War II, were withdrawn.

In his personal memoirs, *Diplomat Among Warriors*, Murphy minimizes the importance of the 400,000 tons of wheat the United States sent to Belgrade three weeks after the settlement was reached.

Only five people in the world knew the truth – the President of the United States, Secretary Dulles, Bob Murphy, Marshal Tito, and the American Ambassadress to Rome, who had started it all.

From Clare Boothe Luce: A Biography *by Stephen Shadegg*
(Leslie Frewin, London, 1973).

MRS CLARE BOOTHE LUCE, on another occasion in Rome, commits a memorable gaffe – to good effect.

After the conclusion of the Austrian State Treaty [ending the post-war occupation by the Allies] in 1955, the United States government was concerned about the need to withdraw its long-range rockets from the former US zone of Austria. They were anxious to persuade the Italian government to agree to the rockets being stationed on Italian soil; but this presented problems, as much opinion in Italy was against any such move. Mrs Luce – as US Ambassador in Rome – was instructed to seek the Italian government's agreement to host the rocket bases.

The ambassador made an appointment with the Italian Foreign Minister and decided to study her brief in the car on the way to the ministry. As the chauffeur slowed down on arrival she looked up from her papers to find that he had taken her, not to the Foreign Ministry but to the President's palace; worse still, the President's equerry had already spotted the big black Cadillac with the US Ambassador's flag flying and was on his way down the steps of the palace to welcome the visitor.

Mrs Luce felt that to withdraw would be more embarrassing than to press on, despite the fact that she had no appointment, and that President Gronchi was newly elected and had received no foreign ambassadors so far. She took a deep breath and told the equerry that she had an important warning to give to the President from the American government. In the circumstances, President Gronchi reluctantly agreed to receive her.

Determined to turn her embarrassment into an advantage, Mrs Luce launched into the subject of the long-range rockets leaving Austria and how exposed this would leave Italy to possible Soviet aggression; she was concerned, she said, for the security of the President's country. She handled her interlocutor so well that by the end of the impromptu conversation Gronchi was suggesting that the US government might be generous enough to consider siting the rockets in Italy; he volunteered to put the proposition in his Foreign Minister. Mrs Luce, for her part, undertook to pass on the President's imaginative proposal to Washington. At the end of the day the US objective was achieved, on what appeared to be an Italian initiative.

Mrs Luce and the US government had reason to be pleased by the outcome of brazening out her mistake. But the Italian *paparazzi*, who of course knew nothing of the content of her talk with President Gronchi, had rumbled the fact that she had called on their President without an appointment, thus apparently jumping the gun in protocol terms. Until the end of her mission the incident was quoted against her as an example of amateurism and arrogance. Mrs Luce is said to have commented: 'I wish all my mistakes were as profitable!'

Compiled from verbal and published accounts available to the editor.

SIR GLADWYN JEBB, the British representative on the Security Council of the UN in 1950, establishes himself as a national television personality in the United States by his forthright resistance to the Soviet policies on the Korean War.

On 31 October 1950, Sir Gladwyn Jebb told his Soviet opposite number on the Security Council of the United Nations that 'for the representative of a country which maintains millions of its own compatriots in slave-labour camps in unspeakable conditions . . . to denounce other governments for alleged misdemeanours as regards political prisoners is just about as nauseating a spectacle as that of Satan denouncing sin'.

It was robust statements and telling phrases like this that appealed to American television watchers across the nation as they tuned their sets to the proceedings of the Security Council in New York. The patrician Englishman with his Oxford intonation, who emerged as the articulate champion of Western values, became – almost overnight – a TV star and popular hero. Thousands of letters of support flocked in every week to Sir Gladwyn's office. People who had never before taken an interest in political debate found the proceedings of the Security Council to be compulsive viewing – out-rating the 'soap operas'. Indeed, the 'Hooper rating' (the accepted criterion for judging the respective popularity of different TV personalities) put Sir Gladwyn as number three on its list, immediately after the comedian Bob Hope.

The Foreign Office in London was rather dazed by the popular success of its man in New York, who had previously been considered more an administrator than a communicator. Sir Gladwyn himself found it somewhat embarrassing to be recognized by taxi drivers and restaurant waiters, some of whom assured him they had switched over from their traditional evening viewing of all-in wrestling to watch the arcane proceedings of the UN. 'A point of order' became a current catch-phrase. Rumours circulated that the Soviet representative had accused Sir Gladwyn (whose head was nodding on his chest) of sleeping through his inordinately long speech, only to be answered by Sir Gladwyn opening one eye and murmuring 'would that he were'! One American accosted him with the words, 'You should run for President, Sir Goldwyn Jeep'.

Not until thirty years later was another diplomat – Sir Nicholas Henderson (British Ambassador in Washington during the Falkands War of 1982) – to achieve a similar star rating on American television. On that occasion, the American viewing public found themselves captivated by the authoritative, articulate but unkempt figure of Sir Nicholas, looking like an Oxford don who had got dressed in a hurry, explaining to them in terms they could understand why the Argentine invasion was *not* an exercise in colonial liberation. Once again, the all-in wrestlers had to give screen space to the diplomats.

Compiled by the editor from published sources and oral tradition.

DAG HAMMARSKJÖLD, as Secretary-General of the United Nations in 1960, defends himself after a vicious attack by Mr Khrushchev for his interventionist policy in the civil war in the ex-Belgian Congo. At the conclusion of the remarks below, the delegates to the General Assembly of the UN rose to their feet and applauded for several minutes. Hammarskjöld's future as Secretary-General was assured, the authority of his office enhanced and his continued intervention in the Congo made possible. Only the Russians struck a jarring note: Khrushchev and Foreign Minister Gromyko banged protestingly on the table with their fists, though not – on this occasion – with their shoes.

I have no reason to defend myself or my colleagues against the accusations and judgments to which you have listened. Let me say only this, that *you*, all of you, are the judges. No single party can claim that authority. I am sure you will be guided by truth and justice. In particular, let those who know what the United Nations has done and is doing in the Congo, and those who are not pursuing aims proper only to themselves, pass judgments on our actions there. Let the countries who have liberated themselves in the last fifteen years speak for themselves.

I regret that the intervention to which I have found it necessary to reply has again tended to personalize an issue which, as I have said, in my view is not a question of a man but of an institution. The man does not count, the institution does. A weak or non-existent executive would mean that the United Nations would no longer be able to serve as an effective instrument for active protection of the interests of those many Members who need such protection. The man holding the responsibility as chief executive should leave if he weakens the executive; he should stay if this is necessary for its maintenance. This, and only this, seems to me to be the substantive criterion that has to be applied.

I said the other day that I would not wish to continue to serve as Secretary-General one day longer than such continued service was, and was considered to be, in the best interest of the Organization. The statement this morning seems to indicate that the Soviet Union finds it impossible to work with the present Secretary-General. This may seem to provide a strong reason why I should resign. However, the Soviet Union has also made it clear that, if the present Secretary-General were to resign now, they would not wish to elect a new incumbent but insist on an arrangement which – and this is my firm conviction based on broad experience – would make it impossible to maintain an effective executive. By resigning, I would, therefore, at the present difficult and dangerous juncture throw the Organization to the winds. I have no right to do so because I have a responsibility to all those states members for which the Organization is of decisive importance, a responsibility which overrides all other considerations.

It is not the Soviet Union or, indeed, any other big powers who need the United Nations for their protection; it is all the others. In this sense the Organization is first of all *their* Organization, and I deeply believe in the wisdom with which they will be able to use it and guide it. I shall remain in my post during the term of my office as a servant of the Organization in the interests of all those other nations, as long as *they* wish me to do so.

In this context the representative of the Soviet Union spoke of courage. It is very easy to resign; it is not so easy to stay on. It is very easy to bow to the wish of a big power. It is another matter to resist. As is well known to all Members of this Assembly, I have done so before on many occasions and in many directions. If it is the wish of those nations who see in the Organization their best protection in the present world, I shall now do so again.

Compiled from UN General Assembly reports, and accounts given to the editor before his own departure for the Congo shortly thereafter.

SIR PAUL GORE-BOOTH, as British High Commissioner to India in 1961, was disconcerted by Prime Minister Nehru giving a press conference attacking British motives and policy in the Congo (the UK was accused of restraining UK forces from acting against the secessionary province of Katanga to avoid damage to British mining interests there). Anti-British sentiment sharpened with the news of Hammarskjöld's death in an air crash in the region, and there were innuendoes suggesting British responsibility. Here Gore-Booth records how he rebutted the charges and criticisms by impromptu action on his own initiative.

Next morning all our fears were realized. The *Indian Express*, not normally hysterically anti-British, said 'Never, even during Suez, have Britain's hands been so bloodstained as they are now.' The Indian language papers followed suit. Our very well-informed and perceptive Press Officer, Ben (Dunelm) Brown, simply said, 'The Press is terrible,' and asked whether I felt I could give a press conference. I asked how much time we had in hand if we were to make the national press effectively the next morning. The reply was 'About ten minutes'.

There was no question of consulting London. A press conference meant repudiating the Prime Minister of India in India before an audience, mainly Indian, of whom many, if not ill-disposed, would be at least sceptical. On the other hand, in terms of Indian public opinion, things were about as bad as they could be, and if nobody said anything, there would be lasting damage to relations. And we had one advantage. Thanks to the Foreign and Commonwealth Relations Offices at home and especially to our very efficient

Ambassador in the Congo, Derek Riches, we were now very well informed and up to date. I would certainly know more about the latest events in the Congo than anyone else present. So I decided to go ahead.

On entering the hall in the High Commission, I invited the assembly to stand for a minute in memory of Dag Hammarskjöld, both as Secretary-General and as a close personal friend of mine (there was no false sentiment about this). I then gave a full statement of British Government policy in the Congo. I recounted the British pledge to work for the unity of the country within the existing boundaries and with Katanga contributing its resources to a united Congo. We had certainly had our anxieties about the use of force in Katanga. So had Mr Hammarskjöld, and that was why the Secretary-General and a British Minister, Lord Lansdowne, were both in the Congo. The decision to go to Ndola to meet Mr Tshombe was Mr Hammarskjöld's own. I confirmed that permission had been given to the Ethiopian aircraft to fly to the Congo and that we objected to 'pirate' aircraft flying round Katanga. It was a long session and there was much more besides. Only the last question was off-side: 'Was I criticizing remarks by Mr Nehru?' 'It is not for me,' I replied, 'to criticize remarks by Mr Nehru.'

We then went home to await results. They were extraordinary. They were also immensely creditable to the Press Trust of India and the individual correspondents and newspapers. The Indian press carried what I had said at length and in detail with good understanding and objective headlines. The heat came off almost instantaneously. The Secretary of State for Commonwealth Relations, Duncan Sandys, sent a heart-warming telegram. Within a week, an understandable interval, the Indian Ministry of External Affairs dissociated itself from any suggestion that Britain had had anything to do with the death of Mr Hammarskjöld. When I next saw Mr Nehru, he was splendidly bland. Of course he had had 'no intention of attacking the United Kingdom'.

So while one cannot in one press conference 'restore' a position which has changed, we in Delhi could allow ourselves a quiet smile over a comment sent to one British newspaper, that: 'the current of anti-British feeling is running in this capital too strongly by now to be reversed by [Sir Paul's] remarks.' If you have never seen a current change, well, I have. And I do not care to think what might have happened to our relations if no one had done anything about it.

From With Great Truth and Respect *by Lord Gore-Booth, GCMG, KCVO*
(Constable, London, 1974).

CHIP BOHLEN, the leading State Department authority on the Soviet Union, is called in by President Kennedy to advise at the outset of the Cuban missile crisis in 1962.

On October 17, as I walked into the President's office to pay my official farewell call [before leaving as US ambassador to France], Kennedy said to me, 'Chip, come here and look at these.' Spread out on his desk were a large number of photographs. They were pictures taken by a U-2 reconnaissance plane of missile bases that the Soviet Union was installing in Cuba. While there had been charges in the Senate and by the press of such Soviet activity, the pictures were the first definite proof of what the Soviets were doing. Until then, the CIA said the Soviets were installing only anti-aircraft missiles with a range of twenty-five miles. I spent a half hour with the President, and the word France was not mentioned. He told me that though the data seemed scanty, our experts could determine the nature of the installations with precision. Invaluable in analyzing the photos was material obtained from Oleg Penkovsky, probably the most successful Western espionage agent who worked in the Soviet Union. The pictures, the President told me, showed sites of twenty-four medium- and sixteen intermediate-range ballistic missiles. The danger these forty missiles posed to much of the United States did not have to be discussed. Once installed and ready to fire, they would amount to nuclear blackmail.

The President had not made up his mind what to do. The CIA pictures, taken on October 14, had been given to the President on October 16, the day before my visit. While he did not know how he was going about it, the President said he was determined to get the missiles out of Cuba. 'We're going to have a pretty tough time ahead of us,' he said, 'and we'll have some hard decisions.'

The President said he was appointing me to a committee, headed by Rusk, to consider the problem. We met until late in the night weighing the options. One group, with which I sided, favored using diplomatic means to the ultimate before turning to force. The other group held that the quickest and surest method of destroying the bases was by bombing. The fact that bombing would kill thousands of Russians installing the missiles did not bulk as large in the minds of this group as it did in mine. I felt that the Soviets might have felt compelled to strike back against so great a loss. The result would have been nuclear war.

The next day, October 18, the committee met again. That evening, forty-eight hours before I was to sail for France, Joseph Alsop, the columnist, gave a dinner at his Georgetown house for my wife and me. The President and Mrs Kennedy attended. After we had dined, the President took me out on the porch and we discussed the missile crisis for almost half an hour. Again we went through the options, but he still had not made up his mind on a course of action.

As we were leaving the Alsop house, I told the President I did not expect to see him again before leaving for Paris. 'I wouldn't be too sure you are leaving,' he said to my wife. 'I think I may ask you to stay.' This remark seemed to be missed by the other guests. After we got home, I warned my wife that she might have to develop a worsening of her back (she had been suffering from a lumbar condition) 'because we are going to have to invent a story for our staying behind here'. I did not tell her and she did not ask me – she was a well-disciplined Foreign Service wife – the reason for the sudden change in plans. Before going to bed that night, I wrote in longhand on a yellow legal pad my suggestions of what the President ought to do about the Soviet missiles in Cuba.

The next morning, my wife called Mrs Alsop, thanked her for the dinner, and said that she was beginning to wonder whether she could leave the United States in view of the condition of her back, which was keeping her in bed. At the State Department, I had a call from Kennedy, who seemed to assume that I was going to attend an important meeting on the missile crisis at 11 A.M. the next day. I then talked with Dean Rusk, and gave him the memorandum I had written the previous night. We both

24

had doubts about the wisdom of canceling my departure plans, including an engagement to speak the next day to the Franco-American Society in New York. Calling off this luncheon of about two hundred people might have alerted the Soviets to the fact that the United States knew about the missiles. Besides, my successor as Rusk's adviser on Russian affairs, Tommy Thompson, had just come back from Moscow and was in a position to give more up-to-date advice on Soviet intentions than I could.

Rusk agreed that my memorandum covered my position fully, and we decided that I should leave as scheduled. Rusk talked with the President, and he apparently agreed. My memorandum, addressed to Rusk for transmittal to the President, said:

TOP SECRET

MR SECRETARY: October 18, 1962

Since the conversation last night was rather general, and I will not be there tomorrow, I feel I owe it to you and to the President to set forth my views on this matter as succinctly as possible. They are as follows:

1. The existence of Soviet MRBM bases in Cuba cannot be tolerated. The objective therefore is their elimination by whatever means may be necessary.

2. There are two means in essence: (a) by diplomatic action or (b) by military action.

3. No one can guarantee that this can be achieved by diplomatic action – but it seems to me essential that this channel should be tested out before military action is employed. If our decision is firm (and it must be) I can see no danger in communicating with Khrushchev privately, worded in such a way that he realizes that we mean business.

4. This I consider an essential first step, no matter what military course we determine on if the reply is unsatisfactory. The tone and tenor of his reply will tell us something but I don't believe a threat of general nuclear war should deter us. If he means it, he would have so reacted even if the strike had come first.

5. I don't feel so strongly about a message to Castro and this could be dropped.

6. My chief concern about a strike without any diplomatic effort is that it will inevitably lead to war with Cuba and would not be the neat quick disposal of their bases as was suggested. Furthermore I am reasonably certain that the allied reaction would be dead against us, especially if the Soviets retaliated locally (as in Turkey or Italy or in Berlin).

7. A communication to Khrushchev would be very useful for the record in establishing our case for action.

8. In general I feel that a declaration of war [against Cuba] would be valuable since it would open up every avenue of military action – air strike, invasion, or blockade. But we would have to make a case before our allies to justify such a declaration of war. But if we acted first and sought to justify it later we would be in a spot of great consequence.

9. Finally, I feel very strongly that any belief in a limited quick action is an illusion and would lead us into a full war with Cuba on a step by step basis which would greatly increase the possibility of general war.

The best course in my view would be a carefully worded and serious letter to Khrushchev, and when the reply is received (if it is unsatisfactory) communicate with our principal allies to inform them of our intention and then ask Congress for a declaration of war with a suitable statement of the reason and all adequate preparations.

Please excuse the handwriting but I have no time to have it typed. If the President asks about my opinion this will constitute it. Good luck.

CHARLES E. BOHLEN

There are of course many other angles – but the above seem to me the essentials. I don't quite see the urgency of military action – if it leaks and we have already initiated diplomatic action we should be able to handle it.

At nine o'clock the next morning, I was paged at Washington

26

National Airport. The call was from Kenneth O'Donnell, the President's appointments secretary, who told me that President Kennedy urgently desired that I attend the 11 A.M. meeting at the White House . . . I asked O'Donnell to put Kennedy on the wire. 'Mr President,' I said, 'I do not see how at this last moment – my plane leaves in fifteen minutes – I can suddenly cancel this flight and engagement in New York dealing with a large audience without running the serious risk of some publicity and a lot of speculation.' Kennedy had not realized that the newspapers had been told about the speech and that a last-minute cancellation was sure to tip off the Soviets that something was up. I was too closely identified with Russian policy for anyone to miss the point. The President wanted to maintain the advantage of secrecy. He had not batted an eye when Gromyko told him the previous day that Soviet activity in Cuba was not related to any offensive intention against the United States. Kennedy immediately saw my point, because he said, 'I guess you are right, Chip. Go on. I guess we will have to do without you.'

From Witness to History 1929–1969 *by Charles E. Bohlen*
(W. W. Norton & Company Inc., New York, 1973).

SIR PAUL GORE-BOOTH, then Permanent Under-Secretary at the Foreign Office in London, describes how friction between Harold Wilson (as Prime Minister) and George Brown (as Foreign Secretary) led to lack of consultation and the possible loss of a chance for Britain to help the US to implement a peace initiative in Vietnam.

In the autumn of 1967, the Americans were in better directed search of something which could be negotiable in terms of North Vietnamese psychology and the real military situation. The prevalent idea was that, if the United States could contrive to make two concessions against one by the North Vietnamese, this could lead towards a cease-fire and negotiation. The idea assumed concrete form in what became known as the 'Phase A – Phase B' programme. Phase A would be a published American cessation of bombing; Phase B would be an assurance of a cessation of North

Vietnamese infiltration into the South in exchange for an American de-escalation of reinforcement for their forces in Vietnam. This approach seemed to hold some prospects of progress.

The story of the end of 1966 and the beginning of 1967 is one of how this plan, largely through administrative muddles, ran into the sand. The principal events from the British point of view were a visit by the Foreign Secretary, Mr Brown, to Moscow in November 1966, and the visit to London of the Soviet Prime Minister, Mr A.N. Kosygin, and his delegation from 6 February to 13 February 1967. . . .

It was on this basis that discussions proceeded on 7,8 and 9 February. By the evening of the ninth (Thursday) Mr Wilson was able to present to an interested Mr Kosygin a text which corresponded with the 'Phase A – Phase B' plan, a text accepted by Mr Cooper [the US government representative] as consistent with United States Government policy and telegraphed back by him 'for information'. It seemed that the ball was now satisfactorily with the Russians who, it was assumed, would see what they could do.

Later on the same evening, Mr Kosygin and party were due to go on the night train to Scotland. At about 10.00 p.m. there was a telephone warning from Washington that an important message was on its way. When it arrived in Downing Street, it was an utterly bewildering shock. Phase A and Phase B had been stood on their heads; the cessation of bombing and the abstention from augmentation of American forces would only take place *after* the North Vietnamese had given assurance that they had actually stopped infiltration.

By the time the new version had been typed out, Mr Kosygin was on the way to the station. Downing Street was faced with a genuine split-second dilemma; should the new version be sent with top urgency to the station to catch Mr Kosygin, or was there any alternative course? If it were sent, any prospect of successful negotiation was pretty certainly dead. If it was not sent, Mr Kosygin would be going off to Scotland under a serious misapprehension and a misleading text might have already gone to Moscow. Mr Wilson accordingly decided that Mr Kosygin must have the new text, and his private secretary got it to him just in time.

Mr Brown is very critical of this decision, which was taken

without his being consulted. With the gift of hindsight, I can see quite clearly what the action should have been. A message should have been sent to Mr Kosygin to say that we had received a worrying message from Washington which we were checking with the Americans; meantime the Soviet Government might wish to suspend any current discussion and action. I was at home and was not consulted either. I am not going to claim that I would in fact have got the answer right had my telephone rung; at the end of a hard tiring week, one is as certain of giving right advice as a footballer in the ninetieth minute of a cup-tie taking a penalty with the score 0 - 0.

Mr Brown is, in my judgement, technically right. But I think the error was not simply technical. I have alluded to strains within the British team at the top level. When such strains exist, there is almost certain sooner or later to be an error of top level decision and this was it.

From With Great Truth and Respect *by Lord Gore-Booth, GCMG, KCVO*
(Constable, London, 1974).

SIR CHRISTOPHER SOAMES, as British Ambassador in Paris in 1969, inadvertently offends President de Gaulle in 'L' Affaire Soames'.

Anglo-French relations were going through a difficult time in the 1960s after President de Gaulle had vetoed the British application to join the European Community; in an effort to establish a personal rapport with the President, Mr Harold Wilson (then British Prime Minister) decided to send Sir Christopher Soames – a prominent former Conservative Minister and the son-in-law of Sir Winston Churchill – as ambassador to France.

Soames was delighted when in January 1969 President de Gaulle took the unusual step of inviting him to an *à quatre* lunch at the Elysée Palace, indicating that he wished to have a serious talk about Anglo-French relations. It was the long-awaited opportunity. Unfortunately Soames was still convalescing after a mild heart attack, and so asked for the occasion to be postponed for a month – a request to which de Gaulle readily agreed.

29

When eventually the lunch took place, it was indeed a significant occasion. Soames reported it fully by confidential telegram to the Foreign Office in London. When his report arrived, the Foreign Secretary was abroad but a copy was immediately shown to the Prime Minister. Mr Wilson was about to have official talks with the West German Chancellor, and felt – understandably – that he should tell the Chancellor something of the recent exchange with de Gaulle in Paris as it was likely to affect the shape of European relations. A garbled report reached the Press and was read by de Gaulle before anyone could tell him what was going on.

President de Gaulle was livid. He felt his confidence had been broken; his proposals had been misrepresented; he suspected British bad faith. He laid the blame on Soames, and refused ever to receive him again. Indeed, if it had not been for de Gaulle's own fall from office soon afterwards, Soames might well have found himself obliged to leave France – his mission a failure, due to clumsy handling by others and unlucky timing.

From a first-hand account of the incident given to the editor in 1993.

DR KISSINGER records how the American reconciliation with Communist China was given initial impetus by the 'Ping-Pong Diplomacy' of the young American table tennis team on their visit to Peking in 1971.

The United States table tennis team was competing in the tournament, the thirty-first World Table Tennis Championship, staged in Nagoya, Japan. The nine young Americans on our team did not know it, but they were about to be players also in a complicated chess game.

On April 6, to everybody's stunned surprise, the Chinese invited the American team to visit China. Graham B. Steenhoven, President of the US Table Tennis Association and manager of the American team, phoned the American Embassy in Tokyo for advice. Without hesitation, the Embassy's China specialist, William Cunningham, who knew nothing of our overtures to Peking except our general desire to improve relations, recommended that Steenhoven accept. Cunningham deserves much credit for his perception and initiative. The Washington bureaucracy was less daring. On April 7 the State Department made sure that it would not be accused of recklessness by reporting to the White House: 'Though we have as yet no way of being sure, the invitation may be intended at least in part as a gesture in response to recent US initiatives.' The visit was an international sensation; it captured the world's imagination, aided no little by Chou En-lai's careful stage management. Peking Radio broadcasts gave pride of place to the team's arrival in China even though several other national teams had also been invited.

The day after the Chinese invitation to the American Ping-Pong team, Nixon gave a speech on Vietnam. While announcing the withdrawal of 100,000 additional American troops between May 1 and December 1 of 1971, Nixon also made a ringing defense of his Indochina policy, including the Laos operation. This had no adverse effect whatsoever on Peking. The United States table tennis players were given a dazzling welcome in China. On April 14, in the Great Hall of the People, they were received by Chou En-lai himself, an achievement that was still an unfulfilled ambition of most of the Western diplomats stationed in Peking. 'You have opened a new chapter in the relations of the American and Chinese people,' said the extraordinary Chinese Premier. 'I am confident that this beginning again of our friendship will certainly meet with majority support of our two peoples.' When the stunned athletes did not respond, the Premier pursued the subject: 'Don't you agree with me?' The Americans burst into applause. They quickly invited the Chinese team to tour the United States. The invitation was accepted immediately.

The whole enterprise was vintage Chou En-lai. Like all Chinese moves, it had so many layers of meaning that the brilliantly painted surface was the least significant part. At its most obvious the invitation to the young Americans symbolized China's commitment to improved relations with the United States; on a deeper level it reassured – more than any diplomatic communication through any channel – that the emissary who would now surely be invited would step on friendly soil. It was a signal to the White House that our initiatives had been noted.

From White House Years *by Henry Kissinger*
(Little, Brown and Company, Boston, 1979).

31

MRS KIRKPATRICK, US ambassador to the UN, by her acceptance of a dinner invitation nearly provokes a row between the United States and Britain at the time of the Argentine invasion of the Falklands.

The Argentine sea-borne invasion force landed on the Falkland Islands on 2 April 1982, to the consternation of the government and people of the United Kingdom and to the surprise of the entire world. Britain expected moral and practical support from its closest ally – the United States. But the US government, and more particularly its ambassador to the UN, Jeane Kirkpatrick, had spent years cultivating Argentina and other Latin American countries and felt that an 'even-handed' policy towards the conflict was called for.

As it happened, Mrs Kirkpatrick and a number of her senior colleagues had – some time previously – accepted an invitation to dine at the Argentine embassy in Washington on the evening of 2 April. Mrs Kirkpatrick saw no reason to cancel her acceptance of the dinner. When surprise was expressed that she was going ahead, she remarked that her country had never taken sides in the Falkland dispute, and 'if the Argentines own the islands then moving troops into them is not armed aggression'.

When Sir Nicholas Henderson, the British Ambassador in Washington, heard what Mrs Kirkpatrick was up to, he commented: 'This is just as if I had dined with the Iranian Ambassador on the night that they seized the American hostages in Tehran – what would they have thought of that?'

When Lord Carrington heard of Mrs Kirkpatrick's action (on the last day before his resignation as British Foreign Secretary), he exploded. It was said to have taken all President Reagan's good relations with Mrs Thatcher to defuse the effect of what many thought of as a diplomatic gaffe.

Compiled from remarks made to the editor by those concerned.

SIR ANTHONY PARSONS, as British Ambassador at the UN in New York during the Falklands War of 1982, uses his intimate knowledge of the workings of the UN and of the personalities involved to confound the Argentines.

Parsons displayed what a UN admirer called 'good old-fashioned diplomatic legwork' to obtain the nine votes he required to have the Security Council summoned on Thursday, 1 April, even before the invasion had occurred. [The British Government had been alerted to the danger only the previous evening.] He announced that an Argentine assault on the islands was imminent and secured an immediate call from the council's Zairean President, Kamanda wa Kamanda, for both sides to show restraint. . . . Invasion would now be in flagrant defiance of a Security Council presidential call.

With the Argentine occupation of the Falklands a fact on the Friday, Parsons once again moved with speed. Thatcher might share with President Reagan the view that the less heard from the UN the better. But no nation likes to go to war without right on its side, and even Thatcher was not averse to the banner of a Security Council resolution fluttering over her task force. Throughout the war, Parsons's strategy was dominated by two considerations. The first was to secure a UN demand for Argentine withdrawal, to 'legitimise' Britain's military response; the second was to avert any subsequent demand that Britain stall or recall the task force.

As soon as invasion was confirmed, the Security Council was again summoned to confront a straightforward British request that it pass a binding resolution ordering the Argentinians to leave the islands. Rather than follow the normal procedure of circulating an advance draft to sound out opinion, Parsons presented a 'take-it-or-leave-it' final resolution. Such 'black drafts' as they are known entitle the presenter to a vote within twenty-four hours. The vote would be held on the Saturday evening. Costa Mendes raced to New York to support Roca, confident he could avert a diplomatic disaster. The Security Council has fifteen members, of whom five are permanent and ten are chosen on rotation every two years. Two-thirds support is needed for a binding resolution, which means a proposer must secure the votes of at least some of the 'non-aligned' members. This seemed a near impossible task for Britain and Costa Mendes's confidence was understandable.

Parsons now set about the challenge. Of the western bloc, he could assume he had the UK, the US, France and Ireland in the bag, as well as Japan. The communist states, China, Russia and Poland, had to be ruled out, as did Latin Spain. Panama had already agreed to sponsor Argentina's case. That meant Britain needed all the remaining five for her two-thirds majority, a mixed bag of Third World nations comprising Jordan, Togo, Zaire, Uganda and Guyana. At times like this a diplomat must draw on every resource at his disposal – an old favour done, a personal contact kept in good repair, a trade deal or cultural exchange in the offing, perhaps simple friendship. Parsons had less than two days for his manoeuvring.

Guyana gave her vote to Britain, agreeing to any resolution which might deter Venezuela from pursing a border dispute with her. Zaire did the same, as the nation of the affronted UN President, Kamanda. France was asked to square the Togo vote, which she did. Uganda remained doubtful until the last minute, but eventually sided with Britain on the grounds of Argentina's 'aggression'. But it was Jordan who found herself in the sort of confusion normally reserved for the US delegation. The Jordanian delegate declared in favour of Britain, but was then instructed from Amman not to vote with any colonialist cause. Parsons tried every pressure, but the Jordanians' hands were tied. Finally he wheeled out his biggest gun. His office telephoned London, tried to reach Carrington, failed and went for the Prime Minister herself. Mrs Thatcher, who had other things on her mind that Saturday, responded to this buccaneering spirit. Parsons had gained her respect (rare in the Foreign Office) when she had previously visited his embassy in Teheran. While Parsons ingeniously stalled for time (even suggesting a retyping of the resolution to include the word 'Malvinas'), she duly telephoned King Hussein and personally pleaded with him to support Britain. Parsons got his ten votes.

From The Battle for the Falklands *by Max Hastings and Simon Jenkins*
(Michael Joseph, London, 1983).

SADDAM HUSSEIN commits a political and diplomatic gaffe which results in his unifying the forces against him in the Gulf War.

When Iraq invaded Kuwait in August 1990, Western governments refused to acknowledge the annexation of the Emirate and declined to close their embassies in Kuwait City as requested by the Iraqi authorities.

The Iraqis responded by surrounding some embassies with troops, thus virtually imprisoning the ambassadors and their staffs; they also cut off supplies of food, water and electricity – confident that this would force the diplomatic missions to close.

But close they did not. The Americans, British, French and others settled down to endure a siege. Vegetables were grown in embassy gardens; swimming pools were converted to reservoirs of drinking water; tenuous lines of communication with the outside world were kept open; a well was dug in one embassy to ensure washing water, and those digging a grave in another struck water too. But unlike the Western legations during the Boxer rebellion siege in Peking, the missions were isolated and could not give succour to each other.

In the world outside, trade embargoes, blockades and military intervention were all being considered as ways to put pressure on the Iraqis to withdraw from Kuwait; the French were particularly uncertain about the wisdom of direct military action.

It was then that Saddam Hussein's forces made a fatal mistake. A military unit forced an entry to the French Ambassador's residence in Kuwait City and seized four French citizens including the Military Attaché of the embassy, thus breaching all the norms of diplomatic behaviour. President Mitterand was furious; he took a proposition to the Security Council of the UN requesting that 'a United Nations mission be sent to Kuwait . . . to restore the normal functioning of the diplomatic missions and secure their inviolability'. Meanwhile, France 'reserved the possibility of taking any measures she might consider appropriate'.

Saddam Hussein had, by his high-handed action towards the French embassy, ensured that French troops would be alongside American and British ones in the campaign to liberate Kuwait.

From an account compiled from press and diplomatic sources.

2

Diplomatic Travellers and Explorers

W HILE IT WAS true in the nineteenth-century high noon of Empire that 'trade followed the flag', it was more often the case in the dawn of European diplomacy that the flag followed the trader. Even if in Renaissance Italy diplomatic envoys often had a predominently political or intelligence role, most of the first European envoys to penetrate the East had a commercial brief: they were sent to explore new markets on behalf of the Muscovy Company, the Levant Company or the East India Company. With Englishmen like Anthony Jenkinson (in Russia and Persia) and Sir Thomas Roe (in Mogul India) their ambassadorial role was grafted onto their market-opening function. Marco Polo also set out as a merchant adventurer but, having reached Cathay from Venice and established his reputation as a shrewd observer of men and affairs, he was then employed on various quasi-diplomatic missions by the Great Khan of China.

For such explorer–diplomats there were few of the traditional safeguards and privileges of diplomatic status. However valid the safe-conducts and credentials they might carry (and these were often sketchy enough), such documents availed them little when they passed out of one ruler's domain and into that of his rival or enemy. Robbery and violence, whether sanctioned by the local authority or not, were constant dangers; so too were the natural hazards of desert and mountain crossings – thirst and hunger were never far away.

But the excitements and novelty must have been rich compensations. The sheer sense of wonder that pervades their accounts of the courts and customs of the orient is infectious, even after an interval of several centuries. It was this lure of the unknown that attracted other diplomatic visitors to the more remote corners of Central Asia as late as the nineteenth century. They also had a formidable diplomatic task to perform: to out-manoeuvre Imperial Russia in the struggle for power and influence in the emirates of Afghanistan, Uzbekistan and Turkmenistan. This was the period of 'The Great Game', when the struggle for empire between St Petersburg and British India was at its height. The Indian Political Service was the diplomatic arm of the Raj, and recruited dashing young army officers with a knowledge of local languages to perform its perilous tasks. One such was Alexander Burnes, who was hacked to death in the Afghan rising of 1841. Another was Colonel Stoddart, the end of whose ill-fated mission to the khanate of Bokhara in 1838 is described in the chapter on Diplomats in Danger. The fact that he was imprisoned in loathsome conditions and later executed despite his diplomatic status, did not deter other like-minded adventurers. Even the young Lord Curzon, at the end of the century, was attracted by the idea of improving his diplomatic and political qualifications by venturing into uncharted territories around the source of the River Oxus.

Some of the most daring and percipient explorers were members of the consular services. Unlike their smoother diplomatic colleagues, such men spent virtually their entire working lives in regions that were often remote from Western values and civilization. It was no doubt for this reason that Richard Burton, after making his celebrated journeys to Mecca and to look for the sources of the Nile, joined the consular service and in that capacity continued his travels both in Brazil and in the Syrian deserts. Other lesser-known Victorian consuls – such as the Mr Wratislaw mentioned in this chapter – were also busy making their contributions to revealing the darker corners of the known world.

The 'lust of knowing what should not be known' persisted into the present century. When Fitzroy Maclean was a junior Secretary at the British Embassy in Moscow in the 1930s, he took off for the Caucasus and Soviet Central Asia on a series of unprecedented infiltrations into closed areas of the country; harried and chivvied by the NKVD (security forces) he managed none the less to tread the Golden Road to Samarkand and write an international best-seller about it afterwards.

Exactly twenty years later – in the late 1950s – I was myself a junior diplomatic Secretary in Moscow and, inspired by *Eastern Approaches* and by encounters with Fitzroy Maclean, I took off by train to Tashkent, Central Asia and the Caucasus. Like Maclean, I wrote up my trip for the Foreign Office (largely to excuse my over-long absence from the Chancery) and was surprised when the Office printed the report in the diplomatic despatches series and thus ensured its preservation.

The despatches, letters and reports of pioneer diplomats are a wholesome antidote to the far more numerous accounts of lives of luxury and obsession with status which characterize so much popular writing about diplomacy.

MARCO POLO, having survived his memorable journey of exploration from Venice across Asia, so impressed the Great Khan of China with his talents that he was sent on a diplomatic mission on the Khan's behalf and won high praise for his powers of observation.

It happened that Marco, Messer Niccolò's son, acquired an impressive knowledge of the customs of the Tartars, their dialects and their letters. It is a fact that before he had been very long at the Great Khan's Court he had mastered four languages with their methods of writing. He was unusually wise and intelligent and the Great Khan was very well disposed to him because of the exceptional qualities that he saw in him. Noting his intelligence, the Khan sent him on an official visit to a country named Kara-jang, which it took him a good six months to reach. The young man fulfilled his mission excellently. He had noticed for himself more than once that when the messengers sent out by the Khan to various parts of the world returned to him and gave an account of their missions, they had very little else to say. Their master would then call them dolts and blockheads, saying that he would rather hear reports on these strange countries and their customs and usages than the official business on which he had sent them. When Marco went on his mission he was well aware of this, and he paid close attention to all the novelties and curiosities that came his way, so that he could describe them to the Great Khan. When he returned he presented himself to the Khan and started with a full account of the business on which he had been sent – he had accomplished it well. Then he went on to describe all the remarkable things he had seen on the journey, in such detail that the Khan and all those who heard him were amazed and said to each other: 'If this young man lives to reach full manhood, he will certainly prove himself a man of sound judgment and worth.' Need I go on? From then on the young man was called Messer Marco Polo; and so he will be called throughout this book. And with good reason, for he was a man of experience and discretion.

From the prologue to Description of the World *by Marco Polo, c. 1300.*

THE MONGOL PRINCE ARGHUN *sends an ambassador to the West.*

In 1285 Arghun wrote to Pope Honorius IV to suggest common action [against the Moslems], but he received no answer. Two years later he decided to send an embassy to the West, and he chose as his ambassador Mar Yahbhallaha's friend Rabban Sauma. The ambassador, who wrote a vivid account of his mission, set out early in 1287. Sailing from Trebizond, he reached Constantinople about Easter-time. He was cordially received by the Emperor Andronicus and visited Saint Sophia and the other great shrines of the Imperial city. Andronicus was already on excellent terms with the Mongols and was ready to help them as far as his dwindling resources allowed. From Constantinople Rabban Sauma went to Naples, arriving there at the end of June. While he was there he saw a sea battle in the harbour between the Aragonese and the Neapolitan fleets. It was his first indication that western Europe was preoccupied with its own squabbles. He rode on to Rome. There he found that Pope Honorius had just died, and the conclave to elect his successor had not yet assembled. The twelve Cardinals who were resident in Rome received him, but he found them ignorant and unhelpful. They knew nothing of the spread of Christianity among the Mongols and were shocked that he should serve a heathen master. When he tried to discuss politics, they cross-questioned him about his faith and criticized its divergencies from their own. In the end he almost lost his temper. He had come, he said, to pay his respects to the Pope, and to make plans for the future, not to hold a debate on the Creed.

From A History of the Crusades: Volume III – The Kingdom of Acre and the later Crusades *by Steven Runciman (Cambridge University Press, Cambridge, 1954).*

FERNÃO MENDES PINTO, a Portuguese trader, soldier of fortune and diplomatic envoy, arrives in Japan as one of the first western visitors in 1556 but finds the Japanese Prince – to whom he wishes to present letters from the Portuguese Viceroy in the Far East – is engaged in a rather improbable sport.

We set out from Funai and at nine o'clock the next morning we came to a place called Fingau, which is about a quarter of a league from the fort at Usuki. Through one of the Japanese escorts I told the oskim, the local commander, how I had got there and that I was part of an embassy from the Viceroy of the Portuguese Far East to the Daimyo [prince] of Bungo. I asked him to find out when the daimyo would want to meet me. The oskim replied straightaway through his son:

'Your arrival, and the arrival of all your companions, is most welcome. I have already sent a messenger to the daimyo who left with a large crowd of people for the island of Saiki yesterday to hunt and kill a gigantic fish, the likes of which we didn't know existed, which has come inshore from the middle of the ocean to feed on a huge shoal of little fish. Now they have it trapped in the bar-mouth and I'd say that the daimyo won't be back here today, unless he arrives after dark.

'Now, if I hear from the daimyo, I will send word to you

41

straightaway. In the meantime I will arrange some good lodging where you can stay and relax and take it easy. You will be provided with everything you need because the King of Portugal himself should feel as much at home in Bungo as he would in his colonies of Malacca, Cochin and Goa!'

Then one of the kamsiu's men, who had been appointed for the task, brought us to a pagoda called Amidam-shu, where we were treated splendidly by the bonzes.

As soon as the daimyo received the news of my arrival he despatched three funces – which are small boats with sails and oars – from the island where they were hunting the great fish. On board one of the funces was one of the daimyo's ministers, one of his court favourites, called Oretandono, who came to the house where I was staying that afternoon.

After we had been introduced he told me why the daimyo had sent him and then took out a letter from inside his robe. He kissed the letter with all the ceremony and courtesy that these people habitually use and then handed it to me. The letter ran as follows:

'Sir, I have been informed of your safe arrival at Fingau but at the moment I am occupied with the sort of business I enjoy very much. However, let me assure you that I am so happy to hear of your arrival that if I had not already sworn to stay here until I have cornered and killed this enormous fish then I would go to meet you myself without delay.

'So now I beg you as a friend that, since I cannot go there to meet you for the reasons I have mentioned, you should come here at once in the boats I have sent to bring you, because your arrival here, and the killing of this fish, will make my satisfaction complete.'

As soon as I had read the letter I set out with my companions, sailing in one funce with Oretandono while our slaves and the gifts for the daimyo came in the other two boats. These funces are very light and swift and in little more than an hour we had reached the island where the daimyo was hunting, which was two and a half leagues away from Fingau.

When we arrived there the daimyo and more than two hundred other men, armed with harpoons, were in sloops chasing a big whale that had followed an enormous shoal of fish into the shore.

The whale was a novelty and a marvel to the Japanese, who had never seen the like of it before.

When the whale had finally been killed and dragged ashore the daimyo's pleasure was so great that all the local fishermen were freed from a tribute they had always had to pay to him and he also gave them titles of nobility; he increased the salaries of some of his favoured noblemen and he ordered the geishos, who are gentlemen-in-waiting, to be given one thousand taels of silver each (which is fifteen hundred cruzados).

So the daimyo received me with a broad smile on his face and then asked me detailed questions about all sorts of things. My answers to some of these questions were embroidered a little because I thought it was necessary for the sake of our reputation and to preserve the high esteem in which the Japanese had held Portugal up until then. At that time they thought the King of Portugal alone could truthfully call himself the King of the World, on account of his lands, his power and his treasure, which explains why our friendship was considered to be so important by the Daimyo of Bungo.

From The Peregrination of Fernão Mendes Pinto *translated by Michael Lowery*
(The Carcanet Press, Manchester, 1992).

ANTHONY JENKINSON, trader and envoy of Elizabeth I of England, describes Christmas day dinner in 1557 with Ivan the Terrible in Moscow.

The 25th day, being the day of the nativitie, I came into the Emperour's presence, and kissed his hand, who sate aloft in a goodly chaire of estate, having on his heade a crowne most richly decked, and a staffe of gold in his hand, all apparelled with golde, and garnished with precious stones.

There sate distant from him about two yardes his brother, and next unto him a boy of twelve yeares of age, who was inheritor to the Emperor of Casan, conquered by this Emperor 8 yeares past. Then sate his nobilitie round about him, richly apparelled with gold and stone. And after I had done obeisance to the Emperour, he with his own mouth calling me by my name, bade me to dinner, and so I departed to my lodging till dinner time, which was at sixe of the clocke, by candle light.

The Emperour dined in a fayre great hall, in the midst whereof was a pillar foure square, very artificially made, about which were divers tables set, and at the uppermost part of the hall, sate the Emperour himselfe, & at his table sate his brother, his Uncle's sonne, the Metropolitane, the young Emperour of Casan, and divers of his noble men, all of one side. There were divers Ambassadors, & other strangers, as well Christians as heathens, diversly apparelled, to the number of 600 men, which dined in the sayd hall, besides 2000 Tartars, men of warre, which were newly come to render themselves to the Emperour, & were appointed to serve him in his wars against the Lieflanders, but they dined in other hals. I was set at a little table, having no stranger with me, directly before the Emperor's face. Being thus set and placed, the Emperour sent me divers bowles of wine, and meade, & many dishes of meat from his own hand, which were brought me by a Duke, and my table served all in gold and silver, and so likewise on other tables, there were set bowles of gold, set with stone, worth by estimation 400 pounds sterling one cup, besides the plate which served the tables.

There was also a cupbord of plate, most sumptuous and rich, which was not used: among the which, was a piece of golde of two yardes long, wrought in the toppe with towers, and dragons' heads, also divers barrels of gold and silver, with Castles on the bungs, richly and artificially made. The Emperour and all the hall throughout was served with Dukes: and when dinner was ended, the Emperour called me by name, & gave me drinke with his own hand, & so I departed to my lodging.

Note, that when the Emperour drinketh, all the company stand up, and at every time he drinketh or tasteth of a dish of meate he blesseth himselfe. Many other things I sawe that day, not here noted.

From Hakluyt's Collection of the Early Voyages, Travels and Discoveries of the English Nation *(R.H. Evans, London, 1809).*

SIR THOMAS ROE, Ambassador of King James I of England to the Great Mogul of India, experiences problems in exchanging gifts with his host.

Early in his stay at the Mogul court at Ajmer in India, Sir Thomas Roe recorded in his journal that the emperor Jahangir clearly 'supposes our felicity lies in the palate' as all the emperor's presents to him – such as the flesh of wild boar and elk that he had killed on hunting expeditions – were edible.

Soon, however, Jahangir proved him wrong by sending other presents, no longer edible but much more embarrassing. First, a male slave who had been convicted of theft but who was considered too handsome and valuable to execute; and then a female slave. When the latter was delivered, Roe recorded in his journal: 'The officers would take no refusal, having command to deliver her to myself, that I was enforced to let one come into my bedside with her . . . I demanded her fault. The officer answered the king bade him assure me she was honest, only she had offended the women.'

But worse than the nature of the gifts he sent to Roe was the way the emperor behaved in respect of the gifts which Roe had brought, on behalf of James I, for Jahangir. A lot of thought had gone into the collection and transportation of these. They included a number of mastiffs and Irish greyhounds. One of the mastiffs had already distinguished itself by attacking a large elephant and hanging on to its trunk while the elephant thrashed the ground with it; this had immensely impressed the Indians, who had never seen such a formidable dog before. Roe had looked forward to making a considerable sensation when he presented them to the emperor.

His chagrin was therefore undisguised when he found that Jahangir had confiscated all his presents and helped himself to them without waiting to be given them. He had even appropriated Roe's own hat. Roe therefore sought an audience with the emperor, who 'began to tell me he had taken divers things that pleased him extremely well . . . and desired me not to be discontent for whatsoever I would not give him I should receive back. I answered that . . . I took it a great discourtesy to my sovereign.' Jahangir then went on to say that even if Roe was now left empty-handed, he would be equally pleased to see him, for it was not his fault that he had no presents left.

Finally, the vexed question of the exchange of gifts ended happily. Jahangir was so delighted with the remaining mastiffs that he allocated them four attendants each to carry them around in palanquins and keep the flies off them – when they were not attacking elephants or enemies of the emperor. And Roe managed to pass on the unwanted slave girl without offence. But as so often in later diplomatic life, exchanging presents had proved a potential minefield.

Compiled by the editor from The Journals of Sir Thomas Roe
(The Hakluyt Society, London, 1899).

ALEXANDER BURNES, a young Indian Army officer seconded to the political service, was sent as a diplomatic envoy from the government of British India to King Dost Mohammed of Afghanistan in 1837. As his task was to consolidate Afghan links with Britain rather than with her powerful northern neighbour – Russia – Burnes was disconcerted by the arrival in Kabul of a Russian emissary – Captain Vitkevich. Here Burnes finds that his professional principles result in his missing a chance to do down his diplomatic opponent.

When Vitkevich first arrived in Kabul, . . . Burnes's star was still very much in the ascendant at the Bala Hissar [the King's palace]. The Russian officer's reception had been cool and unceremonious, as Simonich [the Russian Ambassador in Persia] had warned him it would be. Indeed, at first he had been kept under virtual house arrest, Dost Mohammed even consulting Burnes over the authenticity of his credentials. Had Vitkevich really been sent by the Tsar, he asked, and was the letter from the Russian Emperor genuine? He had sent it round to Burnes's quarters for his inspection, aware no doubt that a copy of it would, within the hour, be on its way to Lord Auckland in Calcutta. It was at this point, Masson [a British renegade living in Kabul] was to claim afterwards, that Burnes made a cardinal error, allowing integrity to overrule expediency.

Convinced that the letter, which turned out to be little more than a message of goodwill, was indeed from Tsar Nicholas, Burnes

46

said as much to Dost Mohammed. Masson, on the other hand, was convinced that it was a forgery, and that it had been composed by Simonich, or perhaps even by Vitkevich himself, to give the Russian mission more weight in its trial of strength with the British. When Burnes pointed to the impressive-looking imperial Russian seal it bore, Masson sent a messenger to the bazaar to buy a packet of Russian sugar – 'at the bottom of which', he claimed, 'we found precisely the same kind of seal'. But by then, Masson added, it was too late. Burnes had thrown away his one and only chance of spiking his rival's guns by not allowing the Afghans – as Masson sardonically put it – 'the benefit of their doubts'.

From The Great Game *by Peter Hopkirk (John Murray, London, 1990).*

SIR RICHARD BURTON, the eminent Victorian explorer, was probably the most unconventional figure ever to adorn the British consular service. In Brazil he took months away from his post to travel the length of the São Francisco river; and in Syria he abandoned the Consulate-General at Damascus to make long camel expeditions with the Bedouin into the desert. On one of these his wife accompanied him, and here describes the scene.

I can never forget some of those lovely nights in the desert . . . mules, donkeys, camels, horses, and mares picketed about, screaming, kicking, and halloaing; the stacked loads, the big fires, the black tents, the Turkish soldiers, the picturesque figures in every garb, and the wild and fierce-looking men in wonderful costumes lying here and there, singing and dancing barbarous dances . . . Richard reciting the Arabian Nights, or poor Palmer chanting Arab poetry, or Charley Drake practising magic to astonish the Mogharibehs . . .

I have seen the gravest and most reverend Shayks rolling on the ground and screaming with delight, in spite of their Oriental gravity, and they seemed as if they could never let my husband go again.

From Life of Captain Sir Richard F. Burton *by Isabel Burton (London, 1893).*

LORD CURZON, travelling as a young Member of Parliament in 1890 to improve his knowledge of the East, encounters difficulties with the Turkish customs officials.

At the very outset of the journey, however, the care with which Curzon had packed his equipment and provisions was frustrated by the Turkish customs officials at Constantinople. On his arrival there from Paris by the Orient express, not even the possession of a diplomatic courier's red passport saved him from the indignity of having every piece of his baggage opened and searched. What particularly aroused Turkish suspicions were boxes full of watches and other trinkets intended as presents for the local potentates Curzon would meet on his travels. His protests that he was a Member of Parliament were brushed aside with scorn. As a commercial traveller in cheap jewellery, he was told, he would have to pay the usual duty in full – an imposition from which he was saved only by the arrival of the Embassy *Kavass* [guard]. He described the episode to Margot Tennant.

> They tore out all my things packed for Persian travel; they swore the saddle was a new one; they crashed into my Liebig soups; they ravished my chocolate; they made me pay special duty on my Waterbury watches, taken out to conciliate respectable Persian Khans. They made me swear, anathematise, curse, blaspheme, condemn them to a thousand hells of eternal fire; and after over an hour of this they let me go panting, lacerated, foaming, unsubdued. As I think of it now I still consign them in my choicest vocabulary to the concentrated flames of a thousand Gehennas.
>
> From Superior Person *by Kenneth Rose (Weidenfeld & Nicolson, London, 1969).*

VICE-CONSUL WRATISLAW, at the outset of a colourful and distinguished career in the (British) Levant Consular Service in 1885, finds himself exploring the hinterland of Macedonia rather more extensively than he had intended, and encountering unexpected hazards.

At this time the shooting round Salonica was quite good, but it was considered dangerous to go out alone, even in the immediate vicinity of the town. The district had a very bad reputation for brigandage, and within the last five years two Englishmen had been carried off and held to ransom. To secure their life and liberty the British Government was compelled to pay £12,000 for one and rather more for the other; and though such captures were almost always the result of deep-laid plans, and the casual one-day excursionist was unlikely to be involved, the countryside was full of bad characters quite ready to murder a sportsman for the sake of his gun and the little money he might have on him, and one only ventured out shooting in parties.

Mr Blunt [the British Consul] got up one of these excursions a month or so after I reached Salonica, which might have ended in disaster to me. We left by carriage early in the morning, drove for a dozen miles, and then proceeded to form line and beat the country. About midday, in pursuit of a covey of partridges in thickish cover, I foolishly allowed myself to get separated from the rest, lost all sense of direction, and before long was as completely lost as a babe in the wood. I did not even know the name of the village where the carriages were left, and had I known it there was not a soul to be seen from whom the way could be asked. The Bay of Salonica was visible in the far distance, and it seemed best to make my way home across country, which I proceeded to do. Two or three miles farther on I came across an Albanian sheepfold, and endeavoured to avoid it by making a detour, but two dogs attached thereto came after me, evidently meaning business. These Albanian sheep-dogs are sufficiently large and savage at any time, but to me in my forlorn condition they appeared of the size of elephants and the ferocity of lions. They got up to me and attacked, one on each side, without uttering a sound, which made their serious intentions all the more apparent. I had not even time to shoulder my gun, but shot one

49

from the hip, with the muzzle almost touching him. The other followed me howling.

Short as had been my sojourn in Salonica, I had already been warned of the awful results of killing these dogs – how their owners would sometimes exact a life for a life, and how the least one could expect was to be severely beaten and pay a heavy fine, calculated in the following way. The defunct was held up by his tail with his nose touching the ground, and corn poured over him until he was completely covered, the value of the corn required for this being the measure of the damages exacted. This had actually happened to a French Consul two or three years before, and who was I to escape when a Consul had succumbed?

From A Consul in the East *by A.C. Wratislaw, CB, CMG, CBE*
(William Blackwood & Sons, Edinburgh, 1924).

LORD CURZON, normally the most punctiliously correct of British grandees abroad, adopts a somewhat bizarre attire for his audience with the Emir of Afghanistan. Although travelling in a private capacity, he was determined to appear important.

Before leaving England that summer [Curzon] had given meticulous care even to the clothes in which he should present himself at the Afghan capital. In 1893, when calling on the King of Korea, he had merely donned the drab blue civil uniform which he was entitled to wear as a former Under-Secretary at the India Office, and had been disappointed at the mediocre figure he cut. Later he recalled how an official of the Indian Political Department engaged on a Boundary Commission in Afghan Turkestan had been received with much deference after having a very broad gold stripe sewn on his trousers and girding a formidable sword at his waist. Curzon likewise decided that if he too were to produce a suitably startling effect in Kabul, he must dispense with the dress regulations laid down by the Lord Chamberlain at St James's Palace.

First he called at Nathan's, the theatrical costumiers in London, and for a modest sum hired a cluster of gorgeous stars of foreign orders, mostly from the smaller States of Eastern Europe. To these he added an enormous pair of gold epaulettes in a case the size of a hat-box. In Bombay he ordered a glittering pair of patent leather Wellington top boots. And while staying with General Sir William Lockhart at his headquarters at Abbottabad, en route for Afghanistan, he borrowed a gigantic curved sword with ivory hilt and engraved scabbard which had been presented to Lockhart in honour of a successful campaign. Someone produced a cocked hat, someone else a pair of handsome spurs, and his baggage was complete.

It was in more workmanlike clothes that Curzon left Peshawar for the ride of 180 miles to Kabul. He crossed the frontier by the Khyber Pass and was met by an escort of seventy men. The Amir had also given orders for relays of horses to await his guest along the route, thus enabling him to maintain an exceptionally high average of twenty-seven miles a day. A little way outside the walls of the capital, a tent had been pitched so that he could change into his ceremonial dress. But it was only after an hour's furtive work with needle and thread that he managed to sew the massive golden epaulettes on to his shoulders. Finally attired in all his splendour, and with an escort that had now grown to 200, he rode into the town and was conducted to the Durbar Hall of the Amir. There was a moment of embarrassment when the Amir asked Curzon for what services or exploits he had received such a galaxy of orders and decorations. 'To these inconvenient queries,' he wrote, 'I could only return the most general and deprecatory replies.' The Amir did not press the point. Apparently satisfied with the social standing of his guest – the only private person he had ever invited to Kabul – he installed him in the most sumptuous suite of his palace.

From Superior Person *by Kenneth Rose (Weidenfeld & Nicolson, London, 1969).*

SIR FITZROY MACLEAN, as a young Secretary at the British Embassy in Moscow in the 1930s, travelled overland through Russian Central Asia to Afghanistan. On the return journey, via Iranian Azerbaijan, he finds himself suspended between two countries.

After some two or three hours we emerged from the light red mountains of Iran into the valley of the Araxes. This marks the frontier between Iran and the Soviet Union and also, in theory at any rate, between Europe and Asia. Far away beyond the Araxes rose the black wall of the Caucasus.

The Customs formalities on the Iranian side did not take long and I soon found myself standing with my two bundles half way across the bridge which crosses the Araxes at this point. I shouted to the sentry at the Soviet end, explaining that I was anxious to enter the Soviet Union. He did not reply, but looked rather pointedly down the barrel of his rifle. After half an hour of more or less continuous shouting neither he nor the frontier guards on the far bank had shown any signs of departing from their hostile attitude. One of the Iranian sentries, who for some reason spoke Italian, said that the frontier seemed to be shut, and advised me to keep away from the Soviet end of the bridge as they did not want a frontier incident. He only wished he could let me return to Persia, but that was unfortunately impossible. It was cold and wet and I had had enough of hovering in uncertainty between Europe and Asia and was trying to devise some safe means of shaking the Soviet sentry's composure, when a car drove up on the Soviet bank of the river and an officer got out who, after a certain amount of parleying, said reluctantly that I might come across, though it would have been better if I could have waited till next day.

I was back in the Soviet Union.

From Eastern Approaches *by Fitzroy Maclean (Jonathan Cape, London, 1949).*

THE EDITOR, while Third Secretary at the British Embassy in Moscow in 1958, makes a crossing of the Soviet–Iranian frontier at the same point as Sir Fitzroy Maclean (in the previous entry) but in the opposite direction and exactly twenty years later; he finds that the hazards of the journey have not diminished.

There are constant reminders that this has always been a frontier area: beside the new wooden watchtowers, regularly spaced and manned with machine-gunners, stand, as often as not, the relics of some former stone or mud tower. The passionate spirit of the frontier-man is indigenous also: a whiskered warrior who invited me to drink to the hackneyed Soviet toast of Friendship ('Druzhba') gave it a local twist by adding, 'This means thy kin will not spill the blood of mine, nor mine of thine'.

But behind the enthusiasm and the bravado, frontier vigilance was a serious matter. MVD patrols with tracker dogs ranged the banks of the River Araxes (which marks the frontier); double rows of barbed wire and a harrowed strip (presumably mined) followed the railway line; armed frontier-guards stood at every door of the train watching for anyone jumping on or off it. At two points – one near Nakhichevan and one near Julfa – where there were Iranian dwellings visible across the river, the Russians had hoisted loudspeakers above the wire and (I was told by the Iranians) broadcast subversive and provocative propaganda directly across the frontier. In Soviet Julfa an officer explained these loudspeakers as being 'for warning purposes' . . . and complained that the Iranians shot at them from time to time. The frontier was practically a front line.

I crossed the frontier at Julfa, or, it would be more accurate to say, between two Julfas, for the Soviet and Iranian villages are divided by a mile of wire, mine-fields and river. There is no telephone between the two and, if there were, it would be of doubtful use since I heard of no one in either village who spoke the other's language. I was escorted by an officer and an armed bodyguard, through the minefields and wire, to the wooden bridge across the Araxes, where the Iranian authorities vented their spleen on the Soviets by keeping us waiting on the exposed bridge in the midday sun for 70 minutes before sending down troops to receive me.

Entering Iranian Julfa, the contrast is immediate. Whereas

Soviet Julfa was a trim little 20th-century village with metalled roads and good brick houses, Iranian Julfa is a ramshackle conglomeration of baked mud houses, dust roads, barking dogs and screaming children which might have belonged to any century. . . . But the Iranian garrison commander received me with a degree of courtesy which I had not met with in any Soviet official in 18 months, introduced me to his wife and family, told his 11-year-old daughter to dance for me, gave me refreshments and invited me to stay.

I declined his offer and, as there was no train for 24 hours, asked his help in finding transport to Tabriz. Eventually a jeep was found, mended and put at my disposal, together with a driver whose recklessness forced me to take over from him. It was already nearly dark when we eventually set out for the five-hour drive over the unmetalled, precarious and lonely mountain road to Tabriz. It was not an uneventful drive. At one point we were pursued and stopped by a mobile Iranian frontier patrol. Two jeep-loads of soldiers, armed with an assortment of weapons, surrounded us and searched us. The situation was not alleviated by my driver describing me (I later discovered) as 'a traveller from Moscow'. The patrol was only finally convinced that I was not a Soviet agent after I had produced such evidences of my nationality as a British passport, a tin of Players and a bottle of Scotch. (The last was most readily understood.)

From a report by Mr John Ure, Third Secretary in Chancery at the British Embassy in Moscow, to the Foreign Office in London in 1958.

3

Diplomats in Danger

NOTHING COULD BE further from the truth today than the conventional image of a diplomat as one who leads a pampered and protected life exclusively in the elegant drawing rooms of sophisticated capital cities. The news media have revealed for all to see the dangers inherent in arbitrating between warring factions in disagreeable corners of the Third World, and in facing kidnap or assassination anywhere from Dublin to Beirut.

But diplomacy was never a particularly safe profession. Leaving aside the risks always associated with travel – ranging from highway robbery to dubiously-serviced local airlines – there are risks peculiar to diplomatic missions. Embassies are a natural focus for the anger of street mobs when relations between the 'host' nation and the 'guest' embassy deteriorate; local police forces are – sometimes by intent – not always prompt to provide the necessary protection or relief force. (I myself well recall being present – and injured – when the Chancery of the British Embassy in Leopoldville was sacked by a violent Congolese mob in 1962 before UN forces could come to our rescue.)

When war breaks out, diplomats resident in enemy countries are supposed to be returned home, often with the assistance of neutral neighbours. But in practice this is seldom a smooth or swift process – as Sir Horace Rumbold discovered in 1914, and as many others have before and since. However improper it may be, there is in the minds of many tyrants an element of the hostage in the very concept of a resident ambassador.

Sometimes diplomats become emotionally involved in personalities or policies in the country where they are serving and court their own danger – like the Swedish quasi-diplomatic Count Fersen, who harboured an affection for Queen Marie Antoinette which led him into performing Pimpernel-like enterprises on her behalf during the French Revolution. Sometimes they are falsely accused of scheming for the destruction of their hosts and – like Bruce Lockhart during the Russian Revolution – arrested and threatened with death, rather then being mildly declared *persona non grata*.

Perhaps the classic case of the whole diplomatic corps in one place being simultaneously threatened with extinction was the Boxer Rebellion in China in 1900. The account of the siege of the legations at Peking on that occasion reads like the reports, half a century before, of the siege of Lucknow during the Indian Mutiny. In both cases the plight of the garrison and the savagery of the assailants forged a strong camaraderie within the compounds; but in the case of Peking the defendants had in common not one nationality but one international profession – diplomacy.

ANTHONY JENKINSON, trader and envoy of Elizabeth I of England, risks starvation, robbery and murder among the Tartars round the Caspian Sea.

Wherefore the 3rd day of September 1558 we discharged our barke, and I with my companie were gently entertained of the Prince & of his people. But before our departure from thence, we found them to be very bad and brutish people, for they ceased not daily to molest us, either by fighting, stealing or begging, raising the price of horse and camels, & victuals, double that it was woont there to be, and forced us to buy the water that we did drinke: which caused us to hasten away, and to conclude with them as well for the hire of camels, as for the price of such as wee bought, with other provision, according to their owne demaund: So that for every camel's lading, being but 400-waight of ours, we agreed to give three hides of Russia, and foure woodden dishes, and to the Prince or governour of the sayd people, one ninth, and two sevenths: Namely, nine severall things, and twise seven severall things: for money they use none.

And thus being ready, the fourteenth of September we departed from that place, being a Caravan of a thousand camels. And having travailed five dayes journey, we came to another Prince's Dominion, and upon the way there came unto us certaine Tartars on horseback, being well armed, and servants unto the saide Prince called Timor Soltan, governour of the said countrey of Manguslaue, where wee meant to have arrived and discharged our barke, if the great storm aforesayd had not disappointed. These aforesaid Tartars stayd our Caravan in the name of their Prince, and opened our wares, and tooke such things as they thought best for their saide prince without money, but for such things as they tooke from me, which was a ninth (after much dissension) I ridde unto the same Prince, and presented my selfe before him, requesting his favour, and pasport to travaile through his countrey, and not to be robbed nor spoiled of his people: which request he graunted me, and intertained me very gently, commaunding me to be well feasted with flesh and mares' milke: for bread they use none, nor other drinke except water: but money he had none to give mee for such things as he tooke of mee, which might be of value in Russe money, fifteene rubbles, but he gave me his letter, and a horse woorth seven rubbles. And so I departed from him being glad that I was gone: for he was reported to be a very tyrant, and if I had not gone unto him, I understoode his commaundement was, that I should have beene robbed and destroyed.

This Soltan lived in the fieldes without Castle or towne, and sate, at my being with him, in a litle rounde house made of reedes covered without with felt, and within with Carpets. There was with him the great Metropolitan of that wilde Country, esteemed of the people, as the Bishop of Rome is in most parts of Europe, with divers other of his chiefe men. The Soltan with this Metropolitan demanded of me many questions, as wel touching our kingdoms, lawes, and Religion, as also the cause of my comming into those

57

parts, with my further pretence. To whom I answered concerning all things, as unto me seemed best, which they tooke in good part. So having leave I departed and overtooke our Caravan, and proceeded on our journey, and travailed 20 dayes in the wildernes from the sea side without seeing towne of habitation, carying provision of victuals with us for the same time, and were driven by necessity to eate one of my camels and a horse for our part, as other did the like: and during the said 20 daies we found no water, but such as we drew out of old deepe welles, being very brackish and salt, and yet sometimes passed two or three dayes without the same. And the 5th day of October ensuing, we came unto a gulfe of the Caspian sea againe, where we found that water very fresh and sweete: at this gulfe the customers of the king of Turkeman met us, who tooke custome of every 25th one, and 7 ninthes for the saide king and his brethren, which being received they departed, and we remained there a day after to refresh our selves.

From Hakluyt's Collection of the Early Voyages, Travels and Discoveries of the English Nation *(R.H. Evans, London, 1809).*

SIR JAMES HARRIS, who was later to become the first Earl of Malmesbury, was one of the great diplomatists of the late eighteenth century; he had won the confidence – and some said the affections – of Catherine the Great of Russia, was an intimate gambling friend of Charles James Fox and was, surprisingly in the circumstances, appointed Minister to the Dutch United Provinces by Pitt. In 1787 the 'Patriots', who supported the French rather than the British alignment of the United Provinces, were in the ascendant and Harris found himself deeply involved and in a tight corner.

The Patriots were not by now capable of any very sober calculations. Their mounting excitement in the towns they controlled threatened dire revenge on their opponents. This was true even at the Hague, now surrounded by the Free Corps, and in a situation, Harris said, like that of Paris at the time of the Fronde. He had sent his family to England for safety and foresaw a grim fate when the Patriots took matters into their own hands. 'If I am *de* witted', he wrote to Carmarthen [the British Foreign Secretary], 'don't let me be *out* witted but revenge me.' His house became the centre of resistance. People of all ranks flocked to him for protection and advice. He destroyed all his cyphers, except the latest one, which he kept ready to burn at a moment's notice, and left no scrap of paper that could implicate either the British Government or any of its friends. He supplied money for arming his supporters in the Hague, and having to keep his house constantly open as a rendezvous, asked for his appointments to be raised from £70 to £100 a week to cover his additional expenses.

He never for a moment thought of quitting the Hague, where his presence, he said, gave confidence to his friends. 'They think the danger less from my being disposed to share it with them; for they reckon, and perhaps very truly, that our antagonists, if driven to despair, will not pay any great respect to the immunities due to a Foreign Minister.' Indeed, some of the Orangists [the pro-British faction] were so panic-stricken that they would not have let him go if they could have stopped him. He advised the preparation of a last foothold, or place of refuge, . . . which was protected by wide branches of the estuary and garrisoned by 900 Swiss and 300 armed Orangist burghers. . . . the Burgomaster promised to defend the town to the last, provided that he was sure of not being abandoned by England, and Harris calculated that it could hold out for two months with the aid of a subsidy of 30,000 florins. As the money was slow in arriving from London he borrowed it on his own private account and had it conveyed secretly to the town by Count Charles Bentinck.

> From Ambassadors and Secret Agents: the Diplomacy of the first Earl of Malmesbury at the Hague *by Alfred Cobban (Jonathan Cape, London, 1954).*

COUNT HANS AXEL VON FERSEN, the Swedish soldier, courtier and diplomat, plays an active and hazardous role in the escape of Louis XVI and Marie Antoinette from the Tuileries in 1791.

Meanwhile Fersen had donned a coachman's livery, and mounting the box of a hackney coach had driven to the Cour des Princes, outside the Tuileries. It was about a quarter-past ten when he took up his position among the line of other cabs. So good was his disguise that his fellow cabbies did not doubt but that he was one of them. His heart was aching with suspense, but he played his part gallantly, cracking jokes and taking snuff with his 'mates' and chatting to them in their dialect.

At about 10.30 the Queen took her children by the hand and led them into an empty room overlooking a courtyard. After waiting some time a tall man, muffled in a big overcoat, with a hat clapped over his eyes, entered, and silently taking the little Dauphin by the hand led him out into the courtyard. The child was not frightened, for he recognised in the tall silent man the friend who was always so kind to him – M. de Fersen. The Queen followed, with her daughter and Mme de Tourzel. It was a bright moonlight night, and the little party carefully crept in the shadow of the carriages that were drawn up along the wall. All except the Queen got safely into the hackney coach: she stole back to the palace.

The 'coachman' mounted the box, cracked his whip and drove them off. Madame Royale writes: 'To throw people off the scent we made several turns in Paris, and returned to the Petit Carrousel, near the Tuileries, to wait for my father and mother. My brother was lying at the bottom of the carriage under Mme de Tourzel's gown. We saw M. de Lafayette pass close by us, going to the King's *coucher*. We waited there a full hour in the greatest impatience and uneasiness at my parents' long delay.'

Their Majesties retired to bed as usual a little after eleven that night. The King went through all the usual ceremony of the *coucher*. Lafayette was present, and the King made valiant efforts to keep up a conversation with him, though it was manifest he was nervous, and preoccupied. It was observed that he went constantly to the window to see what the weather was like. The ceremony over, and all his visitors dismissed, he slipped into his private bedroom and got into bed. His valet drew the bed-curtains and went into an adjoining room to undress previous to going to bed in the King's room.

This was Louis' opportunity. Springing softly out of bed, he carefully drew the bed-curtains and slipped into the Dauphin's empty room. From there he reached the Queen's *entresol*, where he found his disguise for the journey – a large round hat, a grey wig, a brown coat, and a bottle-green overcoat with mother-of-pearl buttons.

The valet meanwhile re-entered the bedroom and went to sleep, never dreaming that his master was not safe and asleep in bed.

Fersen was waiting with his hackney coach in the Petit Carrousel. It was the most anxious hour of his life. He whistled and chatted with the other cabbies, but his soul was sick with suspense. From time to time he got down from his box and walked round the cab as if to examine the horses, but in reality to keep a look-out for the fugitives.

'After waiting for one hour,' writes Madame Royale, 'I saw a woman approach and walk round our carriage. It made me fear we were discovered, but I was soon reassured by seeing the coachman open the carriage door to admit my aunt . . . On entering the carriage she trod upon my brother, who was hidden at the bottom of it; he had the courage not to utter a cry. She assured us that all was quiet at Court, and that my father and mother would soon come. In fact, the King came almost immediately.'

The King seemed very uneasy at not finding the Queen in the carriage. As time went on and she did not appear, he began to fear an accident had happened. It was all the others could do to prevent him from going back to the palace to look for her. At last Marie Antoinette arrived, all breathless from her adventures. She had met Lafayette on his way from the *coucher*, and she had had to shrink into a corner to avoid being seen by him. Also she had missed her way somehow, and it had taken some time to retrace her steps. The King took her in his arms and kissed her tenderly. 'How glad I am to see you here!' he repeated.

They all kissed each other, overjoyed at finding themselves together again . . . Then the coach set off at a brisk pace in the direction of the Porte St Martin.

Madame Royale writes: 'Nothing happened till we reached the barrier, where we were to find the post carriage which was there to take us on. M. de Fersen did not know exactly where it would be; we were obliged to wait a rather long time, and my father got out, which made us uneasy. At last M. de Fersen came with the other carriage, into which we got.'

Having safely installed the Royal family in the *berline*, Fersen seized the horses of the first carriage by their bits and forced them into the ditch. Of course the cab overturned. Fersen smiled quietly as he said, 'When the good people here get up tomorrow morning they will see there has been an accident.' It was now between one and two o'clock.

Fersen mounted the box by the side of Balthazar Sapel, who took the reins. Speed was now the one thing needful. Every moment was precious; every inch of ground covered was a gain.

Balthazar Sapel did not make his horses go fast enough to please Fersen. 'Go on! go on! drive quickly,' he kept on urging, as he cracked the long whip he held. 'Balthazar! your horses are no good! Speed them on! They will have plenty of time to rest soon.'

Fersen knew that in *speed* now lay the only chance of success, and he was burning with a fever of impatience to get the coach on – on! At last the lumbering *berline* and the steaming horses arrived at Bondy, the first stopping-place on the route. Day had just dawned. The early morning light was cold and grey. Fersen and his coachman alighted from the box. The six relay horses stood in readiness in the courtyard of the inn.

The next stage of the drama was about to begin. Fersen had played his part and was now to make his exit. He approached the door of the coach. His eyes shone with a strange light; his voice was very quiet, but it shook a little. The good King, grasping his hand, thanked him for all that he had done, and expressed his hope of soon being able to give him a practical proof of his gratitude. 'We shall soon meet again, I hope, Monsieur le Comte,' he added. The Queen's heart was too full for words. She gave her friend a long understanding look of deep gratitude, and he read the message. The coachman cracked his whip, and they were off.

From A Queen's Knight: the life of Count Axel de Fersen *by Mildred Carnegy (Mills & Boon, London, 1912).*

This same COUNT FERSEN, after his early adventures in France, eventually became Marshal of the Realm in his own country of Sweden where he met an unhappy end, being lynched by a mob on the streets of Stockholm, as is here recounted by a member of the diplomatic corps in that city.

It was in consequence of the death of the young Prince of Holstein-Augustenburg, that Bernadotte had been chosen as Crown Prince of Sweden, and successor to Charles XIII, the childless King.

The Prince of Holstein-Augustenburg died of sun-stroke at a review in Pomerania, and when his body was brought back to be buried at Stockholm, a report was spread that Count Fersen, who had accompanied him to Pomerania, had poisoned him. Consequently, as the funeral crossed the Norrbro, the populace fell on the poor man and literally tore him to pieces. Umbrellas, sticks, and legs of chairs were hurled at him, and all this in sight of the Guards, who never moved to help him. They even wanted to wreak their vengeance on his sister, Countess Piper, who had to fly for her life; and whilst crossing the lake in a boat she heard from the rowers that they were in pursuit of her. She had been bedridden for many years, but the fright restored the use of her limbs, and she lay concealed at Steninge, where her brother's tenantry were faithful to her.

> From Old Days in Diplomacy, *the memoirs of the eldest daughter of Sir Edward Cromwell Disbrowe, GCG (Jarrold & Sons, London, 1903).*

EMMA HAMILTON, wife of Sir William Hamilton, Ambassador to the Court of Naples, writes to the Hon. Charles Greville describing her heroic efforts to succour the Neapolitan royal family on their evacuation from Naples in the face of Napoleon's take-over of the Kingdom.

PALERMO, January 7, 1799.

I have onely time to write you one line as Sir William is not sure he can have a moment to spare today to let you know of our arrival here. We cannot enter in to detail of our being obliged to quit dear Naples. If you are aquainted with Lords Grenville or Spencer

you will know the particulars from them, know onely the *Vanguard*,
Lord Nelson, brought ous off with all the Royal familly and we
arrived here on Christmas day at night after having been near lost,
a tempest that Lord Nelson had never seen for thirty years he has
been at sea the like; all our sails torn to pieces & all the men ready
with their axes to cut away the masts & poor I to attend & keep up
the spirits of the Queen, the Princess Royall, 3 young princesses,
a baby six weeks old & 2 young princes, Leopold & Albert, the last,
6 years old, my favourite, taken with convulsions in the midst of
the storm & at 7 in the evening of Christmas day expired in my
arms, not a soul to help me, as the few women her Majesty brought
on board were incapable of helping her or the poor Royal children.
The King & prince were below in the ward room with Castelcicala,
Belmonte, Grovina, Acton & Sir William, my mother their
assisting them, all their attendants being so frighten'd & on their
knees praying. The King says my mother is an angel. I have been
for twelve nights without once closing my eyes, for 6 nights before
the embarkation I sat up at my own house receving all the jewells,
money & effects of the Royall family & from thence conveying
them on board the *Vanguard*, living in fear of being torn to peices
by the tumultous mob who suspected our departure, but Sir Wm.
& I being beloved in the Country saved ous. On the 21st at ten
at night, Lord Nelson, Sir Wm, mother & self went out to pay a
visit, sent all our servants a way & ordered them in 2 hours to come
with the coach & order'd supper at home. When they were gone,
we set off, walked to our boat & after 2 hours got to the *Vanguard*.
Lord N. then went with armed boats to the secret pallace, got up
the dark staircase that goes in to the Queen's room & with a dark
lantern, cutlasses, pistol &c. &c. brought off every soul, ten in
number, to the *Vanguard* at twelve a' clock. If we had remained to
the next day we shoud have all been imprisoned; but we remained
2 days in the bay to treat with the Neapolitans but alas with such
vile traitors what can you do.

From the letters of Lady Hamilton.

THE CORPS OF KING'S (OR QUEEN'S) MESSENGERS has for long been an élite body of gentlemen carrying diplomatic bags between the Foreign Office and its embassies abroad. They have often been beset by adventures and dangers, but from the record below the early years of the last century seem to have been particularly hazardous.

In September 1797, two messengers (Brooks and Magistri) were drowned off Calais in attempting to land at night, in an open boat, from the *Diana* packet.

In the same year (1797) another messenger (Flint) was killed by a carriage accident near Augsburg, on a return journey from Naples.

In 1807 another (Sparrow) was stabbed by boatmen, who were conveying him along the coast of Sicily, and it was believed that he fell a sacrifice to a most heroic defence of his despatches, which led to a commission in the Army being given to his son by HRH the Duke of York.

In 1815 another (Lyell) was murdered at Madrid; and in the same year another messenger (Shaw) had both his feet amputated owing to their having been severely frost-bitten, and he did not long survive the shock.

In 1820 another (Brown) died at St Petersburg from fatigue and the effects of accidents, after a continuous journey of twenty-three days and nights.

In 1823 another (Bettles) died in consequence of a severe winter in Russia, and the hardships endured on the return journey from St Petersburg in a ship of war.

In 1827 another (Dykes) died from injuries sustained by a fall from his horse between Calais and Paris.

In 1833 another (Latchford) died from an attack of Asiatic cholera, brought on by over-fatigue after a journey of thirteen days and nights to St Petersburg.

In 1836 another (Smith) was drowned at Falmouth, and no doubt many other cases could be mentioned.

There are also numerous instances on record, especially between 1815 and 1834, of messengers having been compelled to cross over from Dover to Calais in an open boat, when the sea was so rough that the captain of the packet could not be induced to risk the passage. The boatmen would appear to have been paid sums varying from £3 5s. to £25 for their services, but on several occasions their boats were dashed to pieces on reaching Calais, when the loss had to be made good by the messengers on behalf of HM's Government. In 1840 a messenger (Barnard) had to pay £35 to a boatman for the loss of his boat, which shows pretty clearly that the boat, in which he had had to cross in the gale, was not a very large or seaworthy one.

From Recollections of the Old Foreign Office *by Sir Edward Hertslet*
(John Murray, London, 1901).

CAPTAIN ARTHUR CONOLLY, who had been sent from India with official British backing to Bokhara to try to consolidate the Central Asian khanates under British rather than Russian influence, was imprisoned by the sadistic Emir together with his fellow envoy, Colonel Charles Stoddart. Their lack of credentials signed by Queen Victoria, and British set-backs in Afghanistan, worsened their plight to the unhappy point which Conolly describes here in writing to his brother.

11th March, 1842   *From our Prison in Bokhara Citadel*

This is the eighty-third day that we have been denied the means of getting a change of linen from the rags and vermin that cover us; and yesterday, when we begged for an amendment in this respect, the Topshee-Bashee, who had before come occasionally as our host to speak encouragingly, set his face like a flint to our request, showing that he was merely a vane to the withering wind of his heartless master, and could not help us thus, so that we need not ask him to do so. This, at first, astonished and defeated us; we had viewed the Ameer's conduct as perhaps dictated by mad caprice; but now, looking back upon the whole, we saw instead that it had been just the deliberate malice of a demon, questioning and raising our hopes, and ascertaining our condition, only to see how our hearts were going on in the process of breaking. I did not think to shed one warm tear among such cold-blooded men; but yesterday evening, as I looked upon Stoddart's half-naked and nail-lacerated body, conceiving that I was the special object of the king's hatred because of my having come to him after visiting Khiva and Kokund, and told him that the British Government was too great to stir up secret enmity against any of its enemies, I wept on entreating one of our keepers, the Gunner's brother, to have conveyed to the chief my humble request that he would direct his anger upon me, and not further destroy by it my poor brother Stoddart, who had suffered so much and so meekly here for three years. My earnest words were answered by a 'Don't cry and distress yourself'; he also could do nothing. So we turned and kissed each other, and prayed together, and then said, in the words of the Kokunders, *My-bish!* Let him do as he likes! he is a demon, but God is stronger than the devil himself, and can certainly release us from the hands of this fiend, whose heart he has perhaps hardened to work out great ends by it; and we have risen again from bed with hearts comforted, as if an angel had spoken to them, resolved, please God, to wear our English honesty and dignity to the last, within all the filth and misery that this monster may try to degrade us with.

We hope that, though the Ameer should now dismiss us with gold clothing, the British and Afghan Governments will treat him as an enemy; and this out of no feeling of revenge. He treacherously caused Stoddart to invite me here on his own Imayut-Nameh; and after Stoddart had given him a translation of a letter from Lord Palmerston, containing nothing but friendly assurances, which he could have verified, with our entire consent, at the Russian embassy, he pent us both up here, because we could not pay him as a kidnapper for our release, to die by slow rot, if it should appear that he might venture at last to put us altogether out of the way. We hope and pray that God may forgive him his sins in the next world; but we also trust that some human power will soon put him down from his oppressive throne at this capital.

From the letters of Captain Arthur Conolly.

SIR RUTHERFORD ALCOCK, the first British Minister and Consul-General in Japan, and his staff at the legation in Edo (Tokyo) are subjected to a gruesome attack during a spate of hostility towards foreigners, arising from resentment at the existence of the so-called Treaty Ports and the privileges they conferred on foreign traders.

The year 1861 began inauspiciously with further alarms of a general massacre. Alcock noted in a despatch to the Foreign Secretary that 'we carry on our relations under a menace which may at any moment be carried into execution'. He doubted if there would be much if any warning, and even if they had time to escape there would probably not be a British ship to which they could escape. On 14 January 1861 news reached Alcock of the murder of Heusken, the Dutch interpreter for the American Legation. He had been waylaid on his return from the Prussian Legation by a band of assassins, and mortally wounded. When Heusken was buried four days later, Harris, the American Minister, was warned by the Japanese authorities that if the Diplomatic Corps persisted in their intention of following the body to the grave, they were likely to lose their own lives. Alcock noted: 'No one hesitated', and all attended.

As the year wore on the security situation seemed to improve and Alcock decided that after a visit he was due to make that summer to Nagasaki the Legation should return to their old quarters in Tozenji at Edo. Alcock reached Edo on 5 July 1861.

That night the Legation was attacked. Alcock wrote dramatically to Lord John Russell: 'We have escaped a massacre but seemingly by the merest chance.' Alcock 'felt incredulous' when Mr Robertson, one of the assistants in the Legation, came to tell him that an attack was taking place. 'I had', he wrote, 'barely time to seize my revolver and advance a few steps, when I heard blows and cries, and the report of a pistol in the passage which runs at the end of my own apartments. The next moment both Mr Oliphant and Mr Morrison (HM Consul in Nagasaki who had come up to Edo with Alcock) staggered forward exclaiming that they were wounded: and I saw the blood flowing profusely from the former, whose left arm was disabled.'

Oliphant's account of how he was wounded in the attack gives

68

a vivid picture of that frightening night. Oliphant's revolver was locked in its case and he could not lay his hands on the key. So he grabbed his hunting crop and stepping past a stray dog who had attached itself to him and who was barking violently at the threshold of his door, exhibiting unmistakable signs of alarm, he proceeded along the passage leading to the front of the house, which was only dimly lit by an oil lamp that was standing in the dining-room. 'I had scarcely taken two steps, when I dimly perceived the advancing figure of a Japanese, with uplifted arms and sword . . . I remember feeling most unaccountably hampered in my efforts to bring the butt-end of my hunting whip to bear upon him, and to be aware that he was aiming blow after blow at me, and no less unaccountably missing me (his sword kept striking a beam), and feeling ready to cry with vexation at being aware that it was a life and death struggle which could only end one way, when suddenly I was blinded by the flash of a shot, and my left arm, which I was instinctively holding up to shield my head, dropped disabled. I naturally thought I had been shot, but it turned out that this shot saved my life.' Morrison, who had been attracted by the sound of Oliphant's struggle, had approached Oliphant from behind and 'placing his revolver over my shoulder, shot my antagonist at the very moment that he had inflicted a severe cut with his long two-handed sword on my left arm, a little above the wrist. A moment after, Morrison received a cut over the forehead and across the eyebrow from another Japanese, at whom he emptied the second barrel of his pistol.'

At about 3 a.m. Oliphant, after Alcock had bound up his wounds, determined to struggle back to bed. 'As I tottered round the screen into the dining-room, a ghastly sight met my gaze. Under the sideboard, completely severed from the body, was a man's head. The body was lying in the middle of the room.' Oliphant was barefoot and found himself slipping about in blood 'and feeling something like an oyster under my bare foot, I perceived it was human eye'.

Alcock exploded when 'after such a night comes a Governor of Foreign Affairs, deputed from the Ministers, gravely to felicitate me on my escape and my return to Yeddo; praying me to accept a basket of ducks and a jar of sugar in token of amity! Your

Lordship will, I am sure, not blame me, that I desired the messenger to take his presents back with him, and tell his principal I desired justice and redress, not ducks or sugar, at the hands of his government.'

From Victorians in Japan *by Hugh Cortazzi (The Athlone Press, London, 1987).*

CARRIAGE ACCIDENTS were a hazard of nineteenth-century life, but possibly more so for diplomats, who had to survive the vagaries of foreign coachmen. Here the daughter of Sir Edward Disbrowe describes an incident when her father was British Minister at the Swedish Court.

Quite early in August my father took my aunt, Lady Harriet Hagerman, and myself for a little northern tour. We started in our light *calèche* with three horses abreast, and with our servant Peter as coachman. I do not recollect what Peter's special post was in the household, but he was most useful as interpreter, also on board the yacht, having been a sailor. Soon after leaving home we had a very steep hill to descend, down which he drove Swedish fashion, as hard as he could go. My father, who was on the box beside him, remonstrated, and asked whether accidents did not frequently happen from such driving. Said Peter, 'I have heard of people being killed, but of nothing worse happening.'

From Old Days in Diplomacy, *the memoirs of the eldest daughter of Sir Edward Cromwell Disbrowe, GCG (Jarrold & Sons, London, 1903).*

MARY CRAWFORD FRASER, the wife of the British representative in Tokyo, describes the security surrounding the Japanese Foreign Minister (to whom she ascribes the title of Viscount) in 1890 in terms which will strike an echo among those modern ambassadors who are subjected to not-dissimilar personal security.

I watched Viscount Aoki drive up to our own door a day or two ago. He was seated in an open victoria with the hood raised, and inside the hood on either hand hung a revolver in a leather pocket, with a heavy chain fastening it to a ring in the carriage frame. The

70

weapons are carefully loaded before the Minister takes his airing, and I fancy that any stranger who tried to stop the carriage or looked into it suddenly would have rather a sensational reception. Three detectives in plain clothes accompany him, as well as a policeman, who sits on the box. The effect is that of a condemned criminal, or a dangerous lunatic out with his keepers. Madame Aoki tells me that the constant watch and guard make life quite intolerable. Wherever she and her husband go, if it be only for a turn in their own garden, the policeman appears, and follows at a not too respectful distance, admiring the flowers and assiduously pretending that he does not hear a word of their conversation. She confided to me that they occasionally amuse themselves by giving their protectors the slip, stealing out like runaway children by a door which opens on a side-street, whence, plainly dressed and on foot, they can take something like a walk. I believe that the consternation is great when it is found that the Minister has really left his own grounds unprotected by the law, and the detectives generally run him to earth and come home with him again.

From A Diplomatist's Wife in Japan: Letters from Home to Home *by Mary Crawford Fraser (Hutchinson and Co., London, 1899).*

THE FOREIGN LEGATIONS IN PEKING were a focal point for the hatred of the Boxer rebels who, determined to drive all foreigners out of China in 1900, first harassed and then attacked the Legations. Having waited in vain for a response to his representations, the German Minister set out to protest to the authorities, and was murdered in the street. The events are described by his diplomatic colleagues who survived the siege of the Legation Quarter.

Sir Claude MacDonald, the British Minister in Peking, described in a letter of 4 September 1900 to the Permanent Under-Secretary of State at the Foreign Office how Baron von Ketteler, the German Minister, who was an impetuous man, had – against the advice of his colleagues – set off with one of his staff, Herr Cordes, to demand an answer from the Chinese authorities to the protests which the diplomatic corps had lodged about the behaviour of the Boxer rebels. What happened on the fatal journey by sedan chair through the streets of Peking was graphically described by Herr Cordes, who himself narrowly survived the attack.

'We were close to the police station on the left of Ha Ta Men street,' Cordes reported. 'I was watching a cart with some lance-bearers passing before the Minister's chair, when suddenly I saw a sight that made my heart stand still. The Minister's chair was three paces in front of me. I saw a banner soldier, apparently a Manchu, in full uniform with a mandarin's hat and a button and blue feather, step forward, present his rifle within a yard of the chair window, level it at the Minister's head and fire. I shouted in terror "Halt!" At the same moment the shot rang out, the chairs were thrown down. I sprang to my feet. A shot struck me in the lower part of the body. Others were fired at me. I saw the Minister's chair standing, but there was no move-ment . . . I affirm that the assassination of the German Minister was a deliberately planned, premeditated murder, done in obedience to the orders of high government officials by an Imperial bannerman.'

The Imperial Foreign Ministry had the effrontery to claim that Baron von Ketteler had fired from his sedan chair into the crowd in the street and thus provoked the attack on himself. The murder and this cynical Chinese response convinced the Western diplomats in Peking that any evacuation plan would be too dangerous; they withdrew into the diplomatic compound; the famous siege of Peking – which was to last for two months – had begun.

Compiled by the editor from contemporary reports published in The Times *and elsewhere.*

AMBASSADOR OSTEN-SACKEN, 'a Russian Courtier of the old – very old – school', finds his family obliged to sacrifice the life of a younger son to the misguided kindness of the Tsar Nicholas I.

Bülow and Ostensacken were speaking of the Czar Nicolas the 1st. B. said that he admired him – but that he had been of a cold unsymp. nature. 'Never were you so mistaken,' cries O. 'He was the kindest hearted man in the world.' To exemplify this O. said that the Emp'r Nicolas had insisted on O's younger brother – a very delicate lad – being sent to the Pages' school – tho' the boy's mother said it would be the death of him. B. didn't see much kind heartedness in this – and asked how the boy got on. O. replied, 'Oh, he died after being two months at the school – but the Emperor sent one of his Aide-de-camps to attend the funeral.'!!!

From the Diary of Sir Edward Goschen, *part of the entry for 14 November 1908 when he was British Ambassador in Berlin.*

ROBERT BRUCE LOCKHART, as a young consular officer, was left in 1917 as the British government representative in Moscow during the Russian revolution. With Britain and her allies becoming increasingly hostile to the Bolsheviks, he here recounts how he was arrested on suspicion of involvement in a plot to assassinate Lenin.

On Friday, August 30th, Uritsky, the head of the St Petersburg Cheka, was murdered by a Russian Junker called Kannegiesser. The next evening a Social-Revolutionary, a young Jewish girl called Dora Kaplan, fired two shots point-blank at Lenin as he was leaving Michelson's factory, where he had been speaking at a meeting. One bullet penetrated the lung above the heart. The other entered the neck close to the main artery. The Bolshevik leader was not dead, but his chances of living were at a discount.

I received the news within half an hour of the actual shooting. It could hardly fail to have serious consequences, and, with a premonition of our impending fate, Hicks and I sat up late, discussing in low whispers the events of the day and wondering how they would affect our own unenviable situation.

We went to bed at one o'clock, and, worn out by months of strain, I slept soundly. At three-thirty a.m. I was awakened by a rough voice ordering me to get up at once. As I opened my eyes, I looked up into the steely barrel of a revolver. Some ten armed men were in my room. One man, who was in charge, I knew. He was Mankoff, the former commandant of Smolny. I asked him what this outrage meant. 'No questions,' he answered gruffly. 'Get dressed at once. You are to go to Loubianka No. 11.' (Loubianka No. 11 was the headquarters of the Moscow Cheka.) A similar

73

group of Cheka agents was dealing with Hicks, and, while we dressed, the main body of the invaders began to ransack the flat for compromising documents. As soon as we were ready, Hicks and I were bundled into a car and, with a gunman on each side of us, were driven off to the Cheka headquarters. There we were put into a square small room, bare of all furniture except a rough table and a couple of plain wooden chairs.

After a long wait I was taken along a dark corridor. The two gunmen, who accompanied me, stopped before a door and knocked. A sepulchral voice said: 'Come in,' and I was brought into a long, dark room, lit only by a hand-lamp on the writing table. At the table, with a revolver lying beside the writing-pad, was a man, dressed in black trousers and a white Russian shirt. His black hair, long and waving as a poet's, was brushed back over a high forehead. There was a large wrist watch on his left hand. In the dim light his features looked more sallow than ever. His lips were tightly compressed, and, as I entered the room, his eyes fixed me with a steely stare. He looked grim and formidable. . . .

'You can go,' he said to the two gunmen, and then there was a long silence. At last he turned his eyes away and opened his writing folder. 'I am sorry to see you in this position,' he said. 'It is a grave matter.' He was scrupulously polite, but very serious. I asked for information, pointing out that I had come to Moscow on the invitation of the Soviet Government and that I had been promised full diplomatic privileges. I made a formal protest against my arrest and demanded to speak to Chicherin [the commissar for Foreign Affairs].

He ignored my protests. 'Do you know the Kaplan woman?' I did not, but I decided that in the circumstances it was better to answer no questions. I repeated as calmly as I could that he had no right to question me.

'Where is Reilly [a British agent and arms dealer]?' was his next question. Again I made the same answer.

Then he produced a paper from his folder. . . . 'Is that your writing?' he asked.

Yet again I replied with studious politeness that I could answer no questions.

He made no attempt to bully me. He fixed me again with a long stare. 'It will be better for you if you speak the truth,' he said.

I made no reply. Then he rang a bell, and I was taken back to Hicks. Again we were left alone. We hardly spoke and, when we did, we talked trivialities. We realised that our conversation was likely to be overheard. I had only the vaguest idea of what had happened. It was obvious, however, that the Bolsheviks were trying to link us up with the attempt on Lenin's life.

From Memoirs of a British Agent *by R.H. Bruce Lockhart (Putnam, London, 1932).*

SIR FITZROY MACLEAN, as a diplomatic secretary at the British Embassy in Moscow during Stalin's purges in the 1930s, witnesses the dangers of extinction or exile to Siberia experienced by those Soviet diplomats who were thought to be in too close contact with foreigners.

The officials at the Commissariat for Foreign Affairs became more inaccessible than ever. They found themselves in a particularly unenviable situation. Contacts with foreigners were notoriously fatal; Tukachevski, it was thought, had been shot for alleged contacts with the German General Staff. Yet it was their duty to see foreigners. If they refused, they were clearly neglecting their duty, or else had a guilty conscience. If, on the other hand, they continued to see foreigners, someone sooner or later was bound to accuse them of betraying State Secrets or plotting the overthrow of the Soviet regime. Theirs was an unhealthy occupation. One after another they disappeared. Their successors were paralysed with fear, for the turnover was very rapid.

One would ring up and ask to speak to Comrade Ivanov. 'He is sick,' an unfamiliar voice would reply nervously, 'he is busy; he has gone for a walk.' 'And who,' one would ask, 'is doing his work?' 'For the time being,' the voice would reply unhappily, 'I am – Comrade Maximov.' 'May I come and see you, Mr Maximov?' one would inquire. 'It is very difficult,' would come the evasive answer, 'I also am very busy.'

Next time, if one could remember his name, one would ring up Mr Maximov. And once more there would be the increasingly familiar answer: 'He is sick; he is busy; he has gone for a walk.' 'For the time being, I am replacing him.' And the chances were that that would be the last that one would hear of Comrade Maximov.

From Eastern Approaches by Fitzroy Maclean (Jonathan Cape, London, 1949).

THE BRITISH EMBASSY IN PARIS and its caretakers survive the German occupation of Paris in the Second World War.

Göring had his eye on the embassy. He came to inspect it and sent for the Americans to open it up for him, which they refused to do. Then one day a German diplomat, accompanied by an officer and soldiers with bayonets, demanded to search the Chancery office. Mrs Spurgeon [the caretaker's wife] recognized him as a frequent visitor in peacetime and boldly told him he had no right to be there. The most alarming experience for the four occupants was when the Germans arrested the two husbands and took them to St Denis. Christie [the other caretaker] remained there five months but the story of the release of Spurgeon is one of the heartwarming incidents of the war. Mrs Spurgeon, a spirited Frenchwoman, had the courage to pester the German Consulate three times a day and, fortunately, the official with whom she so eloquently pleaded was very humane. Herr Johann Leonhard insisted that he was her adversary, not her enemy, and when, finally, she obtained the release of her husband, said that he hoped she would do the same for him should the occasion ever arise. At the time of the invasion, the news of which was whispered through Paris, he even came to ask if they had enough to eat. Leonhard was indeed arrested at the end of the war, and through the Foreign Office Mrs Spurgeon was reminded of her promise. Her recommendation that he was '*un bon Boche*' regained him his freedom.

From The Paris Embassy by Cynthia Gladwyn (Collins, London, 1976).

76

MRS CLARE BOOTHE LUCE, as American Ambassador in Rome, is thought to be the victim of an assassination attempt by arsenic poisoning.

After a little more than a year in Rome, where she was President Eisenhower's glamorous ambassador during the mid-1950s, Clare Boothe Luce noticed she was feeling progressively more unwell; she felt constantly tired and her hair started to fall out. She underwent extensive tests which finally and conclusively indicated that she was suffering from lead or arsenic poisoning.

While she attempted to recuperate in the United States, a team from the CIA arrived in Rome to investigate the possible source of the poisoning. It was known that the Italian Communist party viewed Mrs Luce as their implacable enemy, and at that period no crime seemed too grotesque to lay at their door. There were numerous Italian servants in the kitchen and private apartments of the Luces at the ambassador's residence, the Villa Taverna; all of them came under scrutiny and some under suspicion. Even Mr Henry Luce's relations with his wife were made the subject of discreet enquiry. No word of the investigations was allowed to reach the vociferous Italian Press, but until the potential assassin could be identified Mrs Luce was advised to remain away from Rome.

Eventually, on one of his routine snoops around the Luce's private quarters, one of the CIA sleuths noticed a thick layer of grey dust in Mrs Luce's bedroom. Despite the attentions of the housemaids with their feather dusters, the dust reappeared every day. The dust was sent for confidential analysis in an American laboratory; it contained a proportion of lead which would be highly toxic if inhaled. Mrs Luce slept every night in the room, and often worked in bed. The mystery of what was poisoning her was solved, but not the mystery of how the grey dust got there.

The ceiling above the leaden dust was next examined. It was covered with ornate stucco roses, which had been painted in various delicate shades. The paint had, as was usual at that time, a high lead content. It transpired that whenever the washing machine was switched on in the laundry room above Mrs Luce's bedroom, a layer of lead-laden paint dust was precipitated from the ceiling to the vicinity of her bed – ready to be inhaled overnight.

Nobody had been trying to assassinate the ambassador, but her life had been in danger none the less. The CIA chalked up an (undramatic) success; Mrs Luce returned to Rome; President Eisenhower leaked the story to the Press; Mr Henry Luce – proprietor of *Time* and husband of the ambassador – was furious at being denied a scoop, but published the story all the same.

From contemporary Press reports and other sources available to the editor.

SIR GEOFFREY JACKSON, the British Ambassador to Uruguay in 1971, is kidnapped by Tupamaro anarchist guerrillas in broad daylight on his way to his embassy in Montevideo, being subsequently held in an underground cell for nine months before finally being released.

As always, I was relieved when we turned in from the open corniche into the narrow and crowded side-streets leading to my office, and I was joking with my driver as we edged slowly along the single lane left by the vehicles parked on either side. We were at a point where virtually every day we had to wait for delivery-trucks to finish unloading at one or other of the wayside stores, so I did not pay especial attention to a large red van – certainly of three, possibly of five tons – until it edged out from the kerb as we drew level. There was little room for my driver to swerve, but ample time for the truck-driver to realize and correct his mistake. I knew however that frequently they did not do so till after impact, and was not really surprised when, despite my driver's signals, he bored relentlessly into our left front wing. With a philosophical shrug, and obvious resignation to a coachwork job and some ineffectual insurance activity, Hugo opened his door to climb out and take particulars.

Instead, as the cab-door opened and the truck-driver leapt down, a young man stepped from nowhere and struck Hugo savagely over the head. Simultaneously there was a violent rattle of automatic weapons which continued for what to me seemed an endless time; one of its main constituents originated from a sub-machine-gun concealed in a basket of fruit carried by an apparently innocuous bystander – my captors were very proud of this refinement, of which I was told repeatedly afterwards.

The driver of the truck climbed into my chauffeur's seat, and opened the opposite door for a second young man. A third put his arm round the door-pillar and expertly unlocked the back door from the inside . . . My attackers were not masked – the last human faces I was to see for a long time. They were thoroughly conversant with the idiosyncrasies of the Daimler – its gear-shift, with some rather exotic characteristics for Montevideo; the door-locks; and the power-steering; I found my mind formulating the many circumstances in which this familiarity could have been acquired.

Our driver, whom I could see clearly in the mirror, was, as I have said, a face I had met recently. He had blunt features, a moustache half-way Zapata-style and, again, this rictus of tension, concentration or – I would not blame them – sheer fright. Three of the four I would recognize again instantly, were I to live to be a centenarian.

From People's Prison *by Geoffrey Jackson (Faber & Faber, London, 1973).*

4

Diplomatic Wives and Hostesses

THE POPULAR IMAGE of an ambassadress, or indeed of any diplomatic wife, is traditionally that of a social hostess presiding over lavish entertainments under the cut-glass chandeliers of elegant embassies. Such visions of ideal hostesses usually encompass a range of accomplishments: a familiarity with – at least the more fashionable – foreign languages, a memory for names, a facility for arranging guests around the dining table or around the drawing room, an invariable politeness, and usually an expensive but not-unduly-adventurous wardrobe. Such figures would certainly have been familiar in Paris, Vienna, St Petersburg and elsewhere at most periods between the Congress of Vienna in 1815 and the Maastricht summit of 1991.

But entertaining has seldom been the entire *raison d'être* of an ambassadress. As well as looking after the welfare of her husband and children, she increasingly is expected to administer comfort and succour to the wives of more junior members of the Embassy staff, who may find living in a foreign environment harder to cope with than do their husbands, who have – after all – chosen the career.

An ambassador's wife is likely to find herself seated at dinner between important Ministers or Service Chiefs, while her husband is flanked by their wives, who – in some parts of the world – may still tend to concentrate their conversation on details of their children's illnesses or their problems with domestic staff. In such circumstances, if the ambassador has briefed his wife about his current political and other concerns, she may well find at the conclusion of the evening that she has – with a little adroit steering of the conversation on her part – had a much more productive and fascinating evening than has her husband. Wise diplomats therefore take their spouses into their professional confidence in a way which lawyers and stockbrokers would find inappropriate and extraordinary.

The ambassadress's activities may well extend beyond her family and her husband's staff to include sections of the local community. The days of 'good works' may be waning as more and more diplomatic wives have their own professions, but the notorious Lady Hamilton was neither the first nor the last ambassador's wife to find herself nursing foreign children *in extremis* during an evacuation (as described by her in the chapter on Diplomats in Danger). My own wife had a similar experience when helping with the evacuation of the Portuguese community from Angola after independence in 1974.

One new phenomenon on the diplomatic social scene has been the emergence of the husband who accompanies his diplomat wife. The British Foreign Office has felt it necessary to change the name of The Diplomatic Service Wives' Association to The Diplomatic Service *Spouses'* Association – although not very many male spouses are to be found in the lists of the diplomatic corps in the capitals of the world, and where they do exist they seldom fulfil the hostess function of wives. Inded, special problems can arise. In those few – generally Anglo-Saxon – countries and embassies where the men still stay behind at the dinner table to drink port and swap stories and political gossip while the ladies retire to 'powder their noses', there is marked resentment among lady ambassadors, who are swept upstairs with the wives and miss the post-prandial talk – which can be the most valuable part of the whole evening. The resentment is heightened where a husband stays behind and his diplomat wife does not. Almost invariably, in my experience, the presence of such a couple at a dinner party ensures that the custom is abandoned, as just too difficult to cope with.

Even the most influential and fashionable hostesses, in the mould of Princess Lieven, the Duchess of Dino or Lady Gladwyn,* have to endure the unpleasantness of packing up their possessions and moving round the world. It was the Victorian explorer and Consul-General in Rio de Janeiro, Richard Burton, who on receiving news of a move epitomized this side of diplomatic life in the peremptory telegram he sent to his wife: 'Pay, pack and follow.'

EMMA HAMILTON, wife of Sir William Hamilton, Ambassador to Naples, writes to Lord Nelson with the gossip and intelligence she has been able to glean from the Neapolitan royal family, who were hanging on to their kingdom by a thread as Napoleon threatened them from the Papal States.

NAPLES. June 30th 1798.

DEAR SIR, I take the opportunity of Capt. Hope, to write a few lines to you, and thank you for your kind letter by Capn. Bowen.

The Queen was much pleased, as I translated it for her; and charges me to thank you; and say, she prays for your honour and safety – victory she is sure you will have.

We have still the regicide minister here, Garrat [French Ambassador]: the most impudent, insolent dog: making the most infamous demands every day; and I see plainly the Court of Naples must declare war, if they mean to save their country.

Her Majesty sees and feels all you said in your letter to Sir William, dated off the Faro di Messina, in its true light; so does General Acton [the English-born generalissimo of the Neapolitan armed forces].

But alas! their First Minister, Gallo, is a frivolous, ignorant, self-conceited coxcomb, that thinks of nothing but his fine embroidered coat, ring and snuff-box; and half Naples thinks him half a French-man: and God knows, if one may judge of what he did in making

* Lady Gladwyn, who was the author of *The Paris Embassy* which is quoted on several occasions in this book, was the wife of Sir Gladwyn Jebb (later Lord Gladwyn) and the chatelaine of the magnificent British Embassy in the Faubourg-St-Honoré in Paris from 1954 to 1960.

the peace for the Emperor, he must either be very ignorant, or not attached to his master or the cause commun.

The Queen and Acton cannot bear him, and consequently he cannot have much power: but still, a First Minister, although he may be a minister of smoke, yet he has always something; enough at least to do mischief.

The Jacobins have all been lately declared innocent, after suffering four years' imprisonment; and I know they all deserved to be hanged long ago: and since Garrat has been here, and through his insolent letters to Gallo, these pretty gentlemen, that had planned the death of their Majesties, are to be let out on society again.

In short, I am afraid all is lost here; and I am grieved to the heart for our dear, charming Queen, who deserves a better Fate!

I write to you, my dear Sir, in confidence and in a hurry.

I hope you will not quit the Mediterranean without taking *us*. We have our leave, and everything ready, at a day's notice, to go; but yet I trust in God, and you, that we shall destroy those monsters before we go from hence. Surely their reign cannot last long.

If you have any opportunity, write to us; pray do: you do not know how your letters comfort us.

God bless you, my dear, dear Sir, and believe me, ever, your most sincerely obliged and attached friend,

EMMA HAMILTON.

From the letters of Lady Hamilton.

ADMIRAL LORD NELSON, on the day of his death at Trafalgar, extols the diplomatic activities of Lady Hamilton (as instanced in the previous entry) and argues for her to be maintained by a grateful nation in the event of his death – a request which was totally ignored.

CODICIL TO LORD NELSON'S WILL

October the twenty-first, one thousand eight hundred and five, then in sight of the combined fleets of France and Spain, distant about ten miles.

Whereas the eminent services of Emma Hamilton, widow of the Right Honourable Sir William Hamilton, have been of the very greatest service to our King and country, to my knowledge, without her receiving any reward from either our King or country: first, that she obtained the King of Spain's letter, in 1796, to his brother, the King of Naples, acquainting him of his intention to declare war against England; from which letter, the Ministry sent out orders to then Sir John Jervis, to strike a stroke, if opportunity offered, against either the arsenals of Spain, or her fleets. That neither of these was done, is not the fault of Lady Hamilton. The opportunity might have been offered. Secondly, the British fleet, under my command, could never have returned the second time to Egypt, had not Lady Hamilton's influence with the Queen of Naples, caused letters to be wrote to the Governor of Syracuse, that he was to encourage the fleet being supplied with everything, should they put into any port in Sicily. We put into Syracuse, and received every supply, went to Egypt, and destroyed the French fleet.

Could I have rewarded these services, I would not now call upon my country; but as that has not been in my power, I leave Emma, Lady Hamilton, therefore, a legacy to my King and country, that they will give her an ample provision to maintain her rank in life. I also leave to the beneficence of my country, my adopted daughter, Horatia Nelson Thompson [his natural daughter by Lady Hamilton]; and I desire she will use, in future, the name of Nelson only. These are the only favours I ask of my King and country, at this moment, when I am going to fight their battle. May God bless my King and country, and all those who I hold dear. My relations it is needless to mention, they will of course be amply provided for.

NELSON AND BRONTE

Witness – HENRY BLACKWOOD.
T.M. HARDY.

From the papers of Admiral Lord Nelson.

KING CHARLES XIV OF SWEDEN, the former Napoleonic Marshal Bernadotte, does not impress the young daughter of the British Minister to the Swedish court as being a very martial figure.

The King remained in bed many weeks that winter, not that he was ill, but he was afraid of being poisoned, and part of the time he lived entirely on raw apples, often eating eleven at a time.

We children came in to dessert and saw the King crumbling bread and rubbing his hands with it. We heard him say it was a habit he had acquired, '*Quand j'etais petit lieutenant*', and could not afford anything else to keep his hands white. This did not sound to me like a valiant soldier.

> From Old Days in Diplomacy, *the memoirs of the eldest daughter of Sir Edward Cromwell Disbrowe, GCG (Jarrold & Sons, London, 1903).*

THE DUCHESS OF DINO came to London in 1830 as the hostess for her uncle, Prince Talleyrand, whom some people alleged had once been her lover. The brilliance of their tenure of the French Embassy greatly assisted the Orléans monarchy; as Count Alexis de Saint Priest remarked, 'the July Revolution [which brought the Duke of Orléans to the throne] can sometimes be a little bourgeois, but thanks to Monsieur de Talleyrand, it is carried off in very great style in London. Madame de Dino contributes finely to the total effect.' Here she experiences the rigours of English country-house parties.

She was also introduced to the English week-end house party: 'twenty or thirty persons who know each other but not familiarly are invited to be together for two or three days'. Unfortunately, as the hosts only went to their house to receive their guests and left as soon as they were gone, they themselves had the air of being on a visit which gave the whole party rather an unsettled effect. At Woburn, though they played cards on Sunday, she found that the splendour and size of the house dulled into cold formality everyone except the duchess, who was anyhow notoriously foul-mouthed. At Warwick Castle the great drawing-room was lit only by about twenty candles, like 'will-o'-the-wisps which deceived the eye rather than illuminated the room. I have never seen anything more chilling and depressing . . . I kept thinking that the portrait of Charles I and the bust of the Black Prince would come and join us at coffee . . .' Instead, there arrived Lord Eastnor, a mighty hunter, and his brother, a parson, who had not shaved since Christmas and never opened his mouth except to eat. But not even rigours such as this could dim her affection for the English countryside, which she found richer and more varied than that of France and more sympathetic than that of Germany.

From The Duchess of Dino *by Philip Ziegler (Collins, London, 1962).*

COSSACK NATIONAL DRESS, as worn by a Hetman's wife, arouses some disrespectful comments from a young diplomatic hostess at the coronation of Tsar Nicholas I in Moscow in 1826.

The wife of the Hetman [chief] of the Kossacks was also there. She is very like an ambulating feather bed, mounted on bed posts, wears a dark cloth gown up to her chin, a coloured sash, diamond buttons down the front of her dress, and a blue silk handkerchief tied flat round her head. She has followed her husband in all his campaigns, and it seems to have agreed with her. She says she has retained her national costume because the Emperor Alexander approved of it.

From Old Days in Diplomacy, *the memoirs of the eldest daughter of Sir Edward Cromwell Disbrowe, GCG (Jarrold & Sons, London, 1903).*

PRINCESS LIEVEN, the wife of the Russian Ambassador in London in 1830 and a formidable hostess whose 'house was the most select in London and the one to which the entrée was the most valued', is charged by the Russian Foreign Minister to pass an unpalatable message to Lord Palmerston.

Nesselrode entrusted to Mme de Lieven the delicate task of informing Palmerston that Canning could not be accepted; he was 'un homme impossible, pointilleux, défiant'; there were reasons to believe that he had been guilty of rudeness towards the Tsar, when the latter was still Grand-Duke; Palmerston promised her that Canning should not be appointed, but broke his word, and the Tsar threatened to recall his ambassdor. Madame de Lieven rushed off to Petersburg, and conjured away the danger. The lady, as is well known, was much more the representative of Russia than her husband.

From A Guide to Diplomatic Practice *by the Rt. Hon. Sir Ernest Satow (Longmans Green, London, 1922).*

THE DUCHESS OF DINO does little to disguise her distaste for Lord Palmerston as Foreign Secretary.

No amount of political disagreement or of resentment for his off-hand treatment of her uncle [Talleyrand, then French Ambassador in London] can alone explain the sustained rancour which she bore him or the delight with which she greeted news of his set-backs many years after she had left England for ever. 'It is seldom', she wrote to Barante, 'that a man has a face so expressive of his character. The eyes are hard and pale, the nose turned up and impertinent. His smile is bitter, his laugh forced. There is no dignity, or frankness or correctness either in his features or his build. His conversation is dry, but I confess not wanting in wit. He has on him a stamp of obstinacy, arrogance and treachery which I believe to be an exact reflection of his real character.'

The Prime Minister did what he could to keep the peace between the Foreign Office and the French Embassy. Dorothea [Duchess of Dino] chanced to be visiting Lord Grey the day after Palmerston had offended Talleyrand with a typical piece of ill-manners and lack of consideration. Lord Grey ran down the staircase after her to assure her that Lord Palmerston had had no ill intention and to ask her to make excuses for him to Talleyrand. Dorothea replied that the road to hell was paved with good intentions. 'I promise you to tell Monsieur de Talleyrand that Lord Palmerston is as innocent as an unborn child,' she added dryly, 'but I don't believe a word of it.'

From The Duchess of Dino *by Philip Ziegler (Collins, London, 1962).*

87

MRS PEMBERTON HODGSON, the wife of the British Consul in Nagasaki in 1859, finds that setting up house in Japan is no pursuit for the faint-hearted.

Imagine my terror and disgust, when, on rising from my bed, I was about to touch the mat with my feet, and I saw a – what do you think? – a vile reptile, a detestable serpent within a few inches of me! I shrieked for aid. . . . My maid heard my cry, and summoned one of the Japanese to the rescue. The servant caught the snake, but would not kill it.

Another day, while criticizing some Japanese pictures in my drawing-room, I heard the sound of something falling close to me. Rather alive to the visit of unpleasant guests, I looked whence the sound came, and beheld a really prodigious and ugly round mass gently unrolling its folds. This was another serpent, which had fallen from the roof; and it reminded me too painfully that I was to expect visitors from above as well as below. Before I could hail any one it was gone, after silently looking at me, as much as to say, 'I will call again'.

The centipedes also are my constant and assiduous *admirateurs*. One evening I was playing at *trente-et-un* with some friends, and was rejoicing at my good luck, when one of the gentlemen suddenly rose from his seat, and, without saying a word, most impertinently, as I thought, struck me a heavy blow on the shoulder. Before I had time to ask any questions, he told me 'not to be afraid, for it was only an insect'; but it required the hearty blow of a good sword to exterminate and destroy a very large and thick mailed centipede, which was crawling up my white muslin dress, and would soon have found a road over my neck and shoulder . . .

Four-footed animals gave us nightly entertainments, not of the most musical sort. Rats, as huge as cats, danced and squeaked over my head, either for their own amusement or to escape the pursuit of wild ferrets. Very often have I been awakened at night by fear, thinking the noise was caused by ghosts or some unearthly visitors, and it required some considerable time to accustom myself to these nocturnal orgies.

From A Residence at Nagasaki and Hakodate in 1859–1860
by C. Pemberton Hodgson (London, 1961).

THE DIPLOMATIC WIVES IN PEKING demonstrate their sang-froid when the two-month siege of the Legation Quarter by the Boxer rebels – intent on expelling all foreigners from China in 1900 – ends with the arrival of a relief force of international troops.

Suddenly, at about half-past two, the uneasy torpor of the compounds was shattered. In a dozen languages the cry went up: 'They are coming! They are here!' People rushed up to the Wall; those on the Wall rushed down. Somebody said the troops were Germans. Then, all at once, the tennis-court in the British Legation was covered with Sikhs and Rajputs. As the besieged crowded round them, a kind of sobbing cheer went up, a strange uncontrollable sound like the baying of excited hounds.

Led by their British officers, more and more sepoys poured through the Sluice Gate, up Canal Street and on to the tennis-court – tall, turbanned, sweating men, their legs coated with the mud they had waded through, their faces strained by fatigue. Women crowded round them, touching them, patting them, even trying to kiss them. The soldiers' fierce eyes rolled alarm. '*Pani*', they said humbly, pointing to their mouths, '*pine ki pani.*' Hands shaking with eagerness sought to imperil their souls with champagne.

Of all who recorded their memories of this extraordinary scene, two especially seem to recapture moments of truth. One was the lady who, after eating Mongol ponies for more than a month, was principally struck by 'what a treat it was to see a real horse again'. The other was the youthful Roger Keyes. 'Lady MacDonald looked very charming and nice and might have been our hostess. She said [to Keyes and another officer of the relief force] that she didn't know who we were but was simply delighted to see us.' At that moment firing broke out. A Belgian woman was hit and fell screaming to the ground. 'So then they went in under cover, as one would out of a shower of rain.'

From The Siege of Peking *by Peter Fleming (Rupert Hart-Davis, London, 1959).*

MARY CRAWFORD FRASER, the wife of the British Minister to Japan at the end of the last century – the period of Madam Butterfly – here describes efforts to break the ice with senior Japanese wives in a peculiarly British way.

I think it was in October that I had what the papers called an official tea party, at which we collected all the women of importance in our little world, and asked them if they would care to come to me once a fortnight to hear 'pretty stories' read and talked over. I could give them as an example my English reading society, where twenty or thirty women meet and read and discuss English literature with very keen interest. The idea was new, and pleased them greatly; though I think one or two feared that, as my coadjutor worked so frankly for Christian interests, this might be a scheme to forward them. However, they all accepted, and have been most faithful about coming. Of course there were many things to be thought of and prepared. The first story had to be one which would appeal to their sense of all that was fit and proper. After much deliberation, we fixed on a tale of filial piety, the immemorial 'Exiles of Siberia', with its wonderful story of a daughter's devotion to her parents. Then the translation had to be put into flowery language full of pretty conceits, or else the sensitive ears of these dainty Court ladies would not listen to it for a moment. . . . The long story had to be abridged, and much left out which would have been incomprehensible to our audience; but at last it was ready, and our little ladies gathered in force to listen to it.

From A Diplomatist's Wife in Japan: Letters from Home to Home
by Mary Crawford Fraser (Hutchinson & Co., London, 1899).

MARY CRAWFORD FRASER complains of the rude and patronizing attitude of some of the other diplomatic wives in Tokyo at the turn of the last century towards the same senior Japanese wives whom she herself was seen cultivating so assiduously in the preceding entry.

It has sometimes happened to me to wish that the Japanese ladies understood less than I imagine they do of foreign languages; for some of our colleagues' wives affect an almost brutal rudeness towards them, speaking of them in their presence with sublime contempt, and complaining loudly of an official visit, which perhaps has broken up a more amusing conversation. When, horror-struck, I have expostulated, the reply has been, 'Bah, elles n'y comprennent rien!' I was paying a visit at one of the Legations, when a Japanese great lady, Princess Szem, was announced, and immediately followed the servant who announced her. It was my hostess's reception day, and she should have had a competent interpreter at hand, as we are all supposed to do these occasions. Therefore the Princess, although she can speak no foreign tongue, had not brought one with her. As she entered the room our hostess threw her arms in the air with an expression of despair, and exclaimed (I had better not say in what language), 'Good Heavens, what am I to do with this creature! What an odious bore! Where is So-and-so (the interpreter)? Somebody run and find him! Could anything to be more tiresome?' All this was said at the top of her voice, with gestures which must have made the meaning only too clear to the dignified woman who was thus outrageously received. I did what very little could be done to save the situation; and Princess Szem, like the true lady she is, pretended not to understand it for the few minutes during which she remained. I fled when she said what I fancy will be a long good-bye to our hostess, and for the first time in my life I blushed at being a European.

I met this adornment of diplomacy coming away as I was advancing along the Palace corridor on Thursday, and did not get past her without having to hear some noisy criticisms on the manners of the women she had just left, and who, by the way, have loaded her with kindness. Manners! If they were – as in a measure they may be – the passport to heaven, the Japanese women would certainly have reserved places, and many a 'smart' European would have to take a back seat. Kindness and modesty, a wakeful, real consideration for the feelings of others – surely these make up for a little unwilling ignorance of the higher subjects which most interest us, and which, to tell the truth, are hardly better known to the 'smart' European with her social preoccupations and her rattle of 'chaff', than they are to the little hothouse ladies of the Palace.

From A Diplomatist's Wife in Japan: Letters from Home to Home
by Mary Crawford Fraser (Hutchinson & Co., London, 1899).

LADY TYRRELL proves an absent-minded hostess at the British Embassy in Paris in the early 1930s.

Lady Tyrrell was delightfully vague and the amusing stories about her accumulated. On the arm of the President she once led the procession for dinner in the direction of the ballroom so that everyone was obliged to about-turn. At one of her dinner-parties she sat next to Lord Birkenhead, then Secretary of State for India, and talked to him the whole evening under the impression that he was the Turkish Ambassador. She apologized to a guest for the delay in going to dinner, explaining that they were waiting for the King of Sweden, to whom she was in fact speaking. On another royal occasion she was said to have asked a young man standing near her if he would be so kind as to open the window, unaware that she was addressing the guest of honour, the Duke of York. During this same visit she ran into a figure in the passage and asked anxiously, 'Am I doing all right, Bill?' 'Very well indeed, Lady Tyrrell,' kindly replied the future George VI, whom she had mistaken for the private secretary, Cavendish-Bentinck.

From The Paris Embassy *by Cynthia Gladwyn (Collins, London, 1976).*

LADY CLERK, wife of the British Ambassador in Paris from 1934 to 1937, gives a jolt to Parisian society.

Sir George Clerk was a favourite figure at the Jockey Club in Paris and was fond of entertaining the French aristocracy in considerable style. The only problem was that his wife deplored formality as much as he enjoyed it. He therefore tended to arrange his grander dinner parties at times when she was absent. On one such occasion, however, she returned unexpectedly an hour before one of Sir George's most formal evenings was about to begin.

Lady Clerk's first move was to overhaul the dinner table. Orchids and carnations were swept off the carefully-laid table and ivy was strewn along it, creating a bistro effect. But worse was to follow, after the meal. Instead of allowing the guests to group themselves elegantly for conversation in the drawing rooms, Lady Clerk announced that they would play Musical Chairs. It happened that on this occasion one of Europe's most eminent pianists – Jacques Février – was among the guests; Lady Clerk told him to play and to stop when she hit him. (It was said that his touch never fully recovered.)

The French guests were totally unfamiliar with the game. The first time the music stopped, they sorted themselves out and sat down according to their precedence. Lady Clerk explained that it was a free-for-all: they must fight for their chairs. The French took the injunction all too literally: feet were stamped upon, bruises were inflicted, and even model dresses got torn. One distinguished marquise ended on the floor.

The evening was talked about for a long time. Some of the guests were heard to remark that it confirmed their worst fears concerning the barbarity of the English; others had obviously hugely enjoyed themselves. Sir George Clerk was unamused.

An anecdote told to the editor by Sir Fitzroy Maclean, who was present as a junior Secretary at the Embassy.

FRAU VON RIBBENTROP, the wife of Hitler's ambassador to Britain in 1936, provokes caustic comments from Chips Channon, as does her husband, when they launch themselves on London society.

29 May
The last day of Parliament. Honor [Channon's wife] and I lunched with Laura at Crewe House (which she has taken for the season) to meet Herr Von Ribbentrop und Frau. Frau Von Ribbentrop is distinguished in the Berlin manner, that is she has intelligent eyes, appalling khaki-coloured clothes and an un-powdered, un-painted face. How can the Germans be so silly about things that don't matter, or is it because their women are so unattractive that the race is largely homosexual? He, Ribbentrop, looks like the captain of someone's yacht, square, breezy, and with a sea-going look. Actually he was once a wine merchant. He is not quite without charm, but shakes hands in an over-hearty way, and his accent is Long Island without a trace of Teutonic flavour. Afterwards

the Ribbentrops, Laura and co. left with Lord Londonderry for Mount Stewart for the Whitsun holiday. The Ribbentrops are intimate with the Londonderrys, and he is known as the Londonderry Herr.

From Chips: The Diaries of Sir Henry Channon, *edited by Robert Rhodes James*
(Weidenfeld & Nicolson, London, 1967).

LADY DIANA COOPER was probably the most flamboyant chatelaine ever to hold sway at the elegant mansion in the Faubourg-St-Honoré in Paris (which had been the British Embassy since the Duke of Wellington took it over from Napoleon's sister) when she went there with Duff Cooper at the end of the Second World War. But she was hardly a model ambassadress in all respects.

'I quite agree with Diana that she is not cut out for an Ambassadress,' wrote her old friend Bridget McEwen to her husband.

> Although she is capable of great heroism and devotion she is not capable of enduring boredom: and to endure boredom with the good manners that don't show it is half the duty of an Ambassadress. To be a successful Ambassadress means having a very considerable sense of public duty and public spirit unless you are uncommonly limited yourself. Diana will be no good at all. She will be rude to the bores, and she will wear trousers because they are comfortable, and offend everyone. Only if there is an earthquake or a revolution will she show her true mettle. But who knows, there may be both.

Whether or not Diana could be called a successful ambassadress depends on what one believes an ambassadress is supposed to do and be. Some expect her to be a benevolent mother hen, clucking lovingly over the migraines of the secretaries and the table-manners of the Head of Chancery. This certainly Diana failed to be. She knew the names of hardly any of Duff's staff and tended to ask to the Residence only those whose company she enjoyed – a practice vexatious to the senior members who found themselves neglected. If a typist had been knocked down at her doorstep she would have coped with kindness and competence; but it would never have occurred to her to inquire after the typist's welfare if the accident had happened round the corner. Somebody else would cope with that side of Embassy life and, if they didn't . . . well, a grown human being should be able to look after itself. They gave three large parties the first Christmas: 'one for some French friends and the principal members of the staff, *"très digne"*; one for the whole embassy staff and their friends, a nightmare; one for four hundred little British children, a bad smell'.

Nor was she any more enthusiastic about her role as shepherdess, taking her flock of Embassy women to diplomatic soirées, conducting the wife of a newly arrived member of the staff to call on the other ambassadresses. It was a dreary chore, certainly, and one which gave pleasure to nobody concerned, but her failure to play her part caused embarrassment to younger members of the staff who knew that they ought to be doing *something* but did not feel that they could set about it on their own. Diana's grisliest memory was of a tea-party with Mme de Gaulle. Dutifully she led her crocodile of diplomatic wives into the Elysée Palace, only to find that not one of them was prepared to say a word to their equally taciturn hostess. Then the 'exceedingly vulgar Consul's wife' plunged into the silence and asked Mme de Gaulle whether she had ever been to the Marché aux Puces; if not, she would be delighted to take her any morning. Mme de Gaulle received the overture with disdain and 'a rocket of a look'.

From Diana Cooper *by Philip Ziegler (Hamish Hamilton, London, 1981).*

CAROLINE URE, as the wife of the Counsellor at the British Embassy in Lisbon in 1975, describes her experience as a voluntary helper on an RAF flight undertaking the evacuation of Portuguese refugees from Angola after years of bitter civil war and on the eve of the hand-over of power to a black African government – the sort of unlikely situation which Bridget McEwen (in the previous entry) envisaged would bring out the best in Lady Diana Cooper.

As we taxied to the apron the airport appeared to be encircled by hundreds of glowing red lights. It turned out, on closer inspection, that these were the camp fires of the hundreds of refugees sleeping in the open. The authorities had decided to allow only fare-paying passengers to use the airport buildings, so the refugees were scattered around the perimeter of the airfield living as best they could . . . There were three other aircraft on the tarmac to be loaded before ours and only one airport vehicle for transporting baggage the mile and a half to the plane. I began making enquiries about a truck, and we were surprised when a young man quickly came up offering to let us use a shiny great green monster which appeared almost new. He said anyone could drive it out to the aircraft, and showed no concern about payment for the precious petrol. Our enquiries as to whereabouts on the airfield we should return it were met with, 'Oh, leave it by the aircraft – I'm going on your flight and it is no use to me any more!'

The transport problem for passengers and their baggage having been solved, we returned the mile and a half to the aircraft on foot. We walked through the encampments. I admired the refugees' ingenuity; huts had been made of every conceivable material, boxes, crates, trucks turned on their sides with cardboard doors. One portentous dining table that must surely have been more at home in a gilded hall than in its present role was serving as the roof of a hut sheltering two black women and no less than nineteen children. Two babies were sleeping soundly in a barrel and an old lady was sitting, knitting in the pitch darkness under a brilliantly coloured golfing umbrella.

The flight was seven hours. The passengers were from all walks of life. Amongst them were quite a few black refugees, both educated and uneducated, and there were some mulattoes, but

96

75 per cent were Europeans. There was a bank employee and an agricultural labourer, a builder and a shop-keeper; a few wives travelling alone in the hopes that their husbands would join them later; a very old woman who seemed too fragile to have to undergo such a dramatic upheaval in her life; a wonderfully cheerful man who had lost both legs; two very competent girls aged about twelve who were going to join their grandmother whom they had never seen and for whom they had only the vaguest address. A few had left their houses in a terrible hurry and had travelled for days, or even weeks, to reach Luanda. They were physically exhausted and drawn-looking. . . . They all had between four and seven days to wait for their flight after first requesting to join the airlift. But many hundreds were waiting at the airport for weeks for some personal reason – waiting for missing relatives to turn up, waiting for news of lost luggage, or simply trying to decide whether to leave or stay.

From an article entitled 'A Night to Remember' by Caroline Ure in the Diplomatic Service Wives' Association Newsletter, Spring 1976.

5

Memorable Encounters and Events

DIPLOMACY HAS BEEN defined as the art of building ladders for other people to climb down. This being so, it is surprising how many diplomatic encounters over the centuries have been confrontational.

The early heralds who acted as emissaries and spokesmen between sovereigns were expected to deliver their messages with due deference, and were sometimes liable to forfeit their immunity if they spoke truculently or offensively. But arrogant sovereigns not infrequently sent arrogant heralds to deliver arrogant messages – as did the Dauphin of France to King Henry V of England. War was all too often seen as an extension of diplomacy, rather than as its negation.

However unprovocative or even conciliatory an envoy may be, it still takes two to make a constructive dialogue. Some of the greatest practitioners of the art of diplomacy were contemporaries and interlocutors of Napoleon – notably Talleyrand and Metternich. Yet both of these were driven to some very straight speaking, which resulted in notable explosions, when trying to advise Napoleon and warn him of the dangers of his ways.

Some encounters are of course intended from the outset to be confrontational. When, during a critical moment in the Second World War when the Fascist armies were advancing on British-protected Egypt, Sir Miles Lampson surrounded King Farouk's palace with British tanks and threatened the young king with a demand for his abdication, he was casting aside the velvet glove as an act of policy. The harshness of war had taken over from the niceties of peace-time diplomacy.

Similarly, when Nikita Khrushchev stamped on the American Ambassador's foot at a party in Moscow, or banged his desk with his shoe at a session of the United Nations in New York, he was deliberately violating the norms of diplomacy in favour of shocking those whom he wished to harass or threaten and showing contempt for 'The System'. It could be argued that his actions should find no place in an anthology of diplomacy, but they serve to illustrate the breakdown of the system.

Some encounters founder on language misunderstandings. Mr Harold Macmillan (in one of the following examples) may have failed to make himself understood in French by President de Gaulle; and Marshal Tito (in another example) understood only too well what was being said, despite the attempts of a diplomatic interpreter to pull the wool over his eyes. More usually, diplomatic interpreters are able to ease the intercourse between their principals. In Moscow in the late 1950s, Khrushchev's interpreter – Victor Sukhodriev – would exchange Russian jokes for English ones with me and my colleagues in the Chancery of the British Embassy so that we could interject them at appropriate points in tense exchanges and thus oil the wheels of diplomacy.

Increasingly frequently, diplomatic encounters are not with other diplomats or Foreign Ministers but with the media – journalists and radio or TV interviewers. Lord Gladwyn – as Sir Gladwyn Jebb – was not alone in trouncing his interlocutors from time to time in New York and elsewhere; and Sir Nicholas Henderson's success, as British Ambassador to the US during the Falklands War, in turning the tables on questioners who suggested that he was defending a 'colonial war', was in the style of modern diplomacy. Consequently, rising diplomats are now given instruction in TV interview techniques. For the unskilled, confrontation with a hostile interviewer can be quite as devastating to the morale and reputation of an ambassador as some of the more conventional encounters described in this chapter.

KING HENRY V of England castigates the ambassadors of the Dauphin of France for their impudent message and gift. In Shakespeare's account, the reality of the occasion is probably considerably improved upon.

KING HENRY.   Call in the messengers sent from the Dauphin.

. . .

Enter Ambassadors of France.

Now are we well prepar'd to know the pleasure
Of our fair cousin Dauphin; for we hear
Your greeting is from him, not from the king.
FIRST AMBASSADOR   May't please your majesty to
    give us leave
Freely to render what we have in charge;
Or shall we sparingly show you far off
The Dauphin's meaning and our embassy?
KING HENRY.   We are no tyrant, but a Christian king;
Unto whose grace our passion is as subject
As are our wretches fetter'd in our prisons:
Therefore with frank and with uncurbed plainness
Tell us the Dauphin's mind.
FIRST AMBASSADOR.   Thus then, in few.
Your highness, lately sending into France,
Did claim some certain dukedoms, in the right
Of your great predecessor, King Edward the Third.
In answer of which claim, the prince our master
Says that you savour too much of your youth,
And bids you be advis'd there's nought in France
That can be with a nimble galliard won;
You cannot revel into dukedoms there.
He therefore sends you, meeter for your spirit,
This tun of treasure; and, in lieu of this,
Desires you let the dukedoms that you claim
Hear no more of you. This the Dauphin speaks.
KING HENRY.   What treasure, uncle?
EXETER.   Tennis-balls, my liege.
KING HENRY.   We are glad the Dauphin is so pleasant
    with us:

100

His present and your pains we thank you for:
When we have match'd our rackets to these balls,
We will in France, by God's grace, play a set
Shall strike his father's crown into the hazard. . . .
So get you hence in peace; and tell the Dauphin
His jest will savour but of shallow wit
When thousands weep more than did laugh at it.
Convey them with safe conduct. Fare you well.

[*Exeunt Ambassadors*].

EXETER.   This was a merry message.

From King Henry the Fifth *(Act I, Scene 2) by William Shakespeare.*

ANTHONY JENKINSON, envoy of Queen Elizabeth I, has difficulty with his credentials and his religion on arrival at the court of the Great Sophy of Persia.

Thus comming before his Majestie with such reverence as I thought meete to be used, I delivered the Queen's Majestie's letters with my present, which hee accepting, demaunded of mee of what countrey of Franks I was, and what affaires I had there to doe: Unto whom I answered that I was of the famous Citie of London within the noble Realme of England, and that I was sent thither from the most excellent and gracious soveraigne Lady Elizabeth Queene of the saide Realme for to treate of friendship, and free passage of our Merchants and people, to repaire and traffique within his dominions, for to bring in our commodities, and to carry away theirs to the honour of both princes, the mutuall commoditie of both Realmes, and wealth of the Subjects, with other wordes here omitted. He then demaunded me in what language the letters were written, I answered, in the Latine, Italian and Hebrew: well said he, we have none within our Realme that understand those tongues. Whereupon I answered that such a famous and worthy prince (as hee was) wanted not people of all nations within his large dominions to interprete the same. Then he questioned with me of the state of our Countreys, and of the power of the Emperour of Almaine, king Philip, and the great Turke, and which of

101

them was of most power: whom I answered to his contentation, not dispraysing the great Turke, their late concluded friendship considered. Then he reasoned with mee much of Religion, demaunding whether I were a Gower, that is to say, an unbeleever, or a Muselman, that is, of Mahomet's lawe. Unto whom I answered, that I was neither unbeleever nor Mahometan; but a Christian. What is that, said he unto the king of the Georgians' sonne, who being a Christian was fled unto the said Sophie, and he answered that a Christian was he that beleeveth in Jesus Christus, affirming him to be the Sonne of God, and the greatest Prophet. Doest thou beleeve so, said the Sophie unto me: Yea that I do, said I: Oh thou unbeleever, said he, we have no neede to have friendship with the unbeleevers, and so willed me to depart. I being glad thereof did reverence and went my way, being accompanied with many of his gentlemen and others, and after me followed a man with a Basanet of sand, sifting all the way that I had gone within the said pallace, even from the said Sophie's sight unto the court gate.

From Hakluyt's Collection of the Early Voyages, Travels and Discoveries of the English Nation *(R.H. Evans, London, 1809).*

PRINCE de TALLEYRAND warns Napoleon of a diplomatic gaffe.

To some people the forcible seizure of a Spanish province will seem little better from the moral point of view than the forcible seizure of the Spanish Princes. [Napoleon had turned out the Spanish royal family in favour of his own brother.] But Talleyrand was a man of the world, and he knew which crimes the world will condone and which it can never forgive. He told Napoleon that he had lost more than he had gained by this policy, and when he was bidden to explain himself he did so by an analogy:

'If a gentleman commits follies,' he said, 'if he keeps mistresses, if he treats his wife badly, even if he is guilty of serious injustices towards his friends, he will be blamed, no doubt, but if he is rich, powerful, and intelligent, society will still treat him with

102

indulgence. But if that man cheats at cards he will be immediately banished from decent society and never forgiven.'

So began the rupture between Talleyrand and Napoleon that was never healed. Napoleon was incapable of appreciating the difference between the coup d'état of Brumaire and the coup d'état of Bayonne, and could not forgive Talleyrand who had assisted him in the one for deserting him in the other. Talleyrand, on the other hand, was aware that while it might prove possible to prop up the façade of the Empire for several years, the fate of the Emperor was sealed. At Bayonne Napoleon had committed the unforgivable crime. He had cheated at cards.

From Talleyrand *by Duff Cooper (Jonathan Cape, London, 1932).*

THE QUEEN OF PRUSSIA accompanied her husband to Tilsit in 1807, following the defeat of the Prussian army by Napoleon at Jena, in an attempt to court Napoleon's goodwill; but he declined to pay attention to her, and her humiliation was compounded by having to witness her country being halved both in size and population under the arrangements made – without reference to the Prussian monarchy – between Napoleon and the Tsar of Russia. Her predicament elicited widespread diplomatic sympathy.

July 7th.

The Queen went to Tilsit three days ago; she made a great sacrifice of personal feeling to what she was told might be advantageous to her Country; but the King ought to have sooner given up his Kingdom than have subjected her to the humiliation of courting him who had so cruelly insulted her. If she talks to him upon business, she proves the accusation of her meddling in the politics and affairs of state; if she avoids such discussions, of what possible utility can be her interview with Bonaparte?

July 11th.

You will hear, probably, before the arrival of My letter that Peace is concluded between France and Russia, and Prussia. The King and Queen of Prussia returned here the night before last.

103

The poor Queen is the picture of Misery; she has subjected herself to great humiliation, and has not by the sacrifice of her own feelings obtained any advantage for her country. I shall set off for Petersburgh to morrow or the next day. I am in lower Spirits than I can describe; every thing, both public and private, is as disagreeable as possible.

From The Private Correspondence of Lord Granville Leveson Gower 1781 to 1821
(John Murray, London, 1916).

PRINCE METTERNICH, as Austrian Foreign Minister, confronts Napoleon and provokes a ruthless outburst from the latter.

The famous interview of June 26 1813, which lasted for nine hours, began badly. Napoleon greeted Metternich with the words: 'So you want war? Well, you shall have it. I annihilated the Prussian army at Lützen; I smashed the Russians at Bautzen; now you want to have your turn. Very well – we shall meet at Vienna.' Metternich indicated that the issues of peace and war lay in the hands of the Emperor of the French. 'Well and what is it that you want?' snapped Napoleon. 'That I should dishonour myself? Never! I know how to die; but never shall I cede one inch of territory. Your sovereigns, who were born upon the throne, can allow themselves to be beaten twenty times, and will always return to their capitals; I cannot do that; I am a self-made soldier.' . . . Metternich . . . question[ed] the effectiveness of Napoleon's own troops. 'I have seen your soldiers,' he said to him. 'They are no more than children. And when these infants have been wiped out, what will you have left?' It was this remark which provoked Napoleon's supreme outburst: he flung his hat into the corner and yelled at Metternich: 'You are not a soldier,' he yelled. 'You know nothing of what goes on in a soldier's mind. I grew up upon the field of battle, and a man such as I am cares little for the life of a million men.' Metternich did not offer to pick up the hat which remained in its corner; he leant against a little table which stood between the windows and said calmly to Napoleon, 'If only the words that you have just uttered could echo from one end of France to the other!'

104

Napoleon at this pulled himself together and adopted a quieter tone; he began, as was his wont, to pace round the drawing room . . . talking to Metternich in insistent tones. On his second round he noticed his own hat in the corner and picked it up himself. He spoke more calmly. 'I may lose my throne,' he said, 'but I shall bury the whole world in its ruins.'

It was getting dark; it was already half past eight at night; Napoleon walked with Metternich to the door of the ante-chamber. He was by now calm, almost affectionate. He tapped the Austrian on the shoulder. 'No,' he said, 'you will never make war against me.' 'Sire,' Metternich replied (or says that he replied), 'you are a lost man.'

From The Congress of Vienna *by Harold Nicolson (Constable, London, 1946).*

TALLEYRAND, his advice – that Napoleon should consolidate his position rather than press on with ever more conquests – having been rejected, starts to intrigue against his master as an insurance policy for his own future, should Napoleon overreach himself.

The most sensational event in this campaign of intrigue took place at a reception given in Talleyrand's house in the month of December. For years the rivalry and mutual dislike between Talleyrand and Fouché had been as fixed and as familiar a feature in the political firmament as the hostility between Bonapartes and Bourbons. When, therefore, the name of the Minister of Police [Fouché] was announced at a reception given by the Prince of Benevento [Talleyrand] the other guests could hardly believe their ears and turned to watch with curiosity the encounter of two such adversaries. The sensation seekers were not disappointed. The host limped eagerly eagerly forward to extend the warmest of welcomes to the new arrival, and linking arms with him proceeded to pace up and down through the series of lofty apartments engaged in long and eager conversation, while the rest of Paris gazed and pointed, whispered and wondered.

The next morning the news that this conversation had taken place was on its way to every capital in Europe. Not least swiftly did it travel to Valladolid whence Napoleon was now directing operations in the Peninsula. Had he remained there longer the fortunes of that war would have been changed, but he considered it of greater importance to return to Paris. It was said that he had received reports to the effect that the Austrian Government were taking steps to prepare for a renewal of hostilities, but Napoleon believed that an alliance between Talleyrand and Fouché was more formidable than the mobilisation of Austria.

From Talleyrand *by Duff Cooper (Jonathan Cape, London, 1932).*

DIPLOMATIC LANGUAGE can at times be all the more powerful for observing the formalities. The Spanish Government here ripostes vigorously to notes from the Austrian and Russian Chargés d'Affaires which it considers insulting.

The Spanish Government had always been very tenacious about the interference of foreign Governments in their domestic affairs; and it will no doubt be remembered by many how sharply it resented the conduct pursued by the allied Sovereigns of Austria, Prussia, and Russia, at Verona, in 1823.

In January of that year, notes were addressed to the Spanish Government by the Chargés d'Affaires of those three countries, in which they each, officially, announced the views of their respective Sovereigns assembled at Verona, which were that, owing to the disordered state of the country, they were unable to remain any longer to represent their countries at the Court of Madrid; they at the same time demanded their passports.

To the Austrian Chargé d'Affaires' note, the Spanish Foreign Minister replied as follows:

I have received the note which you were pleased to address to me yesterday, and confining myself, for the present, to informing you that it is a matter of indifference to His Catholic Majesty's Government whether it maintains, or not, relations with that of Vienna, I forward, by Royal order, the passports which you demand.

But to the Russian Chargé d'Affaires' note, a much sharper answer was returned. The Spanish Minister said:

106

I have received the very insolent note which you addressed to me yesterday, and confining my answer to informing you that you have scandalously abused – perhaps through ignorance – the Law of Nations, which must always be respectable in the eyes of the Spanish Government, I transmit to you, by His Majesty's order, the passports which you have demanded, and hope you will be pleased to leave this capital in as short a time as possible.

From Recollections of the Old Foreign Office *by Sir Edward Hertslet*
(John Murray, London, 1901).

BERTIE MITFORD, who was later created Lord Redesdale and was the grandfather of the famous Mitford sisters, served as a diplomatic secretary at the British Legation in Japan between 1866 and 1870. During an incident in the civil war there in 1868, some of the foreign representatives were fired on by one of the warring factions. The chief culprit was arrested and condemned to commit ritual hara-kiri in front of representatives of the Legations concerned. Here Mitford describes in a letter to his father the macabre spectacle which his diplomatic function obliged him to witness.

My dear Father, I was last night sent officially to witness the execution by harakiri (harakiri from hara the belly and kiri root form of kiru to cut) (self-immolation by disembowelling) of Taki Zensaburo, the officer of the Prince of Bizen. He it was who gave the order to fire on the foreign settlement at Hyogo on the 4th of last month. As the harakiri is one of the customs of this country which has excited the greatest curiosity in Europe, although owing to the fact that it had never hitherto been witnessed by foreigners it has seemed little better than a matter of fable, I will tell you what occurred.

The ceremony, which was ordered by the Mikado himself, took place at 10.30 at night in the temple of Seifukuji. . . . A witness was sent from each of the foreign legations. . . . We were seven foreigners in all.

After an interval of a few moments of anxious suspense, Taki Zensaburo, a stalwart man 32 year of age, with a noble air, walked into the hall, attired in his dress of ceremony with the

107

peculiar hempen cloth wings which are worn on great occasions. He was accompanied by a kaishaku and three officers who wore the jimbaori or war-surcoat with gold tissue facings. The word kaishaku, it should be observed, is one to which our word executioner is no equivalent term. The office is that of a gentleman; in many cases it is performed by a kinsman or friend of the condemned, and the relation between them is rather that of principal and second than that of victim and executioner. In this instance the kaishaku was a pupil of Taki Zensaburo, and was selected by the friends of the latter from among their own number for his skill in swordsmanship.

With the kaishaku on his left hand, Taki Zensaburo advanced slowly towards the Japanese witnesses and the two bowed before them; then drawing near to the foreigners they saluted in the same way – perhaps even with more deference. In each case the salutation was ceremoniously returned. Slowly and with great dignity the condemned man mounted on to the raised floor, prostrated himself before the high altar twice and seated himself on the felt carpet with his back to the high altar, the kaishaku crouching on his left-hand side. One of the attendant officers then came forward bearing a stand of the kind used in temples for offerings, on which wrapped in paper lay the wakizashi, the short sword or dirk of the Japanese, nine inches and a half in length, with a point and an edge as sharp as a razor's. This he handed, prostrating himself, to the condemned man who received it reverently, raised it to his head with both hands, and placed it in front of himself.

After another profound obeisance, Taki Zensaburo, in a voice which betrayed just so much emotion and hesitation as might be expected from a man who is making a painful confession, but with no sign of fear either in his face or manner spoke as follows: 'I and I alone unwarrantably gave the order to fire on the foreigners at Kobe, and again as they tried to escape, on the 11th of last month (4 February). For this crime I disembowel myself, and I beg you who are present to do me the honour of witnessing the act.'

Deliberately, with a steady hand, he took the dirk that lay before him – he looked at it wistfully, almost affectionately – for a moment he seemed to collect his thoughts for the last time, and then stabbing himself deeply below the waist on the left hand side he drew it slowly across to the right side and turning the dirk in the wound gave a slight cut upwards: during this sickeningly painful operation he never moved a muscle of his face. When he drew out the dirk he leant forward and stretched out his neck – an expression of pain for the first time crossed his face, but he uttered no sound. At that moment the kaishaku, who still crouching by his side, had been keenly watching his every movement, sprang to his feet, poised his sword for a second in the air – there was a flash – a heavy ugly thud, a crashing fall – with one blow the head had been severed from the body.

A dead silence followed – broken only by the hideous noise of blood gushing out of the inert heap before us which but a moment before had been a brave and chivalrous man. It was horrible.

The kaishaku made a low bow – wiped his sword and retired from the raised floor, and the stained dirk was solemnly borne away, a bloody proof of the execution.

The two representatives of the Mikado then left their places and crossing over to where the foreign witnesses sat called us to witness that the sentence of death upon Taki Zensaburo had been faithfully carried out. The ceremony being at an end we left the temple.

From Mitford's Japan: The Memoirs and Recollections, 1866–1906, of Algernon Bertram Mitford, the first Lord Redesdale *edited by Hugh Cortazzi (The Athlone Press, London, 1985).*

LORD DERBY, whose foreign policy was described as 'floating down a stream occasionally putting out a diplomatic boat-hook to avoid collisions', here takes a firm line in protecting British subjects from abuses abroad.

In 1874 a gross outrage was inflicted on the British Vice-Consul at St. José, Guatemala, and the policy pursued by Lord Derby on that occasion may well be recorded here as laying down an important principle.

Mr Magee was a merchant at San José as well as British Vice-Consul, and on the facts of the outrage being reported to the Foreign Office, Mr Magee, although he had been severely flogged and subjected to other indignities, expressed himself desirous of having no claim for compensation made, publicly or privately, on his account. Lord Derby, however, did not support this view. He said:

Her Majesty's Government consider that Mr Magee has no personal position which can interfere with the exaction of due reparation. His character as a merchant must, in such a grave instance of indignity to the nation of which he is an officer, be merged in his rank as one of Her Majesty's Consular Servants. In such a case the insult extends from the individual to his country, and Her Majesty's Government cannot permit that the honour of Great Britain, and the future security of British subjects in Central America, should be allowed to be compromised in deference to the timidity or private interests of any one person.

Ten thousand pounds were then demanded to be paid as an indemnity, and a salute to be given to the British flag; which demands were complied with.

From Recollections of the Old Foreign Office *by Sir Edward Hertslet*
(John Murray, London, 1901).

SIR EDWARD GOSCHEN, while British Ambassador in Berlin, goes yachting with the Kaiser at Kiel and hears the news of the assassination of the Archduke Franz Ferdinand, which provoked the events leading to the outbreak of the First World War a few months later.

Tuesday 23 June
Reached Kiel 6.23. Had to change into a frock coat and tall hat – and was recd. by Admiral with Guns – Guard of Honour, Band and much pomp all together: *but* I rather enjoyed it as I like all shows! Admiral very kind and nice and pleasant set of Officers. Dined with P'ce and P'cess Henry of Prussia in the evening.
Bunt joined me at Kiel Station.

Thursday 25 June
Had a splendid sail on the *Meteor* – the Emperor [the Kaiser Wilhelm II] very cheery. He rather hoped that I should be seasick

110

as there was a spanking breeze – but I told him that as the representative of a Maritime Nation I was afraid I must disappoint him. Old Tirpitz – Eisendecker – Warrender – Goodenough and I were the guests – besides one or two others. The Yacht did not win. She carried away her main Jackyard Topsail yard on the way down – then lost a minute and a half at the start – and was, I thought, not well sailed in the race. P'ce Henry was of the same opinion and said that HIM had got rid of his English skipper and crew too soon. We had a jolly good lunch after the race.

Sunday 28 June
While the Emperor was racing in *Meteor* she received a wireless to the effect that the Archduke Franz Ferdinand and His Consort had been assassinated at Sarajevo by Servian agitators!

This is a dreadful business and Heaven knows what it may lead to – as the Austrians have for ages been looking out for an excuse to trample on Servia and to punish her for her continual agitation. Personally, too, I am very sorry as the Archduke was always very nice and kind to me – and His Wife was charming. It was a most determined assassination – as the conspirators missed more than once – and a third attempt had been planned if the 2nd had failed. Too awful!

Monday 29 June
The Emperor left Kiel. Ad'l Warrender and I went to see him off at the station. He was very depressed and angry. He told me that the assassination was a dreadful blow to him – both because it was only a fortnight ago that he had been staying with them and seen their happy family life – and because it was such an upset of everything they had planned and arranged together. He didn't know who the next successor was and didn't care – and the Emperor Francis Joseph was so old – the Crown of Austria–Hungary would soon be in the hands of an unknown and inexperienced boy!

From The Diary of Sir Edward Goschen, *1914*.

M. PAUL CAMBON, the impeccable French Ambassador in London in 1914, finds in the weeks before the outbreak of the First World War that it cannot be taken for granted that Britain will enter the arena alongside France. His confidence in Britain badly shaken, he has memorable encounters with Sir Edward Grey (British Foreign Secretary), Sir Arthur Nicolson (Permanent Under-Secretary at the Foreign Office) and the Foreign Editor of The Times.

Nicolson walked, as usual, to the Foreign Office. He was met by the news that Germany had declared war on Russia and that France was mobilising. The Cabinet met again to consider their position and at the conclusion of the meeting Sir Edward Grey again sent for M. Cambon. He informed him that 'France must take her own decision at this moment without reckoning on an assistance which we were not now in a position to promise.' M. Cambon stated that he must refuse to transmit such an answer to his Government. A few minutes later, white and speechless, he staggered into Nicolson's room. Nicolson went towards him and took his hands to guide him to a chair. 'Ils vont nous lâcher, ils vont nous lâcher,' was all that the Ambassador could say. Nicolson went upstairs to interview Sir Edward Grey. He found him pacing his room, biting at his lower lip. Nicolson asked whether it was indeed true that we had refused to support France at the moment of her greatest danger. Grey made no answer beyond a gesture of despair. 'You will render us,' Nicolson said angrily, 'a by-word among nations.' He then returned to M. Cambon. The Ambassador had by then recovered. He suggested that the moment had arrived to produce 'mon petit papier.' This document referred to the 1912 arrangement and made it clear that France, relying on our word, had deprived her northern coasts of all means of defence. Nicolson advised him not to send in an official Note to this effect in view of the high tension then prevailing. He promised, however, to convey the reminder to Sir Edward. An hour later he sent the following minute to the Secretary of State:

53 CADOGAN GARDENS,
August 1, 1914.

SIR EDWARD GREY.

'M. Cambon pointed out to me this afternoon that it was at our request that France had moved her fleets to the Mediterranean, on the understanding that we undertook the protection of her Northern and Western coasts. As I understand you told him that you would submit to the Cabinet the question of a possible German naval attack on French Northern and Western Ports it would be well to remind the Cabinet of the above fact.'

(*Minute by Sir Edward Grey*):
'I have spoken to the P.M. and attach great importance to the point being settled to-morrow.'

E.G. 1.8.14.

M. Cambon, meanwhile, had returned to the French Embassy. He was there visited by Mr. Wickham Steed, Foreign Editor of *The Times*. The latter asked him: 'Que faites-vous, M. Cambon?' 'J'attends de savoir,' he answered, 'si le mot honneur doit être rayé du vocabulaire anglais.' This is the sole recorded instance of an impassioned remark on the part of M. Cambon.

From Sir Arthur Nicolson, Bart., First Lord Carnock: A Study in Old Diplomacy
by Harold Nicolson (Constable, London, 1950).

SIR CECIL SPRING RICE's main task as British Ambassador in Washington during the First World War was to persuade the Americans to enter the war against Germany; any obvious pressure would have encouraged isolationist tendencies; his quiet influence contributed greatly to the achievement of the objective – which he here describes.

I shall never forget a rainy evening in April when I drove down to the Capitol. The Capitol was illuminated from below – white against a black sky. United States troops were collected round it,

113

not for parade, but for defence – and necessary too – and the President came down. I sat on the floor of Congress. The President came in, and in a perfectly calm, deliberate voice he recited word by word, deed by deed, what Germany had said and done. At the end he said: 'I have told you the facts. We have several courses to take. One course we will not take, the course of submission.' I shall never forget the cheer I heard at those words. The die was cast; it was that there was but one course to be taken with honour, and that course was taken.

From The Letters and Friendships of Sir Cecil Spring Rice
edited by Stephen Gwynn (Constable, London, 1929).

SIR MILES LAMPSON's task as British Ambassador in Egypt during the Second World war was an unusual one. There was a huge British army in the country defending the Suez Canal against the German army under Rommel, with a weak and pro-Italian King Farouk presiding over the Egyptian government. In 1942 Lampson – with British tanks surrounding the royal palace – confronted Farouk with an instrument of abdication. It was one of the last manifestations of imperial diplomatic power being exercised on the grand scale.

Owing to this delay we were in Cairo when there occurred the crisis which nearly brought to an end the reign of King Farouk. Everything had been prepared. The cars were ready, the road to the canal was cleared, and at the other end of it was waiting the ship that was to bear the King to his ultimate destination. The experienced hand of Walter Monckton had drafted the abdication, the King had inked his pen to sign it, behind him towered the imposing forms of Miles Lampson and Oliver Lyttelton. The King looked up at them. 'Will you give me another chance?' he asked. He was only twenty-one. They relented. The orders were cancelled. The crisis was off, and when we returned from dining with Mr Kirk, the American Minister, we found most of the principal actors in the hall of the Embassy discussing the evening as people discuss the first night of a play when nobody is sure whether it has been a success or a failure. I am quite sure that those who were responsible for the decision were right. The youthful King expelled by the British would have been a national hero, which there is no danger of the middle-aged King thrown out by his own people ever becoming.

From Old Men Forget *by Duff Cooper (Rupert Hart-Davis, London, 1953).*

ROBERT P. JOYCE of the US Foreign Service stumbles on an unlikely historical connection.

Late in 1945 my wife and I visited from Bern, where I was stationed, Vaduz, the capital of Liechtenstein. We stayed at the inn which was owned and operated by the prime minister. The ruling prince and his young, pretty and gay Viennese wife asked us for dinner at the castle to which we proceeded in one of the taxis owned by the foreign minister. We met an assortment of Liechtenstein princes and their wives and other amiable guests in an informal and relaxed atmosphere.

At dinner I found myself seated next to a very old lady who spoke perfect English. I assumed that she must be a retired governess or other old family retainer and friend. She politely asked me where I had been stationed as an American diplomatic officer. I told her and when I mentioned Belgrade, the following exchange took place:

'Did you did not find the Serbs to be a rather fierce people?'

I replied that they were certainly courageous and fiercely independent as the Austrians found out in 1914 and as did the Germans in the last war.

'Yes, I suppose they are. My brother was visiting Bosnia-Herzegovina many years ago and the Serbs murdered him.'

'Good heavens,' I replied. 'How did that happen?'

'It was most unfortunate,' she continued. 'If I remember correctly it was in June of the year 1914. It happened in the town of Sarajevo.'

She sighed and shook her head gently. 'Franz Ferdinand's murder caused a great deal of political trouble at the time.'

From Tales of the Foreign Service *edited by Ralph Hilton*
(University of South Carolina Press, Columbia, South Carolina, USA, 1978).

115

ERNEST BEVIN – the trade union leader – become Foreign Secretary after the Labour landslide victory in the 1945 election in Britain. He was a surprise choice and the appointment was said to have been made at the prompting of King George VI. This account of his first day in office, by his then private secretary, gives the flavour of the total change of style from Anthony Eden, and of the rigours of having to start the new job by replacing Eden at the Potsdam Conference at the conclusion of the Second World War.

Bevin was appointed that night and received the seals of office at the Palace on Saturday morning. He told us afterwards that he had asked Attlee for the Treasury but had told him that he was prepared to serve where he was most wanted. It was only at 6 p.m. on Friday that he had heard that he was to become Foreign Secretary. At the Palace on Saturday he met Dalton. 'I wanted your job,' he said to Dalton. 'And I wanted yours,' replied Dalton.

Bob Dixon and I met Bevin at Northolt airport on Saturday at lunchtime. Two C 54s were waiting, one for the Prime Minister, the other for the Foreign Secretary. For the send-off to Potsdam there was a small party of wives, a large party of cameramen and an even greater throng of cheering RAF ground crew. We climbed into our plane. It was the first flight Bevin had ever made. He sank into his seat puffing. Bob said, 'You have had a pretty busy morning, I'm afraid.' Bevin said, 'Yes, you see I've had all my Transport House stuff to clear up' – then with a broad grin, 'We never expected this to happen.'

'Fasten safety belts, please,' shouted the steward. Bevin struggled and went on struggling, but the two ends of the belt would not meet.

There was a plenary meeting of the three Powers that night at 10 p.m. Talking afterwards to Bob and me, Bevin said that Stalin struck him as 'a man with too much on his mind and that makes him weak'. He also gave us his views on negotiating with foreigners: 'You see, I've had a good deal of experience with foreigners: before the last war I had to do a good deal of negotiation with ships' captains of all nationalities. These people, Stalin and Truman, are just the same as all Russians and Americans; and dealing with them over foreign affairs is just the same as trying

116

to come to a settlement about unloading a ship. Oh yes, I can handle them.'

We arrived back at the villa to a supper of whiskies and sandwiches. Earlier we had asked Bevin whether he had any views about the food, and whom he would like invited. He clearly was not selective about either – in contrast to Eden.

'I don't care tuppence who you invite to dinner,' he said, 'and I like sandwiches.'

So we had sandwiches for dinner, and various members of the delegation as guests. 'This is a good establishment,' Bevin said, contentedly tucking into the sandwiches. To Alec Cadogan [the Permanent Under Secretary of State at the Foreign Office] he said, 'Ever been to the Communist Club in Maiden Lane?'

'No,' Cadogan replied, as if suddenly charged with murder.

'Ever met Ben Luzzi?'

'No,' he said with equal emphasis.

'He used to be a Trade Union leader in Vienna before the last war. Ever met Pat Lazarus? Used to see a lot of him in Vienna too.'

This went on for some time, but it did not look as though by the end of the evening Bevin and Cadogan would find that they had many old international acquaintances in common. Bevin did not seem surprised or annoyed. He just went on munching and talking happily.

So ended Bevin's first day as Foreign Secretary, which began with a visit to Buckingham Palace and ended with a meeting with Stalin and Molotov. Rarely can anyone have been flung so violently into mid-stream; but Bevin displayed immediately one of his outstanding qualities, confidence in himself and in those who worked most closely with him. He immediately took over the leading role in the British delegation without exciting any resentment from the Prime Minister.

From The Private Office *by Sir Nicholas Henderson, GCMG*
(Weidenfeld & Nicolson, London, 1984).

CHARLES W. THAYER recounts how an American ambassador to Yugoslavia was carried away in conversation by Marshal Tito's charms.

In making oneself charming, Callières [who published a treatise on diplomacy in 1716] warns that one should be careful to avoid getting overcharmed oneself. Shortly before the [Second World] War ended, the military mission which I headed in Yugoslavia was replaced by an embassy. Before I left I drove the newly appointed ambassador – an ex-businessman with little foreign experience – to the White Palace to meet Marshal Tito. Slightly uneasy because of his inexperience, I had made sure that no interpreter other than myself would be present.

On the drive to the palace, the new ambassador kept muttering: 'They say Tito has charm but he won't charm me.'

When we sat down, Tito was in good form and sprayed his charm as though from a perfume flagon. Scarcely ten minutes had elapsed before the ambassador was leaning forward, hanging on every word as the little Balkan Communist vented his usual complaints about how he was misunderstood in the United States.

'Why, do you know, Mr Ambassador, your newspaper people have even called me a dictator!'

The ambassador shook his head perplexed as I translated. 'Tell the Marshal,' he said to me, 'there is only one thing to be done – for Tito to go to Washington and explain his position as he has to me. I know my government will welcome him warmly.'

Aware that the ambassador had no authority to invite Tito and that scarcely anyone at that tense moment would be less welcome in Washington, I paraphrased the ambassador's words, expressing the hope that someday, after he had turned over the reins of government, Tito might find it interesting to come to America and see how we dealt with our problems.

Unfortunately, however, Tito had been taking English lessons and had made considerably more progress than I suspected. He looked at me, smiled, and wagged his finger: 'Colonel, you know very well the ambassador said no such thing.'

From Diplomat *by Charles W. Thayer (Harper and Brothers, New York, 1959).*

SIR GLADWYN JEBB, while British Ambassador to the United Nations in New York during the period of Senator McCarthy's anti-Communist witch-hunt in the United States in the early 1950s, uses a television appearance to point the contrast with political tolerance in the United Kingdom.

As a matter of fact I did once get a word in. On some television programme – I forget which – I was, as usual, being rather harried by Republican news-hawks. This time they concentrated on the Dean of Canterbury who had, I must say, been making even more of a fool of himself than usual in his eulogies of the most important totalitarian slave labour system. First of all I had, of course, to explain that Dr Hewlett Johnson [Dean of Canterbury, dubbed 'The Red Dean' for his Communist sympathies] was *not* the Archbishop of Canterbury, and that even if he had been the Government could not control his political utterances if he chose to make them. But, said my interlocutor, here is a respected Anglican divine, a member of the Establishment, actually preaching Communism which is admittedly the arch-enemy of all the Western democracies. Why don't you *do* something about it in England? I'll tell you why, I said severely. The simple answer to your question is that *England* is still a free country! The newsman was a good chap as a matter of fact. He said afterwards over a drink, 'Sir Gladwyn, I felt as if I had been pole-axed!'

From The Memoirs of Lord Gladwyn *(Weidenfeld & Nicolson, London, 1972).*

NIKITA KHRUSHCHEV was deeply incensed by the discovery in 1960 that the Americans had been flying U-2 spy-planes over the Soviet Union. The US, British and French heads of government had for many months been carefully preparing through diplomatic channels (in which the editor played a minor role in Moscow) for a first-ever summit conference with Khrushchev, in the hope that this would ease the Cold War tensions. But when they assembled in Paris Khrushchev dashed their hopes, as US Ambassador Bohlen here explains.

Khrushchev arrived in Paris on May 14, two days before the conference, and called on de Gaulle and Macmillan, who immediately informed the United States delegation of the conversations. Khrushchev sought to prevail on both to bring pressure on Eisenhower to issue a public apology for the U-2 flights, to pledge not to permit any more of them, and to punish those responsible. Both de Gaulle and Macmillan agreed to transmit the message, but held out no hope of its acceptance and made clear they were giving no support whatsoever to Khrushchev. In fact, I believe that de Gaulle said he did not think such a request was feasible.

As a result of the information received from the British and the French, President Eisenhower was fully prepared for Khrushchev's tirade at the opening session. On our side, there was the President, Secretary Herter, Alexander Akalovsky, an American interpreter, and I, as official note-taker. I had been designated for this because of my knowledge of all three languages. After a cold and formal greeting, a brief handshake, without smiles, between the Americans and the Soviets, the conference opened. Khrushchev took the floor and gave a twenty-minute harangue. Acting the role of the injured party, he asked how anyone could fly over the territory of a friendly country, spying on its most intimate secrets, and not recognize the flight as an act of hostility. He implied that he had not expected such an act from President Eisenhower and withdrew the invitation to the President to visit the Soviet Union. How, he asked, could he explain to the Russian people a visit from the leader of so hostile a country? Then he demanded an apology.

As Khrushchev talked, Eisenhower's bald head turned various shades of pink, a sure sign that he was using every bit of will to hold his temper. De Gaulle then said that while he did not condone espionage, it was necessary. As far as flying over the territory of another nation was concerned, he knew that a number of times a month Soviet satellites, which might contain cameras, crossed over territories of the French Republic. De Gaulle noted that he had not found it necessary to make a public scene over these flights. Macmillan spoke in somewhat the same way, although with more regret in his voice and demeanor. Macmillan had placed a great deal of hope on the summit meeting. He felt, following his visit to Moscow the previous winter, that the conference offered a great hope of peace, and he had possibly exaggerated public expectations of it.

When Eisenhower spoke, he gave no sign of the intense anger that he had obviously felt a few minutes before. He then revealed officially what he had decided a week before, announcing that he had ordered that the aerial spying be discontinued. He refused, however, to apologize. It was hoped on the Western side that Eisenhower's remarks might satisfy Khrushchev, but it soon became apparent that the Soviets would not accept anything but a formal abject apology from the President. The conference adjourned, subject to recall in forty-eight hours.

The next day, a group of us had dinner with the President at the American Embassy. After dinner, we had a long, informal discussion about the prospects of the conference. I voiced skepticism over the possibility of Khrushchev's returning to the conference unless the President issued an apology, which was impossible because the U-2 flights were justified and because the President of the United States could not abase himself. I also expressed skepticism that any substantial progress could be made at the conference even if it should resume. The President asked why. I said I could not see how the Soviets would give up East Germany for the sake of unification of the two sections of the country. They had had many opportunities in the past. By 1960, the East German Soviet regime was fully established. There might have been an opportunity for some progress on Berlin, but I doubted it. Eisenhower was a good listener, asking various people what their views were. Someone suggested that Thompson and I talk with Gromyko to try to work out a settlement of the dispute, but it was decided such a move would be useless. The only problem holding up the conference was the impossibility of the President's making a public

121

apology to Khrushchev. This was never seriously considered.

At the appointed time, the three Western leaders gathered in the Elysée and waited for some sign that Khrushchev would return. When he did not, Macmillan exhorted Eisenhower and de Gaulle to let him make a personal appeal to Khrushchev to return to the conference. With tears in his eyes, Macmillan said that all over the British Isles the day before, simple, trusting people had been praying in little churches for peace. The failure of this conference would be a mortal blow to their hopes and aspirations, and he felt that as leaders of their countries they owed it to their people and to their passionate desire for peace to make one more effort. I was sitting behind the President, and I heard him tell Herter, 'You know, poor old Hal is very upset about this, and I think we might go as far as to meet him on this one point.' I quickly scribbled a note to Herter saying that a personal, emotional appeal was a mistake, that it was not a technique to be used with the Kremlin leaders. While it would not do much harm, I thought it was singularly unnecessary. Before the note could reach Herter, de Gaulle, speaking in his most regal manner in French, said he could not agree with the Prime Minister. The method was too Byzantine, and we must never forget that the Byzantine Empire fell because of addiction to intrigues and similar roundabout methods. His tone was icy and contemptuous. In any event, he effectively killed the idea of another approach to Khrushchev.

From Witness to History 1929–1969 *by Charles E. Bohlen*
(W.W. Norton & Company Inc., New York, 1973).

DR RALPH BUNCHE, who was political Under-Secretary on the staff of the United Nations in 1960, experiences some unexpected problems in the ex-Belgian Congo in the weeks after independence.

The UN was a total novelty to the Congolese. Already on July 10, Bunche had to explain to Lumumba (then Prime Minister of the former Belgian Congo) that the UN would not be in the Congo to fight anyone; and a district administrator in Thysville had asked him, 'L'ONU, c'est quelle tribu?' ('The UN, what tribe is that?').

From Hammarskjöld *by Brian Urquhart (The Bodley Head, London, 1973).*

122

PRESIDENT DE GAULLE is provoked to veto British entry into the EEC by a diplomatic misunderstanding with Mr Harold Macmillan on an unrelated matter.

In late 1962 Mr Harold Macmillan, as British Prime Minister, paid an important visit to President de Gaulle at Rambouillet to review world affairs. The President felt it was an occasion for sharing confidences and drawing closer together. Shortly after the meeting was over, Macmillan flew to Nassau for his now famous meeting with President Kennedy. The latter had just cancelled the Skybolt weapon programme, under strong pressure from the US Treasury to release funds for other purposes. Macmillan was alarmed at the prospect of the UK being left with no credible nuclear deterrent and managed to persuade Kennedy at Nassau that the UK should have Polaris submarines to fill the gap.

When de Gaulle heard of this new agreement, he felt that Macmillan had been distinctly devious in not telling him what he was up to when they had spent so long at Rambouillet talking over world affairs so recently. He told Chancellor Adenauer subsequently that he had been 'insulted' by Macmillan hiding his intentions from him.

It was in this mood that de Gaulle approached the final stages of the British application to join the EEC later the same year, and it was undoubtedly a major factor in deciding him that Britain was more committed to the US than to the EEC, and therefore should be vetoed from entry. The apparent duplicity also helped him to justify his action in exercising that veto.

The irony of the event was that Macmillan thought – and subsequently maintained in his memoirs – that he *had* informed de Gaulle of his intentions about Polaris. The two leaders had had a tête-à-tête, and some reports suggest that Macmillan had talked to de Gaulle in French and that the President had possibly not understood him. The ambassadors were not present, or such a misunderstanding could not have occurred.

From an account given to the editor by a former British Ambassador to France.

DR HENRY KISSINGER, as foreign affairs adviser to President Nixon, aroused wide controversy and suspicion by his secret visit to Peking in 1971 to pave the way for an American rapprochement *with Communist China. Here he justifies that secrecy – which ran contrary to President Wilson's concept of 'open covenants openly arrived at'.*

Had the trip been announced in advance, it would have triggered weeks of speculation to which we could not respond. Opponents would have had an opportunity to raise sinister implications that no reassurances would entirely dispel – especially since we did not really control the agenda of the talks. Even ostensible supporters could embarrass us by putting forward the traditional agenda we were determined to transcend. And some countries with the best claim to being consulted also had the highest incentive to sabotage the trip. To maintain our control over the presentation of the event was synonymous with maintaining control over our policy and its consequences. As the President's Foreign Policy Report of February 9, 1972, conceded, we paid a price for secrecy, but the price was 'unavoidable' and the reasons for it 'overriding'.

The outcome of my trip was not foreseeable; we did not want to risk inflating expectations, generating pressures, and forcing the two sides to take public positions before the results were known. The shock effect of the reversal of positions would have been inevitable no matter how the trip had been handled (witness the Ping-Pong experience). In any event, the report argued, no substantive negotiations with the Chinese would take place until Nixon's trip, before which we would have months to consult with our allies – a promise faithfully carried out.

My colleague Bill Safire found a precedent for our position:

July 19, 1971.

MEMORANDUM FOR: HENRY KISSINGER
FROM: BILL SAFIRE

Here is a quotation about secrecy that you may find occasion to use:

The most dangerous of all moral dilemmas: When we are obliged
to conceal truth in order to help the truth to be victorious.

Dag Hammarskjöld

From White House Years by Henry Kissinger
(Little, Brown and Company, Boston, 1979).

*LORD CARRINGTON was one of the Foreign Secretaries who
was most popular with the British diplomats who served him, and
this story, told to the editor by Sir Richard Parsons, illustrates a* modus
operandi *which ensured good relations between the Foreign Office and
embassies in the field.*

Unlike some other Foreign Secretaries, Peter Carrington realized
that his task would be made easier if he tried to elevate the status
of his own Ambassadors. When I was Ambassador to Spain,
I attended a meeting at Number Ten between Prime Minister
Thatcher and Calvo Sotelo, the Spanish Prime Minister. The
Spanish PM made some request to Mrs Thatcher. 'Do we agree,
Peter?' she asked Carrington. He turned to me. 'Do we agree,
Richard?' he asked. I said we did, Carrington said we did, then
Thatcher said we did. Months later, I told Carrington how much
this incident had helped me with the Spaniards, who now treated
me as a man of influence. 'Of course,' he replied, 'that was the
object of the exercise.'

125

6

Pitfalls of Protocol

THE RULES OF protocol or etiquette were intended to simplify diplomatic life by establishing a code of conduct which would obviate disputes and embarrassments by clarifying procedures and precedence.

Before the Congress of Vienna laid down, for instance, that the seniority of ambassadors should be decided by who had been *en poste* longest, it had been usual for ambassadors to dispute their seniority on the grounds of the seniority of the sovereign they represented; the ambassador of the Holy Roman Emperor claimed precedence over representatives of mere kings, while the ambassador of His Most Christian Majesty of France claimed precedence over the representatives of 'lesser' kings, and so on. There had from time to time been ugly scenes, when ambassadorial carriages raced through the streets to establish the rights of their occupants; accidents and breaches of the peace had ensued. The new order was at once a clarification and a relief.

Unfortunately, however, many of the rules of protocol, based on court procedures, became immensely elaborate. Questions such as how far a host should accompany a departing guest (to the door, to the foot of the stairs, or to his carriage?), or who should leave visiting cards on whom, or which position in a carriage or on a sofa was most honourable, assumed a ridiculous significance in the formalized minuet of eighteenth- and nineteenth-century diplomatic life. As recently as the 1950s, when I joined the diplomatic service, all new entrants were given a book by Sir Marcus Cheke (a former Foreign Office protocol chief) informing newcomers how to behave and including some fairly quaint advice.

When the British government built the India Office in London it was found necessary to construct an audience chamber (which still exists) with four equally grand doors, so that four Indian princes of equal rank could enter the chamber simultaneously without anyone ceding precedence to anyone else. There are well-documented cases of ambassadors leaving dinner tables before the first course because they considered their *placement* to be below their dignity. Before the peace talks over Vietnam, much time was spent designing a table of a shape acceptable to all the participants. The ramifications of protocol are grist to the diplomatic mill, but can strike outsiders as ludicrous or bizarre.

It is for this reason that so much satire has been written on the subject. Lawrence Durrell's *Esprit de Corps* is a classic parody of the vagaries of the diplomatic corps in Belgrade, of which he was once a member. A whole anthology could be devoted to protocol stories.

––––––––––––––

SAMUEL PEPYS records in his diary a violent fracas between the ambassadors of France and Spain over their precedence, and his original editor – Lord Braybrooke – adds a footnote recounting how Louis XIV reacted to the news.

30th September 1661

This morning up by moon-shine, at five o'clock, to Whitehall, to meet Mr Moore at the Privy Seale, and there I heard of a fray between the two Embassadors of Spain and France; and that, this day, being the day of the entrance of an Embassador from Sweden, they intended to fight for the precedence. Our King, I heard, ordered that no Englishman should meddle in the business, but let them do what they would. And to that end all the soldiers in the town were in arms all the day long, and some of the train-bands in the City; and a great bustle through the City all the day.

127

4th October 1661
By coach to White Hall with Sir W. Pen. So to Mr Montagu, where
his man, Monsieur Eschar, makes a great complaint against the
English, that they did help the Spaniards against the French the
other day; and that their Embassador do demand justice of our
King, and that he do resolve to be gone for France the next week;
which I, and all that I met with, are glad of.

Braybooke's footnote:
The Courier sent by d'Estrades to Paris, with the news of his
discomfiture, arrived at the hôtel of the Comte de Brienne (Louis-
Henri de Lomenie, who had succeeded his father, Henri-Auguste,
as Secretary of State) at eleven at night. Brienne instantly repaired
to the King, then at supper with the Queen-Mother, his own
Queen, and his brother, Philippe of Anjou (Monsieur); and,
requesting Louis to appear composed before the numerous spec-
tators, he told him that the Spanish Ambassador's people had cut
the traces of his Ambassador's coach, killed two coachmen, and cut
the horses' bridles, and that the Spanish Ambassador's coach had
taken precedence of that of d'Estrades, whose own son had also
been wounded in the affray. In spite of the caution which he had
received, Louis rose up in such agitation, as nearly to overturn the
table; seized Brienne by the arm, led him into the Queen-Mother's
chamber, and bade him read d'Estrades's despatch. The Queen-
Mother followed in haste. 'What is the matter?' said she. 'It is,'
replied the King, 'an attempt to embroil the King of Spain and
myself.' The Queen-Mother begged him to return to the company.
'I have supped, Madame,' said he, raising his voice. 'I will be
righted in this affair, or I will declare war against the King of Spain;
and I will force him to yield precedence to my Ambassadors in
every Court in Europe.' 'Oh, my son!' replied the Queen-Mother,
'break not a peace which has cost me so dear; and remember, that
the King of Spain is my brother.' 'Leave me, madame,' rejoined
Louis, 'to hear d'Estrades' despatch. Return to the table, and let
some fruit only be prepared for me.' . . . Louis listened to the
despatch, and instantly gave his commands to Brienne, which
were, in substance, to order the Conde de Fuensallagna, the
Spanish Ambassador, to quit France instantly, and to forbid

the Marques de las Fuentes, his intended successor, to set foot on the French territory – to recall his Commissioners on the boundary question, as well as the Archbishop of Embrun, his Ambassador at Madrid – to demand from the King of Spain an apology proportionable to the offence; that de Batteville should be punished in person; and that, in all the Courts of Europe, the Spanish Ambassador should give place to the French: and, on refusal of any part of his demands, to declare war. Louis gained all and every point. After much paper war, and many protocols, Spain gave way. The Baron de Batteville was recalled: the Marques de las Fuentes was sent Ambassador Extraordinary to Paris, to tender apologies; and, on March 24, 1662, in the presence of twenty-seven Ambassadors and Envoys from various Courts of Europe, the Marques de las Fuentes declared to Louis XIV that the King, his master, had sent orders to all his Ambassadors and Ministers to abstain from all rivalry with those of Louis. Louis, turning to the foreign Ministers, desired them to communicate this declaration to their masters. The Dutch Ambassador drily remarked that he had heard of Embassies to tender obedience to the Pope, but that he had never before known of such from one prince to another. . . . A medal was struck by the French to commemorate this great event.

> *From* Diary and Correspondence of Samuel Pepys, FRS, Secretary to the Admiralty in the reigns of Charles II and James II, *with a Life and Notes by Richard, Lord Braybooke (George Allen & Unwin, London, 1848).*

THE EARL OF PORTLAND, as William III's ambassador to Louis XIV, refuses to comply with some demands of French protocol.

The King sent his own first lord-in-waiting to call on Portland with his compliments. Of course this nobleman received the *Door* (greeted at it), the *Hand*, the *Armchair* and the *Coach* (taken to it, put in, and seen off), in fact the whole works. Then came the Marquis de Villacerf representing the little newly-married Duchesse de Bourgogne who, the Queen and the Dauphine being no more, was now the first lady in the land. M. de Boneuil, the *Introducteur des Ambassadeurs* (what is called now *Chef du Protocole* [or director of

129

ceremonial] wanted Portland to go half-way down the stairs to meet Villacerf. Portland refused to budge further than the antechamber. Boneuil flew into a temper and hit the banisters with his cane. Portland took no notice. He and Villacerf then sent messengers to and fro. After a good long time Portland said he would go down two steps and no more. If this did not suit M. de Villacerf he had better withdraw. So up he came. However, there was more trouble when he left; Portland saw him downstairs (the *Door*) but did not wait to see him leave (the *Coach*). Boneuil, beside himself, seized Portland's coat-tails but Portland shook him off and went his way. 'The *Introducteur* made great complaints to me.' Then Monsieur's representative arrived and the same difference arose; and again with Madame's. 'Things may have been very different', he wrote to William, 'when the English King [Charles II] was ruled by the French: but this is no longer the case.' Boneuil, 'confounded and irritated', left the house abruptly, though he was supposed to sup there with Portland. The next day Portland went to Versailles to inform Torcy of these incidents and to tell Monsieur and Madame how very sorry he was that they had occurred. However, Monsieur, 'who knows about these things', said that he had been quite right. Boneuil was reproved; and after that, Portland never had any more reason to protest, all was plain sailing.

From The Sun King *by Nancy Mitford (Hamish Hamilton, London, 1966).*

BENJAMIN FRANKLIN already had an international reputation as a statesman, scientist and co-author of the American Declaration of Independence when he went to Paris to negotiate an alliance with France. When he and his fellow Commissioners were formally received by King Louis XVI at Versailles, Franklin maintained his individual style despite the pomp of his surroundings.

Until March 13 [1778], when Britain was informed, the alliance was still officially a French state secret. Now the moment had come for it to be publicly recognized by the King, who invited the American commissioners to an audience with him at the Palace of Versailles.

Deane, Lee, Ralph Izard and William Lee all rushed to the tailors to order their official court dress as prescribed by the court chamberlain. Not Franklin. He had successfully played the role of the rustic philosopher, the simple, unpretentious Quaker, and he did not intend to change it for the King. He laid out a plain suit of brown velvet, white hose, buckled shoes and a white hat that he would carry under his arm. He could not quite summon the courage to wear his old fur cap.

For a brief moment, he planned to wear a new wig. One did not appear baldheaded before the King of France. According to Paris periodicals of the day, Franklin called in the most fashionable perruquier of Paris, who scurried about measuring Franklin's head, making a dramatic performance of choosing just the right wig. He placed it on Franklin's head and tugged and pulled, but, to his dismay, the wig would not fit.

Franklin mildly suggested: 'Perhaps your wig is too small?'

'No,' shouted the temperamental wigmaker. 'Your head, sir, is too big!' A Paris reporter commented: 'It is true that Franklin does have a fat head. But it is great head.'

Franklin, by now out of patience, dismissed the perruquier and decided to defy custom by appearing before the King uncovered.

When the Americans arrived at Versailles, going first to Vergennes's apartments, the crowd outside set up a rousing cheer and then began to murmur in astonishment when people noted that Franklin was bald and not in court dress. The cheers rose again and they shouted: 'The Apostle of Liberty, Citizen Franklin!'

The chamberlain was shocked at the sight of Franklin and a scandal was narrowly averted when [he was persuaded] to allow Franklin to enter the King's reception room.

No one paid the slightest attention to Deane, Izard and the Lees. All eyes were on the venerable sage as he walked directly to the King, bowing courteously but not low, as befitted a free man.

Louis XVI, after his first surprise at Franklin's costume, smiled graciously. His words, recorded by the Duc de Croy, were simple yet impressive.

'Firmly assure Congress,' said the monarch, 'of my friendship.'

He spoke generously of Franklin's conduct and behaviour in the year he had been in France and thanked him and his colleagues for their efforts.

Franklin spoke for all the commissioners when he told the King: 'Your Majesty may count on the gratitude of Congress and its faithful observance of the pledges it now takes.'

Breaking court etiquette, the crowd of observers cheered as Franklin and the other Americans crossed the courtyard to be introduced to the Cabinet and the nobles of France.

The five Americans were the guests of honor at a banquet offered by Vergennes and then escorted back to the King and Queen for a more informal meeting. Marie Antoinette, now more sympathetic to the American cause, politely asked Franklin to stand by her side. From time to time she would turn to ask him questions about America.

Late that night, his eyes sparkling, the old man, now seventy-two, left the palace. The morrow would bring new crises, new efforts. But that night Ben Franklin savored his triumph at Versailles.

From Triumph in Paris: The Exploits of Benjamin Franklin *by David Schoenbrun*
(Harper & Row, New York, 1976).

LORD GRANVILLE LEVESON GOWER had a distinguished career as ambassador to St Petersburg (1804–7) and Paris (1824–41) and was created a Viscount and finally first Earl Granville. A handsome man who married late, he broke many hearts; he was also an indefatigable correspondent – mostly with ladies whose sympathies he evoked. Here he confides to Lady Bessborough his disgust at the sycophantic and exaggerated protocol of the Russian court.

St. Petersburgh,
Novbre 6th, 1804.

Why did you not write a little every day? Why, I have every Day been employed; I have had to pay visits without End, I have had to go 40 miles into the Country to be presented to the Empress Mother, and I have had conferences with Prince Czartoryski. Your first Question will be, Are you satisfied with yourself? To which I must answer shortly, *No.* In talking upon Business with

Czartoryski, I proceed in French with tolerable facility, but when I am at the Table vis à vis to the Empress Dowager, and that I have to answer long Questions with the Eyes of the whole Room upon me observing narrowly the language of the ambassador, I find a difficulty in squeezing out of my Mouth at the end or beginning of each sentence, Votre Majesté Impériale, and Elle instead of Vous, &c . . . I never was more disgusted than with the mean adulation that she [Lady Warren] has been paying to every body connected here with the Imperial Family – her extravagant and Hyperbolical praises of even the youngest Brothers and Sisters of the Emperor (ce sont des êtres tombés des cieux), positively make me sick. . . .

Nov. 8th.

I am not reconciled to my Situation. Nothing but the occupation of Business can make it tolerable. I am sick of the Punctilio of bowing 3 times to an Ambassador and twice to a Chargé d'affaires, &c., of walking out with the former through all the Rooms to the staircase, and accompanying the latter only to the door of the Ante-Room. There is scarcely a pretty woman to be seen, even Ponsonby's [his diplomatic secretary's] tender heart seems in no danger.

From The Private Correspondence of Lord Granville Leveson Gower 1781 to 1821
(John Murray, London, 1916).

LORD GRANVILLE LEVESON GOWER writes, again to Lady Bessborough but this time about the vagaries of one of his predecessors as Ambassador to Russia.

I was rather amused with a book giving an account of the Embassy of one of my predecessors in the reign of Charles 2d. Lord Carlisle (for that is the name of the Ambassador) seems very anxious to maintain the dignity of his Character; one instance among many others related in this book, notwithstanding my wish upon all occasions to assert the honour of the character with which I am invested, I am by no means disposed to imitate. The Ambassador perceives in walking from his Ship that the Colonel appointed to conduct him takes the right side, upon which he stops short upon the bridge, refuses to proceed another Step, and waits a quarter of an hour in the cold, until the Colonel returns from the Governor to whom he was sent for further instructions upon this important point of Etiquette.

From The Private Correspondence of Lord Granville Leveson Gower 1781 to 1821
(John Murray, London, 1916).

TSAR ALEXANDER I takes offence at the treatment he receives from Louis XVIII of France after the part he has played in defeating Napoleon and restoring the king to his throne.

On April 29 Louis XVIII arrived at Compiègne and on the following day he received the Emperor Alexander in private audience. The interview was not a success. The Tsar had prefaced his visit by a memorial in which he urged the restored monarch to exercise moderation in his government of the French people and to 'husband the memory of twenty-five years of glory'. Louis had not welcomed this advice. He adopted towards the Tsar a gracious rather than a grateful manner. He did not rise from his seat but merely waved the Tsar into a chair beside him. After a few conventional phrases had been interchanged he suggested that the Emperor might wish to retire to his room. A procession was formed and Alexander was conducted through the suite of apartments allotted to the Comte d'Artois, through the suite of apartments allotted to the Duc de Berri, and finally through the suite of apartments allotted to the Duchess d'Angoulême. When at last, by a dark and ill-lit passage, the Tsar reached his own rooms he was outraged by their unimportance. He informed Czernicheff, who had accompanied him as adjutant, that in no circumstances would he remain that night at Compiègne; he would return to Paris the moment dinner had been served. Nor did the meal, when it took place, assuage his indignation. Louis XVIII entered the dining room before him, and when the attendants hesitated with the dishes, the restored monarch called to them, in the high-pitched voice which he adopted when he intended to be rude, 'Me first!' Driving back to Paris that night the Tsar voiced his outraged feelings. 'Louis XIV', he expostulated, 'at the height of his power would not have received me differently at Versailles. One would actually think that it was he who had come to place *me* on *my* throne!' His reaction was immediate. He drove to Rambouillet to pay his respects to Marie Louise; he drove to Malmaison to visit the Empress Josephine; he drove to the Hôtel Cerruti to pay a formal call on Queen Hortense [all members of Napoleon's family]. And when, but a few weeks later, Josephine died of pneumonia, he sent a regiment of Russian guards to honour her funeral. The Bourbons were offended by this demonstration of Bonapartism. And Talleyrand, in spite of the large sums of money which he had received from Alexander's privy purse, decided that the Tsar could never become a stable component in any European pattern.

From The Congress of Vienna *by Harold Nicholson (Constable, London, 1946).*

THE DUKE OF WELLINGTON, as British Ambassador in Paris in 1814, deals crisply with a problem of protocol.

In the midst of these discussions, Wellington had to grapple with a lesser but more awkward incident. Talleyrand came to the embassy to warn him that the Princess of Wales, estranged wife of the Regent, had arrived in Strasbourg and that Louis XVIII wanted to know the Regent's wishes should she turn up in Paris. The Duke devised a quick though brutal solution. He sent a message to the Princess that he could not present anybody to the King of France who was not received at court in London.

From The Paris Embassy *by Cynthia Gladwyn (Collins, London, 1976).*

GEORGE CANNING, when appointed Foreign Secretary in 1822 in succession to Lord Castlereagh, is lampooned for being unable to speak French.

Viscount Fitz-Harris, MP, afterwards second Earl of Malmesbury, was Under-Secretary at the Foreign Office. On his appointment as Foreign Minister, Canning's opponents had accused him of ignorance of French. In a skit of the day he is told to

Brush up your very best jokes, I pray;
And though you can't speak any French, they say,
   Why, as for that matter,
   Fitz-Harris can chatter,
And you can keep out of the way.

From George Canning and his Friends *edited by Captain J. Bagot*
(John Murray, London, 1909).

SIR HENRY BULWER, as a young secretary in Lord Cowley's embassy in Paris in the mid-nineteenth century, discovers the hazards of making enquiries at a diplomatic ball.

Lady Cowley during a ball that was being given at the Embassy observed a face in the crowd of visitors that she was unacquainted with: she accordingly interrogated his Lordship's private secretary and the master of ceremonies but neither could find the slightest clue as to who the gentleman was. Mr Bulwer perceiving Her Ladyship in trouble offered his services to find out the name of the unknown guest and boldly advancing towards him accosted him in French saying, 'I am sent by Lady Cowley to know your name.' Whereupon the stranger replied, 'Before I gratify you with mine perhaps you will let me know yours for your manner is excessively impertinent and you require to be made an example of.' Bulwer replied that his rank as Secretary of Embassy authorised him to make the enquiry as the Ambassadress did not know him. This elicited the stranger's name and address: he was the Marquis D——.

The following morning this nobleman called upon me and mentioned what had occurred the previous evening; he swore that he would run Bulwer through the body for the insult offered him and requested me to be the bearer of a challenge to the offender . . .

From The Reminiscences and Recollections of Captain Gronow *edited by J. Grego*
(London, 1892).

PRINCE VON BISMARCK, having unified Germany and ensured victory in the Franco-Prussian War of 1870, was in a position to offer his master – King William of Prussia – the title of emperor. But the exact nature of that title was to prove a bone of contention between them.

There were difficulties to the last moment. William I wished to be called 'Emperor of Germany' – a territorial title. Bismarck would only allow 'German Emperor' – a glorified presidency. . . . William felt more deeply about this question than about any of the great conflicts he had with Bismarck. He could forgive the making of peace with Austria in 1866 or later the alliance with her in 1879; he could not forgive being saddled with the wrong title. And this was natural. All men care most about the tools of their own trade; and kings are concerned with titles or orders just as a writer is offended by bad grammar or a cricketer by bad sportsmanship. Kings can determine the cut of a tunic or the precedence in a ballroom. They can do little to change the fate of the world – and they do not often try. Bismarck was impatient with the rigmarole. He wrote to his wife: 'The imperial delivery was a difficult one and kings – like women – have strange longings at such time, before they bring into the world what they cannot keep to themselves all the same.' The ceremony of acknowledging William I took place in the great gallery of the palace of Versailles on 18 January 1871. William I tried to cheat at the last moment. He told the Grand Duke of Baden to lead the cheers for 'the Emperor of Germany'. Bismarck intercepted the grand duke on his way upstairs and suggested a safe compromise: cheers simply for 'Emperor William'. William was furious at the trick; and he ignored Bismarck's outstretched hand as he stepped off the Imperial dais.

From Bismarck by A.J.P. Taylor (Hamish Hamilton, London, 1955).

SIR RONALD STORRS, Oriental Secretary to the British Agency in Egypt from 1909 to 1917, points out some of the pitfalls involved in trying to entertain the British community abroad.

Lord Cromer [the British Agent and Consul-General in Egypt from 1883 to 1907], during his last years in Egypt had, after the death of his first wife, and under the weight of his labours and his age, no longer entertained on a large scale; and though the invitations that did issue from him conferred such distinction as to be retained on the mantelpiece long after the entertainment, the complaints of the far more numerous uninvited were as deep as they felt and as loud as they dared. Sir Eldon Gorst [Lord Cromer's deputy], aware of this, assisted by a young and charming wife, with the means and the desire to show a large hospitality, was at great pains to give pleasure by taking the utmost trouble with the numbers, the frequency and the arrangement of his luncheon and dinner parties, which indeed could not have been improved either materially or in the choice and placing of the guests. As a reward for this solicitude the same critics pronounced that it was really no compliment to be asked to the Agency now: you seemed to meet everybody there. And his endeavours to stem the rising flood of insularity by the judicious mingling of elements served but to evoke the classic dialogue: 'Were you at the Agency last night?' 'No; but then you see I'm not a foreigner; I'm only British.'

From Orientations *by Sir Ronald Storrs (Nicholson & Watson, London, 1937).*

LAWRENCE OF ARABIA makes no attempt to exchange pleasantries at diplomatic occasions in Cairo.

Lawrence was not (any more than Kitchener) a misogynist, though he would have retained his composure if he had been suddenly informed that he would never see a woman again. He could be charming to people like my wife and sister, whom he considered to be 'doing' something, but he regarded (and sometimes treated) with embarrassing horror those who 'dressed, and knew people'. When at a dinner-party a lady illustrated her anecdotes with the

Christian names, nick-names and pet-names of famous (and always titled) personages, Lawrence's dejection became so obvious that the lady, leaning incredulously forward, asked: 'I fear my conversation does not interest Colonel Lawrence very much?' Lawrence bowed from the hips – and those were the only muscles that moved: 'It does not interest me at all,' he answered.

I was standing with him one morning in the Continental Hotel, Cairo, waiting for Rūhi, when an elderly Englishwoman, quite incapable of understanding his talk, but anxious to be seen conversing with the Uncrowned King of Arabia, moved towards him. It was hot, and she was fanning herself with a newspaper as she introduced herself: 'Just think, Colonel Lawrence, Ninety-two! Ninety-two.' With a tortured smile he replied: 'Many happy returns of the day.'

From Orientations *by Sir Ronald Storrs (Nicholson & Watson, London, 1937).*

HAROLD EEMAN, as a junior member of the Belgian diplomatic mission in Ottawa in 1920, finds that advantage is taken of his diplomatic privileges by a local resident – on whom the ploy misfires.

During the short interregnum between the departure of the former Consul General and the arrival of his successor – Baron de Sélys – I found myself in charge. This fact seemed, to a millionairess friend of mine, then travelling in the States, a golden opportunity to save money. Writing to me from New York, she added, as an afterthought, the following Post Scriptum: 'I have just bought a statue at Tiffany's worth $1000, and to save customs duty I have had it sent to you since I hear you are now in charge.'

I had already found out that the New Rich, while throwing pounds away quite recklessly, were often inclined to scratch for pennies. But it was too bad of my friend to face me with a *fait accompli*. The statue was on its way. What could I do? As I had received a great deal of hospitality from Miss X.'s family, it would have been ungrateful to betray her. On the other hand it was outrageous that I should be forced to cheat the Customs in her favour.

The arrival of my new chief took my mind off this problem. But not for long. Owing to the inscrutability of the ways of Providence, I am unable to explain why the statue was timed to turn up on the most unsuitable day: that when Baron de Sélys assumed his office. He had only been sitting a few minutes at his desk when he was informed that a large case containing a statue and addressed to The Belgian Consul General in Ottawa had arrived at the Customs. He naturally disclaimed all knowledge of any statue and sent word to the Customs that there must be some mistake and that the statue was probably intended for the Consul General of another Nation.

When, a few minutes after this message had been sent, I entered my chief's study, I found him still ruffled by what he called the carelessness of the Canadian Administration. Blushing, no doubt, to the roots of my hair, I told him – alas, too late – how the matter stood. Reddening in turn with righteous indignation, he exclaimed: 'How monstrous of that girl to make use of you in that way! It would serve her right if we exposed her.' But on second thoughts he agreed that the Canadian officials would hardly thank us for placing them in the embarrassing position of having to condone a misdemeanour or set the law on a member of so influential a family. 'It goes against the grain,' he said, 'but we must now tell the Customs that the statue was ordered by you while you were in charge. They may smell a rat, but their suspicions will be allayed when they find that the statue remains in your possession. *For keep it you must*, until such time as you leave this country.'

The Consul General remained adamant. The statue could not be delivered to its owner and was to remain in my possession to my embarrassment for the next three years.

From Diplomatic Bag: Memoirs of a Junior Diplomat *by Harold Eeman*
(Robert Hale, London, 1980).

MARCUS CHEKE, when Vice-Marshal of the Diplomatic Corps in London in 1949, wrote a short book of guidance on 'foreign usages and ceremony' for members of the British diplomatic service going abroad on their first appointments. It was an extraordinary mixture of useful tips and out-dated pomposity, addressed to an imaginary 'Mr John Bull' in an imaginary 'Mauretania'. The extracts below give something of its flavour.

We may seize the present opportunity to lay down what is one of the most useful rules for Mr John Bull to follow in his relations with his colleagues. If he is faced, in any small matter, by two alternative courses of action – the one easy, but appearing somewhat over-familiar, and the other more respectful, but appearing somewhat pompous or old-fashioned – let him always plump for the latter rather than the former. For instance, if he hesitates between ending a letter 'Yours ever' and 'Yours sincerely', let him plump for 'Yours sincerely'. If his wife is hesitating whether to appear at the beach picnic of the Counsellor's wife (who has been most friendly to her) with or without stockings, let her (if she is unable to telephone and ask) wear stockings. This preference to the over-respectful rather than the over-familiar in the first Golden Rule.

In this connection the author of these pages will venture to relate a personal anecdote. When he was first appointed to the staff of an Embassy abroad, it happened one day that he spent an afternoon helping his Ambassadress arranging books in her library. At half past four she dismissed him, saying that she had to go out to a tea party at the house of the Counsellor. Now he himself was invited to the same party where many 'Mauretanians' were to be present, and so it happened that a quarter of an hour later he walked into the Counsellor's drawing-room to find his Ambassadress already taking tea and talking to one of the Counsellor's foreign guests. As he had spent the whole afternoon with her, and had only taken his leave of her a quarter of an hour earlier, it did not occur to him that he ought to pay his respects to her.

The next day he was summoned by his Chief, a diplomatist of experience and sagacity, who reproved him for his act of omission.

He hastily explained the circumstances: 'But I had spent all the afternoon arranging books with Lady R——, I had left her only a quarter of an hour previously. . . .'

'That may well be,' answered the Ambassador, '*but the people at the party did not know that.*'

In conversation with Mauretanian University men or press-men – indeed, in conversation with *all* Mauretanians – Mr Bull must bear in mind, first, that he is not himself a private individual, and that the Mauretanian in question is bound to regard him primarily as a member of the British Embassy. Thus, the Mauretanian, who may have some political axe of his own grind, may tell him things which Mr Bull will be well advised to accept with a pinch of salt, for the world is full of humbugs. For instance, the Mauretanian, if he is in opposition to the existing régime, may inform him that such-and-such a prison is crowded with the victims of tyranny. If he is a Latin, with the Oriental imagination of certain Southern peoples, he may add some horrific and picturesque details which seem to carry the stamp of absolute veracity. 'The Director of the Petunia Laundry,' he will say in a grave whisper, 'which does the personal washing of the Prison Governor, was telling me only last Tuesday that some articles of clothing evidently belonging to the prisoners had got muddled up with the Governor's possessions, and had come to her in the same laundry basket. One of the things was a grey woollen shirt stained with blood.' Such statements, if the informant is hostile to the authorities, must be accepted with reserve.

Mr Bull should remember that there is such a thing as speaking a foreign language, even French, *too well*. Many racy, colloquial phrases go suddenly out of fashion, and if an Englishman shows off his knowledge of a language by employing them he lays himself open to ridicule. The same thing applies to the foreigner. A certain great foreign hostess, who wished to do especial honour at her dinner-table to a British Ambassador, once made a sign for silence, and raising her glass and looking across at her distinguished guest said, 'Chin, chin!' It is safer to stick to a safe, correctly grammatical path. After all, as a foreigner he is not expected to speak a foreign language like a native; to speak it with a certain diffidence may even have a charm for a foreign ear while, on the other hand, a perfect glib-ness may be antipathetic. 'Méfiez-vous toujours', Bismarck once remarked, 'd'un Anglais qui parle trop bien le français.'

Mr Bull must remember that whereas most Latins have a sense of humour, their humour is entirely different to the British variety. The late Prince Arthur of Connaught rightly instanced the follow-ing lines as an example of humour that every Englishman delights in, but which is unintelligible abroad:

> I was playing golf
> The day the Germans landed,
> All our troops had run away,
> All our ships were stranded,
> And the thought of England's shame
> Nearly put me off my game.

The humour of these lines depends on the fact that England's ships are *not* all stranded. England has not been invaded for a thousand years, and 'he jokes at scars who never felt a wound'. But there are many foreign countries which know only too well what defeat and invasion are, and for them it is not a subject for joking at all.

If ever you fail to penetrate a man's personal attitude towards yourself or towards the business you have in hand, the following tactics will often give results; say your farewells, and then, at the last moment before you are to vanish from his sight – at the very last instant before the door closes upon you – *cast one last rapid glance back*. The expression which you will catch on the face of a man with whom you have just been conversing is sometimes absolutely devastating. On a face which throughout your interview has been wreathed in smiles, whose mouth has been full of expressions of friendship towards your country, you may catch a look of malig-nant disgust; or a startlingly complacent smug air will have superseded the stern glance which had accompanied his indignant statement that a proposal that you had made was utterly unaccept-able! *Vice versa*, if Mr Bull is not to lay himself open to the same simple manoeuvre, he will do well, when escorting to the door some almost unbearable bore, to retain his proper expression of civility until after the door closes.

From Guidance on foreign usages and ceremony, and other matters, for a Member of His Majesty's Foreign Service on his first appointment to a Post Abroad *by Marcus Cheke, His Majesty's Vice-Marshal of the Diplomatic Corps (The Foreign Office, London, 1949).*

SIR OLIVER FRANKS, as British Ambassador in Washington in 1948–52, is embarrassed by an American radio station. This story was described by Lord Franks to the editor as one which 'occasionally surfaced in the press, but was not altogether accurate'.

A US radio station telephoned Sir Oliver Franks at the British Embassy shortly before Christmas one year and said they were seeking interviews with some of Washington's leading ambassadors. After a number of questions about international affairs, they asked Sir Oliver what he would like for Christmas. The ambassador, thinking they might intend to send him a gift in recognition of his help with the programme and not wanting to ask for anything of embarrassingly high value, gave a suitable reply.

To his discomfiture, on Christmas eve he heard the programme announce that they had invited the Russian, French and British ambassadors to tell the world what they most wished for this Christmas. The Russian had said: 'Peace and understanding between all the nations of the world.' The French ambassador had said: 'A more civilized attitude to world problems and the spread of French culture.' The British ambassador said: 'That's extremely kind of you – a small box of crystallized fruit would be very nice.'

MRS CLARE BOOTHE LUCE, on her first diplomatic appointment as American Ambassador to Italy in the 1950s, inadvertently makes a protocol gaffe.

Clare's first state dinner . . . took place at the Spanish Embassy. In a city of late dining the Spaniards sit down last of all. Dinner began at ten, ended at eleven-thirty. As the guests gathered in the drawing-room, Clare wondered how soon she could leave. 'State' had briefed her about the protocol. 'Quite simple. No one leaves before the guest of honour.'

So Clare watched British Ambassador Sir Victor Mallet, Senior Ambassador of the diplomatic corps.

Time crept slowly but relentlessly by. Sir Victor, big-nosed, grey-haired, the very picture of an English diplomat, chatted urbanely and endlessly on. Twelve-thirty. One. One-thirty. Clare felt like putting matchsticks under her eyelids. Finally she whispered desperately to the Spanish Ambassadress, 'What time does Sir Victor usually go home?'

'When the guest of honour leaves,' was the frigid reply.

'But who is the guest of honour?'

The Señora's eyes were like black ice as she answered, 'You are!'

It took the Luces forty-five seconds flat to make their adieux and get out of there.

From Clare Boothe Luce: Ambassador Extraordinary *by Alden Hatch*
(William Heinemann, London, 1956).

GEORGE BROWN, as Foreign Secretary in the 1960s, had a reputation in London diplomatic circles for outrageous behaviour, an example of which is here recorded by Sir Richard Parsons, who was one of his private secretaries.

When I was briefly in George Brown's private office, someone used to come in each morning to tell Murray MacLehose [the Principal Private Secretary] and me the latest horror story. In particular, George was notorious for his habit of peeking down the bosom of his diplomatic hostess when, as all too often, he dined out at one of the Embassies in London. On one such morning, nobody came to report anything. Murray and I became concerned . . . perhaps, this time, it was too awful even for us to know. I made enquiries. It transpired that the evening before, George had dined at one of the Scandinavian Embassies; the Swedish, I think. George had caused enormous offence there. The Ambassadress in question was not young – and George had not troubled to peek down her bosom. Prepared for the experience, she had been deeply mortified by his failure to come up to scratch.

145

7

Views of the Foreign Office

THERE HAS ALWAYS been some element of built-in tension
between embassies abroad and the Foreign Office in London,
a tension which is by no means unique to the British diplomatic
service. Until after the First World War this tension was heightened
by the fact that the Diplomatic Service was an entity quite distinct
from the staff of the Foreign Office: there were two different careers,
members of the former only serving abroad and the latter only (with
rare exceptions) at home. So, not unnaturally, diplomats who spent
all their working lives (41 years in the case of Sir Horace Rumbold)
living among foreigners found the 'clerks' in London excessively
insular in their views and unrealistic in their expectations; while
those permanently in Whitehall found their 'superior' colleagues
(the Diplomatic Service, unlike the Foreign Office, required a
private income) tiresomely inclined to see the foreigners' point of
view and out of touch with priorities and sentiments at home. (The
mutual suspicion was not dissimilar to that between the captain of
a warship at sea and the seemingly-remote Lords of the Admiralty
in London.) Now that the services are united, and officers are
regularly and rapidly interchangeable between embassies and head
office, the mistrust has largely evaporated. But acerbic comments
still occasionally fly in each direction.

Other types of mistrust of the Foreign Office still persist. The
public and the press affect to believe that 'just as the Ministry of
Agriculture looks after farmers, so the Foreign Office looks after

foreigners'. Mrs Thatcher, as Prime Minister, was not alone in her feeling that the FO (or FCO as it now is, with the inclusion of 'Commonwealth' into the title) was too ready to argue the foreigners' case – be it on behalf of the European Community or the Argentines – at the expense of British self-interest. Winston Churchill also made snide remarks about 'the Office' in this sense. Sometimes the criticism was justified: highly-educated and intelligent diplomats, trained to see both sides of every question, tend to produce too 'balanced' a view for domestic consumption.

The British public's scepticism about the FO is compounded by their ambivalent approach to their own embassies abroad. If visitors are not greeted with the warmth they had hoped for, or to which they feel their position entitles them, they quickly assume they have been snubbed: 'the Embassy was too busy chatting up the local grandees to bother about a simple businessman like me . . .'. If on the other hand the Embassy roll out the red carpet and entertain the visitor generously, there can be an equally familiar reaction: 'these chaps in the Embassy live like lords – flunkies and duty-free booze which the likes of us don't see at home . . .'. It can be a delicate matter to get the balance of hospitality right.

The normal tension between the Foreign Office and its embassies abroad can – on occasion – extend to a personal antipathy between a Foreign Secretary and senior ambassadors. Lord Derby was not alone in mistrusting Lord Curzon. Many ambassadors in the 1960s felt that Mr George Brown as Foreign Secretary had no conception of their proper role, and he in turn thought of many of them as 'stuffed shirts' who could be insulted with impunity. On the other hand, often there is a real rapport between Foreign Secretaries and the service over which they preside: Ernest Bevin was deeply loved by his Foreign Office staff, and in turn was a stalwart champion of the diplomatic service at home and abroad.

Douglas Hurd has noted that 'diplomacy is unfashionable in the world of knee-jerk reaction and the dogmatic sound bite on television'. But whatever the views of the Foreign Office from the British public or from their own missions abroad, a sense of humour is never very far away: *Carlton Browne of the FO* is essentially a figure of fun. It is probably healthier that he should remain so.

HORACE WALPOLE, the celebrated letter-writer and younger son of the Prime Minister, maintained a long correspondence with Sir Horace Mann when the latter was British Minister in Florence. Here he complains in 1764 about the inadequacies of diplomatic representatives abroad.

I am sorry for what you tell me in your letter of the 18th, that Lord B. does not please in Russia; for his own particular I am very indifferent, but I have great regard for his aunt, Lady Suffolk, and know how much it will hurt her if she hears it. That he should be pert *mal à propos*, does not surprise me. He would never have been my choice for such an employment, which ought so little to be given by favour, and is so seldom given for any other reason – is so seldom given to a Sir Horace Mann. You know it is my opinion, that the reason of sending so many fools about Europe from all parts of Europe, is, that such are elected whose capacities resemble most the heads of those they are to represent. Adieu! It is time to finish when I attack the *Corps Diplomatique* and the *Patronanza*, though writing to a minister.

From The Letters of Horace Walpole, 4th Earl of Orford, 1764–1766
(The Clarendon Press, Oxford, 1904).

KING WILLIAM IV intervenes with Lord Palmerston to secure a consular appointment for a former comrade-in-arms. The irregularity of the action upset the Foreign Secretary but does not appear to have injured the public service.

When H.R.H. the Duke of Clarence (afterwards King William IV) was in the Royal Navy, but serving in 1814 as a volunteer in the Army, and Mr W. Smith was a subaltern in the Army, they were present at some action together, when a shot was fired, which struck H.R.H.'s belt, and, glancing off, inflicted a slight wound on Mr Smith, upon which the Duke went up to him and said,'My dear Smith, that shot was meant for me; now, if I ever become King, I hope you will remind me of this day. I will not forget it, and here's my hand upon it.' Years rolled on, and on June 26, 1830, H.R.H. the Duke of Clarence became King. Mr Smith had then left the Army, and was very anxious to obtain some civil appointment. In 1834 the consulship of Lisbon fell vacant, and by the advice of his friends, Mr Smith very reluctantly determined to endeavour to obtain an audience of the King. He accordingly went to the Palace, and explained the object of his visit to the Equerry-in-Waiting. The equerry went to the King, and returned in a few moments, saying, 'His Majesty will see you at once.' On being ushered into the King's presence, His Majesty held out his hand and said, 'My dear Smith, I am delighted to see you again, and I hope you have come to ask me for something.' To which Mr Smith replied that he had ventured to trespass upon His Majesty to ask whether it would be possible for him to assist him in obtaining the appointment of H.M.'s Consul at Lisbon, which post, he had heard, was then vacant. The King at once replied, 'Certainly, you shall have it, I will write to Lord Palmerston without delay,' and His Majesty did so. Lord Palmerston was exceedingly annoyed at the King's interference with his own especial patronage, and for a time resisted His Majesty's appeal on Mr Smith's behalf, but he was ultimately compelled to yield, and Mr Smith obtained the much-coveted consular post (June 2, 1834). Lord Palmerston, however, it is said, never forgave Mr Smith in his heart; still, he held the post of Consul at Lisbon with great credit for over thirty-one years, and died at his post, at the age of seventy-two, on November 11, 1865.

From Recollections of the Old Foreign Office *by Sir Edward Hertslet*
(John Murray, London, 1901).

VISCOUNT GRANVILLE, as British Ambassador in Paris, is reprimanded by George Canning, as Foreign Secretary, for writing slovenly despatches. The remarks were probably intended to be taken in good part and are not quite as sharp as they sound, since Granville was a notable liberal and a close personal friend of Canning, to whom he largely owed his advancement to the rank of viscount.

Already in his first conversation with the King, the Ambassador had failed to make clear an important point by omitting a key word, and when he wrote of the 'specific' policy of the Tsar instead of the 'pacific' policy, Canning advised him to read over his despatches before signing them. Also they were too short and did not always make sense. One report 'leaves me at the conclusion entirely uninformed whether you accomplished the object stated at the beginning'. Then, 'the perpetual recurrence of dinner is exceedingly distressing. But did it never enter your mind that you might evade the force of that not unexpected impediment by beginning to write at a time of day when it does not usually present itself? Try that device.'

From The Paris Embassy by Cynthia Gladwyn (Collins, London, 1976).

SIR EDWARD HERTSLET and his father between them occupied the post of Librarian and Keeper of the Archives of the Foreign Office for almost the entire period between 1801 and 1896. One of the moments in all that time which he recalled as being the most memorable was the preparation for defending the library against the Chartist rioters in 1848.

As it was feared that an attack might be made on the Foreign Office, the windows of the MS. Library, on the ground floor, facing Downing Street, were filled with books, loopholes being left to pass muskets through, should they really be required; but there never was a greater farce. A few muskets of the old Brown-bess pattern were fetched from the Tower of London – it should be remembered that there were no rifles in those days – and sent into the office, but, so far as I could ascertain, without ammunition; and there was not a soul in the office who had ever handled one of these clumsy weapons before, or knew how to fire it off, as it was long before the commencement of the volunteer movement. A few navy cutlasses were also supplied by HM's Government, but they looked, for all the world, as if they had been borrowed from Astley's theatre. There had been no previous attempt at drilling, nor was anyone instructed what to do in the event of the rioters making their appearance, probably owing, in a great measure, to the jealousy which existed among the officials in the Government offices in the immediate neighbourhood of Whitehall. At the Foreign Office the dispute between the permanent Under Secretary of State and the Chief Clerk waxed so warm that the latter was reported to have said to the former that if he meddled in matters which did not belong to his province in the office, but were solely within that of the Chief Clerk, he would shoot him!

From Recollections of the Old Foreign Office *by Sir Edward Hertslet*
(John Murray, London, 1901).

SIR HUGH CORTAZZI describes the working conditions for a junior 'clerk' in the Foreign Office in the mid-nineteenth century, as they were experienced by Bertie Mitford before his first posting to Japan.

We complain today of the old-fashioned style of the Foreign and Commonwealth Office building, with its immensely high ceilings and network of corridors like a rabbit warren, but things were far worse in Mitford's day. He wrote: 'The old Foreign Office in Downing Street (knocked down in 1864) was a dingy building enough, with a sort of crusted charwomanly look about it, suggestive of anything but Secretaries of State, Ambassadors and suchlike sublimities. The Dei Majores occupied tapestried chambers facing St James's Park, but the great mass of the rooms in which the clerks worked looked out upon nothing but Downing Street on one side and on the other a rookery, so richly caked with soot and dirt that the very windows must long since have ceased to let in a ray of light – a nest of squalid slums.' Mitford noted that there was always 'plenty of work', but there were compensations.

151

The clerks did not begin work until twelve, or even later, although they were often still 'copying for the mails until after seven o'clock' (not late for an official in the Foreign Office today!). The Foreign Office clerk in those days thus had his mornings off, when, like Mitford, he could take some exercise. In the evenings there were parties galore. As Mitford put it, 'A clerk in the Foreign Office at that time carried with him a passport to all that was best in political, diplomatic, literary and artistic society. The best clubs from the Travellers downward opened their doors to him.' Mitford indeed frequented the Saturday-night parties given by Lady Palmerston at her house in Piccadilly (now the Naval and Military Club), which went on until the early hours of Sunday mornings.

Mitford started work in 'the slave trade or African Department'. His head of department, Dolly Oom, detested 'work in any shape'. Mitford described him as sitting there 'supping weak soda water and brandy'. His eccentricity was to insist that all words ending in 'c' such as 'public' should have a final 'k'! After two years spent tracing slave-trade ships and similar tasks, Mitford was transferred to the French Department. This was the most important and hardest-worked department in the Office, according to Mitford. Every despatch of any importance had to be copied to Paris where the Embassy 'was looked upon as a sort of branch of the Foreign Office'.

From the introduction to Mitford's Japan *edited by Hugh Cortazzi*
(The Athlone Press, London, 1985).

SIR THOMAS SANDERSON, Permanent Under-Secretary at the Foreign Office from 1894 to 1906, was known as 'Lamps' to his contemporaries on account of his thick-lensed spectacles, and had a reputation as 'a martinet of the old order'. His particular obsession was correct office procedures, but these extracts from his memorandum on this show that his schoolmasterly view of the Office was tempered with wit.

It is useful occasionally to remind oneself that Secretaries of State are human beings like ourselves, more oppressed with business and interruptions, liable to occasional attacks of fatigue, possibly even to headaches (of an august kind), and with eyes only differing from our own in that they have had longer, and have daily harder, usage in the service of the State than most of ours. For whereas our work is mostly with official papers, the Secretary of State's day generally begins with the perusal of a quantity of private letters in more or less illegible handwritings.

Still more, that the Sovereign is a lady who during a long reign has conscientiously and continually devoted herself to a large amount of work which to most women would be almost intolerable.

To take care that they are not wearied and blinded with faint or half-legible copies of important papers seems to me, quite irrespective of all questions of loyalty and respect, a duty of simple humanity and consideration.

It is true that a long experience of suffering has made most Cabinet Ministers patient in the matter of handwriting, but there are limits; and at times mutterings have reached me that the calligraphy for which the Foreign Office was once so celebrated has woefully deteriorated.

The handwriting of the Foreign Office was excellent in the days of Mr Pitt. But it was brought to its perfection by Lord Palmerston, who himself wrote a magnificent hand – firm, round, flowing, and to all appearance never hurried or fatigued. He expected the same of his subordinates, and even when Prime Minister took an interest in the writing of the Foreign Office despatches, sending across short minutes of criticism, of which I remember three: 'The handwriting of one of the Secretaries at Berlin resembles nothing but a set of dilapidated park palings.' 'The handwriting of the present day, and particularly the official handwriting, is rapidly deteriorating, but it is difficult to account for the moral obliquity which insists on constantly substituting an "u" for an "n".' 'If the gentleman who writes these interesting despatches would use goose quills instead of his own quills, and ink as black as his feathers, it would be more agreeable for his readers.' We are neither greater men, nor busier men, than Lord Palmerston, and I do not know why we should affect to disregard that which he, rightly as I think, considered so important. It is not a small matter. Handwriting once thoroughly formed or deformed is not easily altered later in life; and it is almost impossible for the reader to give full attention to a paper when half his mental power is occupied in decyphering it.

A despatch is certainly not made more attractive by being, so to speak, swathed with sheets and half-sheets of note-paper, and a sort of Joseph's coat of ragged slips of many colours. And I think that at all events what I should call departmental and inter-departmental conversations might safely be destroyed. I find occasionally in the interstices of despatches slips asking somebody whether he remembers something, to which the reply is generally strongly in the negative – a confession which need not be preserved. The request of the Chief of the Department for previous papers, the confession of the Junior that they are missing, the stern reply that they *must* be found, the despairing rejoinder that it is impossible, and the ejaculation of gratified surprise three weeks later when they are discovered in some entirely inappropriate lurking-place – all these seem to me to be merely of temporary interest, and unnecessary for the information of the New Zealander of the future.

In the putting by of papers the prime necessity is regularity and method. The fundamental principle of a well-managed Department is that a certain amount of trouble should be systematically taken in order to avoid recourse to violent and ineffectual effort upon an emergency. To leave papers to accumulate till the mass becomes intolerable, and then to have a grand clearing up, is a direct contravention of this elementary rule. In this and in other matters erratic genius is not a quality well suited for a public office. Squibs and sky-rockets are very brilliant things, but they are more in their place out of doors.

There was in former times a Senior Clerk in the Office, a man of some celebrity, whose habit was, when a paper could not be found, to rush to the press and, with some eloquent expressions, to scatter violently the whole contents upon the floor. This drastic but generally effective method of treatment had been discontinued before I joined. I still remember, however, with some discomfort my finding several superior officers on all fours searching vainly for some correspondence on the navigation of the Danube which I had arranged in a pigeon-hole of my own contriving. Their remarks did not encourage me to repeat the experiment.

It is, perhaps, a matter of prejudice that I dislike the too frequent use of the expression 'I beg leave' in letters to foreign Representatives. It is a merely conventional expression, but the Foreign Minister of England deals with other countries, even the greatest, on terms of equality, and I do not see why he should beg anybody's leave except his own Sovereign's. I do not wish to taboo the phrase, but I think it is not to be squandered.

You should not begin a sentence without knowing, more or less, how you are going to get out of it.

But above all things endeavour to think and to take an intelligent interest in the work. A good deal of it is dull, but it has its interesting side – which is the less official one. I should be glad to think that I could at any moment refer to any member of the Chinese Department for the respective whereabouts of the Provinces of Honan and Hunan, or ascertain from a Junior of the Western Department what are the sizes of the various islands in the Samoan Archipelago, and whether the inhabitants do, or do not, wear trousers. But I am afraid that to many of us Samoa only represents copying and sections of blue print. This I think is a misfortune; it turns our daily bread into dry bones, and after a time the steel pen enters into the soul, and the individual becomes a mere official (who is a very dismal creature), or loses all vigour, and sinks into hopeless mediocrity.

From a memorandum entitled Observations on the Use and Abuse of Red Tape for the Juniors in the Eastern, Western, and American Departments *by Sir Thomas Sanderson, October 1891.*

THE EARL OF DERBY, presiding over the Paris Embassy at the conclusion of the First World War, finds relations with Lord Curzon, as Foreign Sceretary, somewhat strained.

Things were less easy for him when a new Foreign Secretary was appointed with whom he had had petty differences in the past. As Minister of War he had taken Curzon to task for wasting government petrol on his weekend guests. Then, during the excitement of the Armistice, he returned one day from a brief call at the Elysée to discover the embassy invaded by cheering tommies brought there by a musical comedy actress who ran their Leave Club. Derby arrived just in time to see Curzon concluding a speech from the porch and being kissed warmly by Miss Decima Moore while the soldiers sang 'For he's a jolly good fellow' under the impression that he was the Ambassador.

Even when separated by the Channel the envoy and Secretary of State continued to bicker. One evening Malcolm Bullock was handed a letter by his father-in-law with instructions to get it off by that night's bag. It began, 'My dear Curzon, I have always known you to be a cad. I now know that you are a liar.' Perturbed by the opening sentence, Malcolm consulted the minister, who advised him just to leave the letter in the tray. The next morning the Ambassador seemed distinctly relieved to learn that it had not gone and dictated another in a milder vein: 'My dear George, You and I have known each other too long to quarrel over so small a matter.'

From The Paris Embassy *by Cynthia Gladwyn (Collins, London, 1976).*

ROBERT BRUCE LOCKHART bemoans the tasks the Foreign Office lays on its young diplomats in St Petersburg during the First World War.

At last, a large white door with an iron bar across it opened, and a tall, athletic, and extremely good-looking man of about thirty came out. It was 'Benji' Bruce, the Head of the Chancery and the inevitable and indispensable favourite of every Ambassador under whom he has ever served. Telling me that the Ambassador would see me in a few minutes, he took me into the Chancery and introduced me to the other secretaries. Later, I was to know them better and appreciate their merits, but my first impression was of a typing and telegraph bureau conducted by Old Etonians. At uncomfortably close quarters in a large room, blocked with tables, sat half a dozen young men busily engaged in typing and ciphering. That they did their task well, that 'Benji' Bruce could type as fast as any professional typist and cipher and decipher with astonishing speed is beside the point. Here was a collection of young men, all of whom had had thousands of pounds spent on their education, who had passed a difficult examination, yet who, in the middle of a great war in which their special knowledge might have been used to their country's advantage, were occupied for hours on end in work which could have been performed just as efficiently by a second-division clerk. This system, now fortunately abolished, was typical of the want of imagination, which reigned in Whitehall during at any rate the first two years of the war. Any side-show mission – and in Russia there must have been a score – could command an almost unlimited supply of money from the Treasury. The professional diplomatists, who, whatever their shortcomings may have been, knew their job better than the amateurs, were left to carry on as in peace time, not because of any danger of secrets being divulged, but merely because this system had been in force for generations and because, in the Chief Clerk's Department in the Foreign Office, there was no one with sufficient elasticity of mind or force of character to insist on its being altered. No wonder that, after the war, many of the younger diplomatists, weary of this senseless drudgery, sent in their resignations. Bruce was a case in point. A man of strong and attractive personality, an excellent linguist, and a firm disciplinarian with a real genius for organisation, he ran his Chancery with remarkable efficiency. If a trifle obstinate as becomes an Ulsterman, he served his various chiefs with passionate loyalty. When he resigned soon after the war, the Foreign Office lost perhaps the best-equipped of its younger diplomatists.

From Memoirs of a British Agent *by R.H. Bruce Lockhart (Putnam, London, 1932).*

THE FOREIGN OFFICE as perceived in popular mythology.

An Englishman was walking down Whitehall looking for the Foreign Office, where he had an appointment, on a foggy night in the black-out during the Second World War, when he bumped into another Englishman.

'Excuse me,' he said, 'could you tell me which side the Foreign Office is on?'

'I don't know, mate,' came the answer, 'but I believe in the last war they were on our side.'

From a familiar after-dinner story.

WINSTON CHURCHILL fulminates against the Foreign Office to his private secretary, John Colville, during the Second World War.

Churchill had no love for the Foreign Office, one of the very few Departments of which he had never been head. He suspected them of pursuing their own policy, irrespective of what the Government might wish, and he mistrusted their judgment. One evening, after he had abused the Foreign Office (which was my own Department, and for which I felt both loyalty and affection) with unusual vehemence, I reminded him that during the afternoon he had been equally harsh about the Treasury. Which, I asked, did he dislike the most? After a moment's thought, he replied: 'The War Office!'

From Action this day: Working with Churchill *edited by Sir John Wheeler-Bennett (Macmillan, London, 1968).*

SIR GLADWYN JEBB, as British Ambassador to France in 1956, finds that his advice and the entire 'diplomatic machine' is ignored by a British government determined to use force against Egypt to resolve the Suez crisis.

From July 1956 onwards till the end of the year, the whole scene was, however, overshadowed by the Suez crisis . . . There were agitated conferences and I was among those who favoured, in principle, some kind of direct action to bring the Canal back under the control of the Company, always provided that we and the French had enough forces available. For it seemed to me that unless we did so we should lose every position that we held in the Middle East – on which point at least I was not far out. I have no doubt now that I was wrong in so advocating in the heat of the moment. And as the crisis wore on; as the attitude of the Americans and others was revealed; and as we became involved in what was in effect a process of negotiation, I personally became gradually persuaded that force was out. Not that my advice was requested. For it was fairly soon apparent that something was happening completely outside the diplomatic machine of which I had no inkling. . . . When Eden and Selwyn Llyod [Prime Minister and Foreign Secretary, respectively] came over to Paris on 16 October and had a meeting of several hours from which all officials were excluded, this became even more obvious. My increasingly vigorous protests against being kept completely in the dark about the Government's intentions were, however, ignored save, at the very last moment, for a vague hint of what was impending . . .

The whole eventual plan, secretly concerted with the Israelis, was based on the assumption that the Americans would not intervene against us in the UN or elsewhere and that any Soviet opposition could be disregarded. Events proved that the first part of this basic assumption was not valid. But even had it been valid, how could we have avoided the consequences of 'success', such as condemnation in the UN, the break-up of the Commonwealth and the sheer impossibility of occupying Egypt for very long?

From The Memoirs of Lord Gladwyn *(Weidenfeld & Nicolson, London, 1972).*

LORD CARRINGTON explains his own perspective on the role of the Foreign Secretary when he was occupying that post in 1982. Ironically, he felt obliged to resign eleven days later over the invasion of the Falklands, not because he considered he or his Department had been responsible for the disaster, but because he felt that his continued presence in the government was not an asset at that moment.

I was looking the other day at the photographs of my predecessors hung on the walls of the Private Office. I have known fifteen of them. At first blush, and indeed at second blush, they seem a disparate lot. Bevin and Eden, Halifax and Morrison. What on earth have they and the others got in common? Quite a few of them do not seem to have been much interested in foreign affairs until they were made Foreign Secretary. After all, it is pot luck whether you become Foreign Secretary or not. The appointment may depend more on the political balance in the party or the clash of personalities in the Cabinet than on anything else. But, rum lot though they all may have been, I suspect that when they arrived in the Foreign Office and sat down and thought about what was to be done, they all approached it from much the same stand-point.

It is a truism, attributed to Palmerston, that a Foreign Minister's job is to further his nation's interests. It was the Duke of Wellington who proclaimed that 'interest never lies'. The proposition has largely survived the growth of political ideologies which claim to replace national interest with an internationalist conception of the common good. I have never heard, and never expect to hear, a communist leader define the interests of the working people of the world in a way which does not precisely coincide with the immediate interests of his government.

But to say that the job of Foreign Secretary is to further British interests begs the question of what those interests are. Here we come much closer to the point. The real role of a Foreign Secretary is to define this country's overseas interests, to choose between those that may conflict; to decide on the methods needed to further the major interests; and then to see that those decisions are carried out.

My decisions, if they are to be sensible ones, need to be based on the right information and on expert advice. With this I am copiously supplied: indeed as I read the press and look through my post I often suspect that, with the possible exceptions of the Prime Minister and the Chairman of the England Cricket Selectors, I am the most advised man in the country.

There arrives each day a constant stream of telegrams from posts abroad. And there is a not inconsiderable flow also in the other direction. As you know, each of these telegrams, however mundane its subject, is addressed to me over the Ambassador's signature, or vice versa – a convention which can produce curious results if its logic is pursed to extremes. One Ambassador infuriated his staff with his excessive punctiliousness in this respect. They got their revenge when circumstances one day allowed them to send a telegram which read 'I regret to report that I have fallen down the lift-shaft and am still unconscious'.

All this makes for a busy life, but that is not new. At the beginning of the century, Grey moaned: 'For a Cabinet Minister who is head of a big department of State there is no real holiday, the work follows him like his shadow, presses upon him like a perennial stream.' I sympathise with him. The same despatch boxes that ate into his sleep follow me wherever I go. Even the most enthusiastic Foreign Secretary has on occasion been known to tire of them. There is a story that Ernie Bevin was once confronted with a pile of red boxes one Friday evening with a note from his Private Secretary reading: 'The Secretary of State may wish to look at these over the weekend.' He scrawled underneath: 'A kindly thought, but erroneous.'

From a lecture by Lord Carrington entitled My Job *delivered at Chatham House on 25 March 1982 on the occasion of the bicentenary of the establishment of the office of Foreign Secretary in 1782.*

8

Diplomatic Eccentrics

MOST PROFESSIONS BREED some eccentrics, but the diplomatic profession has traditionally bred more than most. There are probably several reasons why this is so.

Until relatively recently, the diplomatic profession tended to be peopled by aristocrats whose families often had a recurring streak of eccentricity (or worse) and who not infrequently felt they were a law unto themselves. Henry Labouchère probably thought there was nothing odd about proposing to remain in Baden-Baden while holding the post of minister in Buenos Aires. And Baron Stroganoff found it less boring either to live lavishly (if he were feeling rich) or like a recluse (if he were not) than to subscribe to the middle-class values of prudence and good-husbandry. The Lords Lyons and Bertie, during their respective terms as ambassadors to France, saw no reason to compromise their essential Englishness in order to pander to continental conventions or susceptibilities. Aristocratic eccentricity was often a close cousin to arrogance: Lord Palmerston's high-handed attitude to foreigners made him as many enemies abroad as it brought him admirers at home.

Another breeding ground for eccentricity is the intellectual life, and as the diplomatic corps of the world became less aristocratic they tended to exercise a natural attraction to intellectuals. 'Donnishness' became a recognized feature of some chancelleries and embassies, and a conspicuously artistic temperament of others. Benjamin Franklin, with his odd clothes and round spectacles, was a notorious case in point at the court of Louis XVI; Paderewski with his long, untidy hair was similarly conspicuous at Versailles; and Pablo Neruda – the Chilean Nobel-prize-winning poet – cut a quaint figure in Paris as Allende's ambassador to President Pompidou.

Perhaps it is living abroad from an early and impressionable age that encourages eccentricity – 'an undue taste for foreign habits and usages', as Sir George Staunton described it (in a passage quoted in a later chapter). And foreign wives – as Sir George would doubtless have agreed – can often aggravate the situation. There was one distinguished British ambassador's wife in my own time who dismayed the Ministry of Works representatives by painting black the interior of every residence she occupied. When questioned about the suitability of this colour scheme, she replied that she never rose until after sun-down herself and liked her houses to resemble the Levantine night-clubs she recalled from her youth. The Ministry of Works man is reputed to have retired defeated.

At an early stage in my career I remember being astonished on a working visit to Afghanistan to find the then ambassador, complete with a goatee beard and a monocle, sitting on a large pouffe in the shade of a Banyan tree in the Kabul embassy's delightful rose garden, dictating despatches to a secretary who sat on a smaller pouffe under a smaller tree, while liveried and turbaned Pakistani footmen brought him his papers from the Chancery on a silver salver.

'My predecessor', he confided to me later at dinner, 'was really not up to this job.'

I waited, expecting revelations of professional incompetence or indiscretion.

'No,' said the ambassador, 'the poor man had no idea how to graft roses.'

Although I did not realize it at the time, the ambassador was a worthy successor to a long line of diplomatic eccentrics, and would no doubt have felt at home with Labouchère or Lord Bertie.

BENJAMIN FRANKLIN, as American Minister Plenipotentiary to France, finds his spectacles an aid to understanding French.

His sober unembroidered brown coat, with a fur collar in cold weather, became almost his uniform. He carried his crab-tree stick wherever he went, and always wore glasses. By August 1784 he could not, without them, 'distinguish a letter even of large print'. Before that year he had used 'two pair of spectacles which I shifted occasionally, as in travelling I sometimes read and often wanted to regard the prospects. Finding this change troublesome and not always sufficiently ready, I had the glasses cut and half of each kind associated in the same circle.' That is, he invented bifocals. 'This I find more particularly convenient since my being in France, the glasses that serve me best at table to see what I eat not being the best to see the faces of those on the other side of the table who speak to me; and when one's ears are not well accustomed to the sounds of a language, a sight of the movements in the features of him that speaks helps to explain; so that I understand French better by the help of my spectacles.'

From Benjamin Franklin *by Carl Van Doren (The Viking Press, New York, 1964).*

BARON STROGANOFF'S extravagances are described in a letter from a British colleague in St Petersburg in 1805.

A Baron Stroganoff, who is appointed Minister in Spain, passes thro' London on his way to Madrid; I shall give him a Letter of recommendation to you and your Sister. He is really a clever man, and he has shewn himself an adept in one art in which you have excelled, though not to the same degree as your Sister: I mean that of spending Money. His Extravagance here three or four years ago is proverbial; his fêtes are represented as exceeding in magnificence what we read of in fairy tales. When his money was exhausted he sent his wife and children to travel, and he shut himself up out of all society, and has been reading indefatigably.

From The Private Correspondence of Lord Granville Leveson Gower 1781 to 1821
(John Murray, London, 1916).

LORD LYONS proves an eccentric British Ambassador in Paris between 1867 and 1887.

Lord Lyons had a strong sense of the importance of representation and the embassy was run in the grandest style, even if the Ambassador was consumed with so great a shyness that, as he dared not look his servants in the face, he had to recognize the footmen by their stockinged legs. He kept the finest carriages in Paris, a good cellar though he never drank wine, an excellent chef. Some compensation for loneliness was found in excessive enjoyment of food which, together with a dislike of exercise, contributed to his vast dimensions. The farthest he was known to walk was to and from the church over the road, and even for this brief excursion away from British territory he never failed to carry his passport.

From The Paris Embassy *by Cynthia Gladwyn (Collins, London, 1976).*

HENRY LABOUCHÈRE epitomizes the approach of the amateur diplomat.

Henry Labouchère twice provoked Lord John Russell into dispensing with his services. He survived the first occasion when he justified his failure to remove himself from Europe to South America by telling the Secretary of State that he would have gone to Paraná if he had been able to find out where it was, but was dismissed when he volunteered to fulfill his obligations at Buenos Ayres from the residency at Baden-Baden.

From The British Diplomatic Service 1815–1914 *by Raymond A. Jones (Wilfrid Laurier University Press, Waterloo, Ontario, Canada, 1983).*

LORD SALISBURY, as Prime Minister and Foreign Secretary at the same time, clearly relishes telling Queen Victoria in 1879 about the curious goings-on at the British Consulate-General at Bangkok.

There is another post which it will be necessary to fill up shortly – the Consul-Generalship in Siam. There has been a curious trouble at Bangkok (the capital of Siam) which has brought over the little

Envoy that was presented to Your Majesty two days ago. Mr Knox the present Consul General had a natural daughter by some Siamese woman – the young lady who went by the name of 'Miss Fanny' was very wilful and given to falling in love. A great Siamese nobleman, Governor of a province, had embezzled the gold in some gold mines committed to his care to the amount of £200,000: and was in great distress because he expected to be found out and was certain in that case to lose his head. His name was Phra Phri Cha. It seemed to him that he might save himself by means of Miss Fanny. He made love to her and proposed for her hand: but Mr Knox refused. Thereupon he persuaded her to elope and to sleep one night with his other wives of whom he had a large number on board his steam yacht. After that the young lady being compromised Mr Knox was compelled to give his assent. But the Siamese government took offence at this cavalier proceeding towards a foreign Representative and Phra Phri Cha was ordered to be publicly flogged – thirty stripes. Mr Knox however did not take this reparation to his wounded honour in good part. On the contrary he was furiously angry at the insolence of the Siamese Government (1) in taking notice of his domestic troubles and (2) in flogging his son-in-law. He demanded an immediate apology and the release of Phra Phri Cha – whose proceedings at the gold mine had intermediately transpired and who was kept in custody. On the refusal of the Siamese government he ordered up one of Your Majesty's Men of War and if luckily Lord Salisbury had not heard of the matter in time to stop him by telegraph he would probably have proceeded to strong measures. The Siamese Embassy was sent over to complain of these proceedings and Mr Knox will come home to explain himself. But it is scarcely possible that he can return to Bangkok after this scandal. The last that has been heard of the matter is that Phra Phri Cha has put all the papers that might compromise him about the gold mine in Miss Fanny's charge and she refused to give them up to the tribunals, declaring that she is under British protection.

From a letter from Lord Salisbury to Queen Victoria, dated 25 August 1879
(Royal Archives).

LORD BERTIE maintains his Englishness as British Ambassador in Paris during the First World War.

Lord Bertie was a dynamic envoy who gave the impression that nothing awful could happen while he was in charge because he could be counted upon to prevent it. When asked why he, who spoke fluent French, had never perfected the accent, he replied, *'C'ay pour montray que j'ai la flotte Anglayse derrière moi.'*

From The Paris Embassy *by Cynthia Gladwyn (Collins, London, 1976).*

LORD KITCHENER, long after his earlier conquests in the Sudan, was appointed British Agent and Consul-General in Egypt. Although he was virtual ruler of the country, he was disappointed not to have been made Viceroy of India (where he had earlier been Commander-in-Chief and quarrelled with Curzon), and he arrived in Cairo in 1911 determined to stand no nonsense from anyone.

During Kitchener's first week in Cairo I was informed on good authority that a number of British officials might be tendering their resignations; some from old dislike of him, others in order to forestall compulsory retirement. When (without mentioning individuals) I warned him of this tendency he significantly tapped a drawer in his desk and said: 'You'd better go down to the Club and let it be generally known that I've always kept printed acceptance forms for resignations, only requiring the name to be added to become effective.' I duly circulated this news and need hardly say that, for whatever reason, not one single resignation was submitted. Next day, curious to see how the forms ran, I opened the drawer, and found it to contain a box of cigars.

In dealing with an outstanding problem or a crisis (and in those days in Egypt when there was not one it was because there were both) Lord Kitchener had two habits at first disconcerting to a subordinate. He would invite opinion as to the course to be taken, deride it with merciless wit and not infrequently bring forward next day a solution of his own indistinguishably similar. Or he would gravely propound fantastically improbable choices of action, solely for the purpose (and sometimes for the malicious pleasure) of observing whether – and how – they were countered

From Orientations *by Sir Ronald Storrs (Nicholson & Watson, London, 1937).*

SIR HAROLD NICOLSON, who resigned from the Diplomatic Service in mid-career in the 1930s, always thought that his light-hearted sketches of diplomatic life in Some People *detracted from his reputation as a serious professional. Here he recounts with verve how he and his colleagues treated the Head of Chancery at the British Embassy in Tehran in the 1920s.*

Titty, who was senior to all of us, was head of the Chancery. He was almost incredibly incompetent, and yet he would endeavour in a forceless way to live up to his position. He told us on one occasion that it was his duty and not ours to open the red despatch-boxes that came down from the Ambassador. We took full advantage of the occasion thus afforded. We had a store in the Chancery of card-board folders backed by a strong clamp or spring: if one bent the folders backwards an aperture was disclosed which, when released, gripped any papers inserted as in a vice. We discovered that if one reversed those folders inside out and carefully closed upon them the lid of a despatch box, they would, when the despatch box was unlocked, leap gaily three or four feet into the air. The effect was increased if one inserted on the top little boxes of nibs, or paper-clips, or, best of all, a tin of tooth-powder. We would in the early morning prepare one or two of these destructive engines, and attach a label marked 'Chancery: urgent.' We would then place them among the boxes that had come down from the Ambassador over-night. When Titty, who was invariably late, arrived in the Chancery we would all be working hard at our respective desks. Titty would approach the boxes with a calm, ruminating manner such as he had seen adopted by other high officials in the past. He took hours turning over his key-ring until he found the proper key. He had a habit of locking up all his squalid little possessions, so that there were a great many confusing keys to select from. The first box contained a telegram, and he would read it through very slowly four or five times. Then he would exclaim suddenly in a startled voice, 'I say, you fellows, here is a telegram to go off,' and he would then place the telegram under some newspapers, or lock it up again in the box he had just opened, or devise some other original means by which it might be mislaid. The second box, we knew, was the one to startle him. Our suspense was increased by the fact that it was again necessary for him to search laboriously through his bunch of keys. But when at last the key was inserted and turned, our mechanics seldom failed to have their effect. The folders would spring into the air with immense vitality, scattering nibs and paper-clips like a handful of flung gravel. 'Oh, I say!' Titty would exclaim, 'you fellows must have been playing a joke on me.' And then very slowly, swinging his keys on a steel chain, he would absently leave the room. The full joy of this entertainment was to be found, however, not so much in his reception of one of our explosive boxes, as in his attitude towards a box which was, in fact, authentic. He would circle doubtingly around it, fiddling with his keys, and then keep his hand very firmly down on the lid when he had at last unlocked it. Very gingerly he would relax the pressure and then, on finding that the contents were of a static and not of a dynamic nature, he would open the lid in a detached and offhand manner, as if he had known from the first that there was merely a sheet of folded foolscap inside. Alternately, when he was feeling a little below the mark, he would avoid the boxes altogether, leaving them to languish unopened for hours on end; so that in the interests of the public service this particular pastime had to be discontinued.

From Some People *by Harold Nicholson (Constable, London, 1927).*

CLEMENCEAU encounters Paderewski for the first time.

When the Peace Conference assembled in Paris after the conclusion of the First World War in 1919, Georges Clemenceau – the French Prime Minister – noticed across the room a bizarre and flamboyant figure whom he had never seen before.

169

'Tell me,' he said to his secretary, 'who is the gentleman over there with the extraordinary hair?'

'But Your Excellency, that is Monsieur Paderewski, who was the greatest pianist in the world and is now the Prime Minister of Poland.'

'*Quelle chute!*', was Clemenceau's only comment.

Told to the editor by John Julius Norwich, who in turn heard the story from his father Duff Cooper (sometime ambassador to France, and 1st Viscount Norwich).

SIR HAROLD NICOLSON recounts a disconcerting departure by Lord Curzon's drunken valet, Arketall.

I did not witness his departure. I merely heard next morning that he had gone. While having breakfast I received a message that Lord Curzon wished to see me urgently. I found him in his dressing-gown. He was half angry and half amused. 'That indefinite Arketall,' he said, 'has stolen my trousers.' 'Not *all* your trousers?' I asked in some confusion. 'Yes, *all* of them, except these.' Lord Curzon was wearing his evening trousers of the night before. I glanced at my watch. There was still an hour before the meeting of the Conference, but by this time Arketall must have reached Pontarlier. I ran for Bill Bentinck and told him to telephone to the frontier police: 'Don't say trousers,' I shouted after him, 'say "quelques effets."' I then secured the manager and proceeded to Arketall's room. We looked in, over and under the cupboard and into the chest of drawers: I peered under the bed; there were three more bottles of Benedictine against the wall, but otherwise the space was empty. The manager and I looked at each other in despair. 'C'est inénarrable,' he muttered, 'complètement in' é-narrable.' I sat down wearily on the bed to consider our position. I jumped up again immediately and pulled back the bed-spread. Upon the crumpled bed-clothes lay a trouser-press bursting with Lord Curzon's trousers. I sent the manager to stop Bill Bentinck telephoning; myself, I clasped the trouser-press and returned in triumph to Lord Curzon. He was seated at his writing-table, his pencil dashing across sheets of foolscap, his lips moving. I stood there waiting. When he had finished four or five sheets and cast them from him he turned to me indignantly. His face relaxed into a smile and then extended into that irresistible laugh of his, that endearing boyish sense of farce. 'Thank you,' he said, 'I shall now complete my toilet. There will only be Leeper to dinner to-night, and as a reward I shall give you my celebrated imitation of Tennyson reciting "Tears, idle tears".'

From Some People *by Harold Nicolson (Constable, London, 1927).*

LORD KILLEARN was one of the last great British pro-consular figures in Egypt. Although his hospitality was princely (according to Churchill, who stayed with him during the war) he had habits which disconcerted some of his other visiting compatriots, as is seen here.

Sir Miles Lampson, who was elevated to the title of Lord Killearn during his time as ambassador in Egypt in the Second World War, was a man of immense physical stature – six foot four inches tall, broad and stout. He had little respect for King Farouk and the Egyptian government and court, who were too sympathetic to Fascist Italy for comfort.

On one occasion he is said to have accompanied the Permanent Secretary of some Whitehall department to an audience with Farouk. In the course of conversion with the king, the Whitehall official crossed his legs as he was sitting on the sofa, only to receive a sharp blow from Killearn's hand across his knee-cap and the audible reprimand: 'Don't cross your legs in the presence of His Majesty!'

Totally disconcerted by this incident, the official faltered but continued to the end of the audience; once back in the yellow embassy Rolls-Royce with Killearn, the official apologized for his gaffe and explained he had no idea his conduct would seem discourteous. 'Don't give it another thought,' roared Killearn. 'I often do that: it impresses these wops!'

On another occasion, it was however Killearn who was disconcerted. Soon after his elevation to the peerage, a visiting British minister was received by him at the embassy and opened the conversation with the words: 'I'm so glad to find you here, Lord

Killearn, because I was told that your predecessor Lampson was an awful shit!'

From an account given to the editor by one of Lord Killearn's successors as ambassador in Cairo.

KHRUSHCHEV displays undiplomatic behaviour at the United Nations and elsewhere.

In September [1960], Khrushchev was still carrying on. He proposed that the United Nations be reorganized, and went to New York to offer the plan in person. The plan did not amount to much – substituting a 'troika' (a three-man commission) for a single secretary-general and moving the United Nations headquarters to Switzerland, Austria, or the Soviet Union. It was Khrushchev's behaviour that drew the most attention. He shouted and laughed during the speeches, and took off a shoe and banged it on his desk – interrupting Macmillan's address.

Earlier, in Moscow, Ambassador Thompson had been subjected to a number of embarrassing moments. At a reception, Khrushchev began to shout at Thompson about the U-2. To illustrate his point, he said, 'Do you think it is all right to do this?' and stepped heavily on the Ambassador's foot. Afterwards, he told Thompson, 'I didn't mean to hurt you'.

From Witness to History 1929–1969 *by Charles E. Bohlen*
(W. W. Norton & Company Inc., New York, 1973).

RAB BUTLER, as Foreign Secretary in the 1960s, is described by Sir Richard Parsons as teasing his officials by disconcerting behaviour at Foreign Office meetings.

By the time Mr Butler became Foreign Secretary he was somewhat disillusioned and he liked to tease his advisers. Once at a large meeting in his room, he sat at his desk, tilting his chair back so that he could put his feet up. It looked most precarious. All the ambitious diplomats sat on the edge of their own chairs, intent on rushing forward to save the Foreign Secretary's skull, if he should fall backwards. But he failed to do so. Afterwards, I heard him mutter to Nicko Henderson, then his Principal Private Secretary, 'It keeps them on their toes'.

MR R.A. BURROUGHS, as British Ambassador in Algeria in 1971, reports at some length to a colleague in the Foreign Office about the eccentric behaviour of the Spanish Ambassador. Such light-hearted reports were a regular feature of the more leisured days of British diplomacy, and (like this one) were not infrequently printed and given a wide distribution within the Diplomatic Service to brighten the working day of hard-pressed officials.

Having sent you in my previous letter an account of the Opening of the Judicial Year, I realise that I should have written to you somewhat earlier about the Affair of the Spanish Ambassador's Suitcase; an affair which has passed into local diplomatic legend.

It took place on the night of 19/20 June. The 19 June is a day which is always celebrated in Algeria as marking some event, which I have forgotten, in the Struggle for Independence. This year it was decided that against the background of the quarrel with the French Government over oil, the celebrations should most appropriately take place at Hassi Messacud in the Sahara, where oil was first struck by the French. A pleasing note of additional insult would be given to the occasion by celebrating also the nationalization of French oil interests on 24 February of this year.

For the purpose it was of course necessary to have all foreign Ambassadors present. I am never sure whether this insistence on our presence springs from a misplaced but delicate desire to give us pleasure, or whether it is an expression of Algerian xenophobia. The way these affairs are organised may be not the result of inefficiency but rather of fiendishly clever planning designed to torture the bloody foreigners. The previous year was, by all accounts, of such prolonged horror that it could only have been effected by design.

As 19 June approached the Corps began to speculate about what

173

might lie in store for us. By the 17th nothing had been revealed. Protocole Department would only smile roguishly and say that it was to be a surprise. Indeed, when we were all informed of what had been arranged for our delectation it was a surprise; rather a pleasant one. It might have been another steel-works entailing a 5.00 a.m. start, and a return home at 3.00 a.m. on the following morning. Instead we were to be flown down to the desert at the civilized hour of 4.00 p.m., and beds were to be provided for the night.

As the special 'plane was due to start at 4.00 p.m., we were instructed to be at the airport at 3.00 for the traditional ceremony of standing on the tarmac for an hour or so in the blazing sun. We arrived variously equipped. Most Ambassadors brought brief cases containing a tooth-brush, razor and pyjamas. A few brought rather elegant little dressing cases, and a certain Ambassador's case gave out the sound of clinking whisky bottles every time he put it on the ground.

The only exception was the Spanish Ambassador, who is a Lieutenant-General 'still on the active list, my dear', as he assures everyone. He brought, not a brief case, but an enormous, splendid and expensive portmanteau, made of heavy leather with gold fastenings, and bound with elegant straps each with a heavy gold buckle. He arrived late, panting and sweating profusely as he deposited his case on the tarmac.

Having stood around for an hour and a half the Chef de Protocole looked at his watch, asked Their Excellencies to group themselves before him, clapped his hands and said 'Prenez vos places dans l'avion. Vite, vite.' He urged us up the ladder at a gallop, wringing his hands and saying, 'Nous sommes déjà en retard, Excellences'.

The Spanish Ambassador grabbed his suitcase and joined the rush. He got it half-way up the steps, fell over it and said something very rude in Spanish. With the Chef de Protocole yapping around the heels of the pack we pressed forward, stepping over the suitcase and round the Spanish Ambassador, who is of a shape that makes this operation difficult. Finally he was left alone on the gang-way ascending slowly backwards and dragging the suitcase up step by step.

He was installed in the rear, with his suitcase occupying the neighbouring seat. The doors closed and we took off. We were comforted by the announcement that as it was a day of National Celebration, this type of aircraft was being flown for the very first time by an all-Algerian crew. Some of us were more touched by this delicate attention than others.

Apart from one or two rather dashing tight turns designed to show off the burning flares at various oil well heads, we had none the less a comfortable and safe journey, punctuated by offers of bottles of Coca-Cola with the tops wrestled off by an air-hostess of quite remarkable plainness. There is much to be said for the wearing of the veil.

We landed at an airstrip in the desert, and the Spanish Ambassador had found the answer. It was easier this time to descend backwards sliding his suitcase towards him. Naturally, we had all been speculating about the contents. Some Ambassadors leaned to the view that it contained several gold-braided uniforms and loads and loads of medals. Others thought that he had brought a white tie and tails. The Greek, however, believed that he had brought his wife 'en cas de besoin'.

Standing on the sand, the Spanish Ambassador ran round and round his suitcase demanding to know where was the orderly who was to carry his baggage. He was ignored by the Chef de Protocole and the welcoming party. Rather we were told that our presence was urgently required in the salon d'honneur for a lecture on the oil-field and its operation. 'Where is the salon d'honneur?' we asked. 'Over there,' we were told, and a small hut in the far distance was indicated to us. 'Vite, vite Excellences.'

We trudged off through soft sand for our lecture, with the Spanish Ambassador losing contact with the pack, and leaving a furrow behind him like a light plough. We heard our lecture. In Arabic, a language with which the speaker was himself not too familiar. Most of the Ambassadors identified it as Arabic simply because it wasn't either French or English.

As question time started, the Spanish Ambassador appeared through the door, clutching a couple of hernias acquired between the aircraft and the salon d'honneur.

For the next lecture, we had to move to another hut, mercifully quite near this time. Then into a bus to be conducted to our air-conditioned aluminium huts, 'Pour une demi-heure de repos, Excellences. N'oubliez-pas vos baggages.'

By this time it was black-dark with one or two oil-flares on the horizon. Our sleeping huts were scattered among oleander bushes in the artificial oasis created by the oil-engineers. They were numbered from 1 to 60 on what appeared to be a totally random plan, and each Ambassador was issued with a numbered ticket.

As the most recently accredited Ambassador I was allocated Hut No. 60, which was the most distant and the most obscure. When I finally found it and opened the door it was already occupied by the Greek Ambassador, in the process of removing his trousers. I showed my ticket with the number 60 printed on it. He extricated his ticket from his trouser-pocket around his ankles, and it too bore the number 60. There ensued a diplomatic negotiation in which I made great play of the fact that since he had presented his credentials a full hour before me, I was obliged to yield him precedence. Plainly therefore he should be in Hut No. 59. Having satisfied himself that HM Government was a signatory of the revised Vienna Convention which reaffirms the rules of diplomatic precedence, the Greek Ambassador had no alternative but to pull up his trousers and depart into the Saharan darkness.

We had been instructed to parade at a certain spot among the oleander bushes at 8.30 p.m. The Chef de Protocole had insisted that we should be there 'exactement a l'heure prevue'. He need not have bothered. We were full of impatience to see the Spanish Ambassador, and to learn what his suitcase contained. Would he be in full military uniform, or were the theories about the evening dress and the diamond studs and the insignia of many Spanish and Catholic orders to be confirmed? Perhaps he had been made a Field Marshal and would arrive with a little jewelled baton.

We assembled. The Chef de Protocole lined us up and counted us. A prolonged wait, while we considered who might be missing. It was the Spanish Ambassador. 'He 'ave great trouble with 'is corsets', said the Bulgarian. 'No soldier to give the pull.' But he was wrong. At long last the Spanish Ambassador arrived through the bushes, and to confound us all, wearing the suit in which he had started out.

'Vite, vite,' said the Chef de Protocole. 'We will now proceed to have *un meshaoui*.'

A meshaoui consists of a recently slaughtered sheep, impaled on a long pole and roasted slowly over charcoal. Its head, its hooves surmounted by short woolly socks, and what the Bible delicately describes as 'the appurtenance thereof' are all included in the dish. Having been escorted to a vast open tent in the desert where we passed between us convivial, family-sized bottles of Pepsi-Cola, and listened to numerous speeches, the meshaoui finally arrived.

The ration was one sheep to every three Ambassadors. I shared mine with two African Ambassadors. I had the head end and the horns kept catching my sleeve as I pulled pieces of hot meat away with my fingers. His Excellency at the rear end made a grap for the 'appurtenances' and rolled up the sleeves of his robe. He was nearly up to his shoulder in the interior of the animal, and kept saying, 'Le gout de dedans est meilleur'. As the meal progressed I became more and more alarmed. He showed every sign of disappearing up the rear end of the sheep, and I had visions of having to seize a pair of black ankles to recover His Excellency.

A nationalistic play was succeeded by hours of greatly entertaining music. Much of it consisted of three old nomads blowing down flutes which had been imperfectly constructed and which allowed air to escape from cracks in the side. The effect was rather peaceful and wistful. The bit I liked best, however, was the appearance of a Western style orchestra. It was not the excellence of its rendition, but rather the fact that it contained a left-handed violinist. There is something satisfying about the concerted sweep of violin bows. But it is as nothing to the excitement of a row of violinists containing a Southpaw fiddle. The quick bits are the best, when his right-handed neighbour has to keep on ducking like a demented woodpecker.

I will not trouble you with the rest of the night's entertainment, full though it was of delightful vignettes. We managed to get three hours' sleep in our air-conditioned huts before reporting at our aircraft shortly after dawn.

The sun rose with its accustomed splendour over the desert horizon. The Spanish Ambassador made a parallel track in our wake through the sand with his suitcase. [He] left immediately thereafter for leave in Spain. He has only returned within the last few days and no one has seen his wife. Was the Greek Ambassador's theory perhaps right and has the Spanish Ambassador lost the keys of his expensive suitcase? It is clearly a highly-prized object, and it must have given him great pain to bore air-holes through that expensively grained leather.

9

Pomp and Circumstance

DIPLOMACY HAS ALWAYS been connected with ceremonial. It has usually been considered important to impress on envoys the power and wealth of the rulers they are visiting or to whom they are accredited. When Agamemnon received envoys in the *Iliad*, he toasted them from golden chalices; Ivan the Terrible's chancellor took Anthony Jenkinson aside to see the tsar's jewels and sables; ambassadors arriving at Versailles were deliberately subjected to being dazzled by the Sun King's splendour. Even today, monarchs – and, to a lesser extent, presidents – receive ambassadors with the full panoply of carriages, guards of honour, bands and formal court ceremonial.

Ambassadors for their part are conscious of representing the person of their sovereign or head of state. They grow accustomed to being treated deferentially – at least by courtiers, officials and fellow diplomats – and can quickly assume that any slight on them is a slight against their sovereign or their country. They are generally granted precedence above most people in the country where they are accredited; they often have stately residences, and invariably large and prestigious cars.

These trappings can all too easily lead to a sense of self-importance. Happily there are various antidotes, of which the Press (no respecter of persons), the ambassador's own children, and an occasional posting back home (like prophets, ambassadors are without honour in their own country) are usually the most

179

effective. But the annals of diplomacy remain studded with tales of pomposity. Lord Curzon was said to answer his telephone in the Foreign Office with the words 'It's Lord Curzon himself'. One British ambassador is reputed to have received Edward VII on the steps of his impressive residence with, 'Welcome, Your Majesty, to my humble house', allegedly to be put down with the response, '*My* humble house, if you don't mind, Ambassador.'

Honours have traditionally played a part in the formal minuet of courts and embassies. Most countries allow – and indeed encourage – their diplomats to accept the foreign decorations which are often offered at the termination of a mission; hence the fact that many European and Latin American ambassadors are covered in stars and sashes on ceremonial occasions. In Britain this has not been permitted since Queen Elizabeth I declared that her 'sheep' should not be branded 'with any other mark than my own', and – on another occasion – that 'my dogs should run in my collars'. This had the – probably intended – effect of increasing the significance of indigenous honours for British diplomats. Although the bi-annual honours list is now again under review, at present the Order of St Michael and St George is almost exclusively the preserve of the Diplomatic Service, and the old joke about the initials of the different grades of the order persists: CMG ('Call me God'), KCMG ('Kindly call me God') and GCMG ('God calls me God'). In recent times it has been strictly taboo – and doubtless counter-productive – to lobby for British honours, but the letters of eighteenth- and nineteenth-century diplomats suggest that this was not always the case. Embarrassing as these letters are, they could probably be matched by those of politicians and soldiers of the same period: Lord Cardigan's protestations of his case for the Garter after the battle of Balaclava are positively blush-making.

Pomp and circumstance are a diminishing part of diplomatic life in all except the popular conception of the profession; and even there, multi-lateral diplomacy in Brussels and New York and Landrover-diplomacy in the Third World are correcting the image.

CARDINAL WOLSEY impresses on the Venetian Ambassador that he alone is directing English foreign policy.

Wolsey did not adopt a modest pose, and make a pretence of being only a humble adviser to his King, as many powerful ministers have done. He did all he could to impress both his subordinate officials and the foreign ambassadors with his own power, with his wealth and ostentation, and the grandeur of his house at Hampton Court. He wrote to Gigli [the Cardinal Bishop of Worcester, who lived in Rome and had never visited his diocese] that neither Henry nor the English nobles would ever allow him to resign. When Giustiniani, in August 1516, asked to have an audience with Henry, who was away from London on a progress in Dorset, Wolsey told him that Henry did not wish to be troubled with foreign policy; and Giustiniani, fearing to offend Wolsey, agreed to transact the business with him and not with the King. When Giustiniani returned to Venice in October 1519, and reported to the Senate on his four years' mission to England, he said that when he first arrived in London in 1515, Wolsey would say: 'His Majesty will do so and so.' A few years later, he would say: 'We will do so and so.' By 1519 he was saying: 'I will do so and so.'

From Henry VIII *by Jaspar Ridley (Constable, London, 1984).*

ANTHONY JENKINSON, trader and envoy of Elizabeth I of England, is shown Ivan the Terrible's treasures so that he can report back to England on the Tsar's magnificence.

The 14th of April in the morning when M. Gray and I were ready to depart towards England, the Chancellors sent unto us and willed us to come to their office in the Chancerie, where at our comming they shewed us a great number of the Emperor's jewels, and rich robes, willing us to marke and beholde them well, to the end that at our arrivall into England, we might make report what we had seene there.

The chiefest was his majestie's crowne, being close under the top very faire wrought: in mine opinion, the workmanship of so much gold few men can amend. It was adorned and decked with rich and precious stones abundantly, among the which one was a rubie, which stood a handfull higher then the top of the crown upon a small wier, it was as big as a good beane: the same crown was lined with a faire blacke Sable, worth by report 40 robles.

Wee sawe all his majestie's robes which were very richly set with stones, they shewed us manie other great stones of divers kindes, but the most part of them were uneven; in maner as they came out of the worke, for they doe more esteeme the greatnesse of stones, then the proportion of them.

We saw two goodly gownes which were as heavie as a man could easily carrie, all set with pearles over and over: the gards or borders round about them were garnished with saphires and other good stones abundantly. One of the same gownes was very rich, for the pearles were very large, round and orient: as for the rest of his gownes and garments, they were of rich tissue and cloth of gold and all furred with very blacke Sables.

When we had sufficiently perused all these things, they willed master Gray at his arrivall in England, to provide if he could, such jewels and rich clothes as he had seene there, and better if he could, declaring that the Emperour would gladly bestow his money upon such things.

So we tooke our leave the same time, and departed towards Vologda immediatly.

From Hakluyt's Collection of the Early Voyages, Travels and Discoveries of the English Nation *(R.H. Evans, London, 1809).*

QUEEN ELIZABETH I forbids her diplomats to wear or accept foreign decorations.

Queen Elizabeth objected to her subjects wearing foreign *insignia* of knighthood. Two young Englishmen, Nicolas Clifford and Antony Shirley, had been admitted by Henry IV to the Order of St Michael as a reward for their services. On their return to England they appeared at Court in the city displaying the *insignia* of the order, which provoked the Queen's anger, because the French king, without consulting her, had allowed these her subjects

182

to take the oath to him on their admittance, and she threw them into prison. Nevertheless, she was too merciful to put the law in force against them, seeing that they were ignorant youths, and also because she entertained a special goodwill towards the King of France, who had conferred so great an honour upon them. She therefore ordered that they should return the *insignia* and take care to have their names removed from the register of the Order.

Queen Elizabeth is reported by Camden to have said, in connexion with [another] case: 'There is a close bond of affection between princes and their subjects. As it is not proper for a modest woman to cast her eyes on any other man than her husband, so neither ought subjects to look at any other prince than the one whom God has given them. I would not have my sheep branded with any other mark than my own, or follow the whistle of a strange shepherd.'

From A Guide to Diplomatic Practice *by the Rt. Hon. Sir Ernest Satow*
(Longmans Green, London, 1922).

CASANOVA, who was not averse to undertaking spying commissions in the intervals of philandering, receives a dubious decoration from the Pope.

Feeling highly flattered at the favour the Holy Father had shewn me, I put on the cross which depended from a broad red ribbon – red being the colour worn by the Knights of St John of the Lateran, the companions of the palace, *comites palatini*, or count-palatins. About the same time poor Cahusac, author of the opera of Zoroaster, went mad for joy on the receipt of the same order. I was not so bad as that, but I confess, to my shame, that I was so proud of my decoration that I asked Winckelmann whether I should be allowed to have the cross set with diamonds and rubies. He said I could if I liked, and if I wanted such a cross he could get me one cheap. I was delighted, and bought it to make a show at Naples, but I had not the face to wear it in Rome. When I went to thank the Pope I wore the cross in my button-hole out of modesty. Five years afterwards when I was at Warsaw, Czartoryski, a Russian prince-palatine, made me leave it off by saying,

'What are you doing with that wretched bauble? It's a drug in the market, and no one but an impostor would wear it now.'

The Popes knew this quite well, but they continued to give the cross to ambassadors while they also gave it to their *valets de chambre*. One has to wink at a good many things in Rome.

From The Memoirs of Jacques Casanova de Seingalt, *Vol. IV, translated by Arthur Machen (Putnam, London).*

HORACE WALPOLE writes a letter of introduction to the British Minister in Florence, with an elegance which suggests his more leisured age.

TO SIR HORACE MANN

Arlington Street, May 11, 1765.
Mr Stanley, one of the Lords of the Admiralty, has done me the honour of desiring a letter of recommendation to you, as he is going to pass the summer in Italy. His character and abilities must be too well known to you to make my interest in your friendship necessary, even if he should wish for greater share in your acquaintance than your constant attention and good nature direct you to offer to your countrymen in general: yet it is so flattering to me to seem to contribute to your connection, that when I beg you to exceed your common civilities on his account, I am determined to please myself with thinking that you do it on mine.

From The Letters of Horace Walpole, 4th Earl of Orford, 1764–1766
(The Clarendon Press, Oxford, 1904).

HORACE WALPOLE, who – as well as asking occasional favours for visitors – keeps the interest of Sir Horace Mann in the forefront of the government's mind in London, here writes to inform him, that the vacancy in the Order of the Bath for which he had hoped is to be given to Clive of India.

Your red riband is certainly postponed. There was but one vacant, which was promised to General Draper, who, when he thought he felt the sword dubbing his shoulder, was told that my Lord Clive could not conquer the Indies a second time without being a Knight of the Bath. This, however, I think will be but a short parenthesis, for I expect that *heaven-born hero* to return from whence he came, instead of bringing hither all the Mogul's pearls and rubies. Yet, before that happens there will probably be other vacancies to content both Draper and you.

From The Letters of Horace Walpole, 4th Earl of Orford, 1764–1766
(The Clarendon Press, Oxford, 1904).

LORD GRANVILLE LEVESON GOWER, in a letter to Lady Bessborough, deplores the self-importance of his predecessors at the British Embassy in St Petersburg.

November 12th, 1804

I believe I before told you of my Dissatisfaction at the conduct of the Warrens; I believe all originated with her love of Pomp and his low ambition to be made a Peer. He flattered himself that a Convention must be the fruit of his Diplomatic Labour, and a Peerage the Reward of concluding a Convention. We went to Court in his Coach together, and could you believe it possible that, upon my getting into the Coach first and sitting forwards, he asked me if I wd. not sit backwards, meaning that till I had presented my Credentials I was so much his inferior that I ought not to sit upon the same seat with him.

From The Private Correspondence of Lord Granville Leveson Gower, 1781 to 1821
(John Murray, London, 1916).

LORD GRANVILLE LEVESON GOWER, who finds much to disapprove of in the present as well as the past, is appalled at the cost of keeping up ambassadorial state in St Petersburg in 1804.

The mode of Life I propose to myself is to receive the world. I have made up my Mind to being ruined; the expense of this Place exceeds all calculation. I have 10 Servants out of Livery in fine uniform – Gold Lace Coats, and 7 or 8 in Livery. I have horses for the night, I shall have sledge Horses, and I have my own Eight I brought from England. It is said that it is worth while to be Ill in order to know the value of Health; it may be, perhaps, also worth while to live in such society as I find here, in order to estimate properly that which I have been accustomed to in England.

From The Private Correspondence of Lord Granville Leveson Gower, 1781 to 1821
(John Murray, London, 1916).

SIR GEORGE STAUNTON peevishly complains that a lack of friends in the Cabinet has deprived him of the recognition due for his service as a a British representative at the court of Peking.

If I had a personal *friend* in the Cabinet, he would . . . have contended that an individual who had been pronounced by the authorities in China (who beyond all question were the most competent judges) to have 'maintained our national honour and promoted our commercial interests, by his decision and sound judgement, under circumstances the most trying, when less firm minds might have bent under the weight of the responsibility he incurred', was justly entitled to some reward. He might have further contended that this reward was doubly due to him, when those who had taken the opposite and less praiseworthy cause, and whom his conduct alone had saved from actual disgrace, were, nevertheless, from whatever cause, honoured and promoted; and he would finally have scouted the idea of what had been the *usual practice* being pleaded as a bar to reward in a case so absolutely peculiar and unprecedented. When, some years after, Mr Henry Ellis and Mr Holt Mackenzie were made Privy Councillors, neither previous services nor usual practice were regarded. It was quite sufficient that the one was the friend of Lord Ripon, and the other of Lord Glenelg. They are both most estimable and talented individuals, but I apprehend that there can be no question that this is the true history of their promotion to that honour.

From Memoirs of the Chief Incidents in the Public Life of Sir George Thomas
Staunton, Bart. *(L. Booth, London, 1856).*

LORD SALISBURY, as Prime Minister and Foreign Secretary,
adopts the attitudes of Lord Pamerston.

Four days later, on 7 January 1896, Salisbury was giving a dinner
party at Hatfield when a red despatch box was brought to the table.
He asked the permission of Princess Christian, a daughter of Queen
Victoria, to open it, and studied the short message it contained.
Then he scribbled for a moment or two and had the box removed.
The Princess asked him what it was. He replied that the German
Emperor had landed 150 men at Delagoa Bay, in Portuguese East
Africa, the only access of the Boers to the sea other than through
British territory. 'What answer have you sent?' the Princess
enquired. 'I haven't answered,' Salisbury said, 'I have sent ships.'

From Superior Person *by Kenneth Rose (Weidenfeld & Nicolson, London, 1969).*

LORD CROMER was British Agent and Consul-General in Cairo
from 1883 to 1907 and established a total predominance over Egypt
during that period – a predominance which his successors, such as
Kitchener and even Killearn, were to continue to enjoy. Not infre-
quently, as described below, he allowed his mastery of the local scene to
spill over into his relationships at home.

Of his influence on the home front I saw later many proofs. Lord
Salisbury had been Prime Minister as well as Foreign Secretary;
redoubtable as either, omnipotent as both. I found a telegram
addressed to him by the British Consul-General thanking him for
instructions but informing him that the previous Cairo telegram
had been intended to announce, not what he proposed doing, but
what he had already done. Only once was his authoritative impatience of ceremony rumoured to have sustained a reverse. Arriving
in London on leave from Egypt he applied for an audience with
the King. It was granted – for three days later. Lord Cromer
intimated to the Private Secretary that he had hoped to be received
that very afternoon, in order that he might catch the night train for
his holiday in Scotland. 'He seems to take me for the Khedive,'
answered King Edward.

From Orientations *by Sir Ronald Storrs (Nicholson & Watson, London, 1937).*

187

SIR EDWARD GOSCHEN, as British Ambassador in Berlin, returns with the Kaiser for the funeral of King Edward VII and provides a reminder of how close the English and German royal families were, right up to the outbreak of the First World War.

Friday 20 May

King Edward's funeral . . . On arrival at Windsor we found lots of carriages and were driven straight up to the Chapel and both took our places in the Nave – where we had to wait an hour and a half before the Procession came: but during the wait the organ played beautiful funeral marches – Beethoven – Schubert's and others. Then we heard the muffled drums coming nearer and nearer and we had a chokey moment. Then came the procession and the remains of our dear old King. One can scarcely imagine him *gone*. The Queen (Alexandra) was a pathetic figure – swathed in crape and with a white set face. With her came the King [George V], then the Emperor [Kaiser Wilhelm II] and Duke of Connaught – and then about 8 other Kings. Amongst these was King of Bulgaria who rather spoilt solemnity by mopping himself all the way up the Chapel . . .

Tuesday 24 May

Had an audience with the King after seeing the Emperor off. Latter told me how nice everybody had been – how sympathetic he had found the King and how he had admired the decorum and reverence of the enormous crowds who had assembled to see the Procession. 'England sh'd be proud of her people *and* her police.'! The King was charming and talked to me for an hour – he seemed quite up in For. Aff. and spoke most sensibly about them. He said that nothing could exceed the kindness and thoughtfulness of the Emperor during the visit – adding that he should do his best to keep up the best private and public relations with Germany.

From The Diary of Sir Edward Goschen *(1910).*

SIR ERIC PHIPPS, British Ambassador to Germany during the rise of Nazism in 1934, reports a visit to Göring's sporting estate which he finds both ludicrous and disturbing.

The Head Ranger of the Reich, Hermann Göring, appeared to his guests in a variety of costumes, ranging from aviator's garments of india-rubber with top boots and a large hunting knife stuck in the belt, to white tennis shoes, white flannel shirt, and a green leather jacket with a large harpoon-like instrument in his hand . . .

The chief impression was that of the almost pathetic naïveté of General Göring, who showed us his toys like a big, fat, spoilt child: his primeval woods, his bison and birds, his shooting-box and lake and bathing beach, his blonde 'private secretary', his wife's mausoleum and swans and sarsen stones, all mere toys to satisfy his varying moods, and all, or so nearly all, as he was careful to explain, German. And then I remembered that there were other toys, less innocent, though winged, and these might some day be launched on their murderous mission in the same childlike spirit, and with the same childlike glee.

From a report by HM Ambassador at Berlin to the Foreign Office in June 1934.

THE NATIONAL SALUTE TO THE SULTAN OF MUSCAT AND OMAN forms the subject of a memorable despatch from Her Majesty's Consul-General in Muscat to the Earl of Home, then Foreign Secretary.

British Consulate-General,
Muscat,
August 27, 1960.

(No. 10. Confidential)
My Lord,
 I have the honour to refer to your Lordship's despatch No. 8 of July 29, in which you requested me to ascertain, on behalf of the Lords Commissioners of the Admiralty, whether the B♭ clarinet music, enclosed with your despatch, was a correct and up-to-date

189

rendering of the National Salute to the Sultan of Muscat and Oman.

2. I have encountered certain difficulties in fulfilling this request. The Sultanate has not since about 1937 possessed a band. None of the Sultan's subjects, so far as I am aware, can read music, which the majority of them regard as sinful. The Manager of the British Bank of the Middle East, who can, does not possess a clarinet. Even if he did, the dignitary who in the absence of the Sultan is the recipient of ceremonial honours and who might be presumed to recognise the tune, is somewhat deaf.

3. Fortunately I have been able to obtain, and now enclose, a gramophone record which has on one side a rendering by a British military band of the 'Salutation and March to His Highness the Sultan of Muscat and Oman'. The first part of this tune, which was composed by the bandmaster of a cruiser in about 1932, bears a close resemblance to a pianoforte rendering by the Bank Manager of the clarinet music enclosed with your Lordship's despatch. The only further testimony I can obtain of the correctness of this music is that it reminds a resident of long standing of a tune, once played by the long defunct band of the now disbanded Muscat infantry, and known at the time to non-commissioned members of His Majesty's forces as (I quote the vernacular) 'Gawd strike the Sultan blind'.

4. I am informed by the Acting Minister of Foreign Affairs that there are now no occasions on which the 'Salutation' is officially played. The last occasion on which it is known to have been played at all was on a gramophone at an evening reception given by the Military Secretary in honour of the Sultan, who inadvertently sat on the record afterwards and broke it. I consider, however, that an occasion might arise when its playing might be appropriate; if, for example, the Sultan were to go aboard a cruiser which carried a band. I am proposing to call on His Highness shortly at Salalah on his return from London, and shall make further enquiries as to his wishes in the matter.

5. I am sending a copy of this despatch, without enclosure, to his Excellency the Political Resident at Bahrain.

I have, &c.

J.F.S. PHILLIPS

10

Diplomacy and Espionage

S PYING HAS BEEN linked with diplomacy from the earliest days of resident embassies. The emissaries of the Italian city states reported on each other's defences and intrigued in a way of which their contemporary Machiavelli fully approved. Queen Elizabeth I of England was deeply suspicious – with good reason – of the activities of the Spanish and French embassies in her country: the messages relating to the plotting around Mary, Queen of Scots usually passed through these missions.

This was the case despite the fact that the concept of diplomatic immunity had only developed in a rather erratic way. As Garrett Mattingly has pointed out in his admirable *Renaissance Diplomacy*, ambassadors were on occasion deemed to be subject to the jurisdiction of the Princes to whom they were accredited if they broke the fundamental laws of Christian society by conspiring to treason or assassination. The immunity of diplomatic communications was even more open to question, and Cardinal Wolsey authorized the violation of diplomatic bags on at least one occasion. But from the early seventeenth century onwards, ambassadors and their staff were generally protected from any worse fate than expulsion – being declared *persona non grata* – if they were caught scheming against the rulers of the country where they were posted, spying out the defences of the 'host' country, or recruiting agents among the local population to act as informers.

One Venetian ambassador in the sixteenth century remarked that 'there is no government on earth which divulges its affairs less than England, or is more punctually informed of those of others'. Sir Francis Walsingham set up an efficient secret service for Elizabeth I, but was not above cooking the evidence if it served his purposes – such as incriminating Mary, Queen of Scots explicitly in the Babington plot to kill Queen Elizabeth. He also had a team of expert code breakers, since most incriminating correspondence tended even then to be sent in some sort of cipher. Walsingham's service combined the tasks of penetrating the networks of foreign spies, plotters and agents at home with aggressive intelligence gathering abroad – the former activity being that allocated in our own century to M.I.5, and the latter to M.I.6.

Code-breaking has its own problems. One of the hazards of doing anything so ungentlemanly as to read other people's letters is that the temptation to refer to them – or even to remonstrate about them – can be overwhelming. H.J. Bruce quotes a case where the Imperial Russian foreign minister made one such gaffe and got away with it. At a more tragic level, it is widely believed that Churchill was aware of the details of the air-raid the Germans planned on Coventry before the event, because his cryptologists at Bletchley had broken the German ciphers; but he dared not deploy the RAF to defend Coventry for fear that the source of his advance knowledge should be evident, and consequently dry up for the rest of the war.

Throughout the first half of the eighteenth century, a high priority for British intelligence was monitoring the activities of the Jacobite court, in Rome and elsewhere. Sir Robert Walpole and his successors had a most effective network of agents and informers, and it was with the greatest difficulty that Prince Charles Edward Stuart eluded them – slipping away unnoticed from a hunting party – to travel to the Channel and embark on the Forty-five uprising. One of the principal tasks laid on the British diplomatic ministers in Florence and elsewhere after the Forty-five was to warn London of any evidence that another uprising was being planned.

When Napoleon and Tsar Alexander I met on a barge on the

river at Tilsit in 1807, the British government are believed to have had an agent on board who could give them a report of all that passed. In present times that eavesdropping function would have been provided by a microphone or an electronic bugging device of the sort discovered at the American embassy in Moscow. The objective remains the same; only the instruments have changed.

There are many who think that sophisticated civilian espionage is too frequently concerned with penetrating the espionage machine of other countries, rather than with discovering material secrets: a 'mole' inside one country's intelligence service may be able to give information about a spy inside somebody else's country, but may not be able to tell much about the policies or military plans of that country. Military intelligence – it is argued – is more solid. But when this argument was put to Sir Maurice Oldfield, a one-time head of M.I.6, he is said to have commented that 'military intelligence has the same kind of relationship to real intelligence as military music has to real music'.

There have always been two sorts of spies: those who work for payment, and those who work for principles. In Walsingham's day, the members of the Roman Catholic community in England were potentially disaffected, and natural suspects in any plot against the Crown. In our own times, Communism has been an active faith that has seduced followers from different nationalities, classes and cultures. Burgess, Maclean, Philby and Blunt were all recruited to the ranks of the Communist Party in the 1930s at Cambridge, and their pernicious effect on British diplomacy took forty years to work itself out of the system. Probably one of the most harmful aphorisms of modern times has been E.M. Forster's remark: 'If I had to choose between betraying my country and betraying my friend, I hope I should have the guts to betray my country.' It was much quoted by Burgess. Sir Cecil Spring Rice – of 'I vow to thee my country . . .' – was a truer representative of his profession.

CARDINAL WOLSEY flagrantly violates diplomatic immunity.

It was perhaps because of [the Emperor Charles V's] set-back that Wolsey ventured to commit a very provocative act against him in February 1525. Charles's Flemish ambassador in London, Praet, sent a dispatch to Charles by his courier, who set out for Plymouth, intending to take ship for Spain. The courier was stopped late at night near Brentford by a party of constables under the command of Sir Thomas More, who detained the courier, opened his packet, and read the letter to Charles, despite the courier's protest against this violation of diplomatic immunity. More sent the letter to Wolsey. Praet had criticised Wolsey and his policy in the letter, and Wolsey summoned Praet before the King's Council, upbraided him for writing it, placed him under house arrest, and forbade him to write to the Emperor. Henry and Wolsey then complained to both Charles and Margaret of Austria that Praet had been sending lying reports which damaged Charles's relations with Henry. They asked Charles to recall Praet and replace him by another ambassador.

The diplomatic immunity of ambassadors was not so clearly established in 1525 as in later centuries; but both Praet and Charles regarded it as a breach of international usage, and a grave affront to the Emperor's honour. It was probably Wolsey, not Henry, who was responsible for the action against Praet. Never again, during the rest of his reign, did Henry ever intercept diplomatic correspondence and arrest a foreign ambassador, even when he was dealing with ambassadors and their sovereigns who were far more hostile to him than were Praet and Charles in 1525. But Wolsey would not have acted without Henry's knowledge and authority; and after Praet had been detained, Henry officially backed Wolsey's action. He spoke on the subject to the ambassadors of Margaret of Austria, and wrote in person to Charles to demand Praet's recall, taking the opportunity, in his letter, to emphasize his high regard for Wolsey.

Charles blamed Wolsey for the incident. He thought it wise to suppress his anger for the time being, and agreed to replace Praet; but he told Praet that he wished he were in a position to punish Wolsey.

From Henry VIII *by Jaspar Ridley (Constable, London, 1984).*

SIR FRANCIS WALSINGHAM, head of Queen Elizabeth I's secret service, intrigues to implicate Mary, Queen of Scots in plotting against Elizabeth's life, and thus justify Elizabeth in signing her death warrant and removing a threat to the throne and to Protestantism in England.

Walsingham took the opportunity of the move from Tutbury to Chartley to mount a new stage in his campaign to incriminate the Queen of Scots. His aim was of course to provide England – and Elizabeth – with sufficient evidence to prove once and for all that it was too dangerous to keep Mary alive. Already the bond of Association passed through Parliament the previous year meant that a plot had only to be made in favour of the Queen of Scots – rather than by her – and she would by English law merit the death penalty. Now Walsingham, through his many and devious agents, set about enmeshing Mary in two separate conspiracies against Elizabeth, which together made up the complicated and in part bogus machinations which are known as the Babington plot. . . . The assassination plot against Elizabeth, which is at first sight a dastardly conspiracy to kill the English queen, changes character as it becomes clear that much of the plot consisted of mere provocation by which Walsingham hoped to entangle Mary.

[Mary received compromising correspondence through the French embassy in London, including letters from Anthony Babington.]

Babington in his letter had talked of the killing of Queen Elizabeth. There can be no doubt but that Mary in her reply took this prospect briefly into consideration, weighed it against the prospect of her own liberty, and did not gainsay it. From first to last, in this letter, she quite understandably viewed the matter from her own point of view, but when she wrote: 'Orders must be given that when their design has been carried out I can be *quant et quant* got out of here', it was clear to the recipients of her letters – as it was to Walsingham – that the design of which she wrote and thus tacitly accepted was that same design of which they too had written, the assassination of the English queen. . . .

There was no wonder that Phelippes drew a gallows mark on the outside of this letter when he passed it on to Walsingham. Mary

had fallen plumb into the trap which had been laid for her. . . .
Even so, Walsingham was not totally satisfied with Mary's reply:
he added a forged postcript to the end of the letter, also in cipher,
in which she was made to ask for the names of the six gentlemen
who would perform the deed. It would, he felt, represent the climax
of her guilt, as well as providing the English government with some
additional useful information. This forged postscript provides
the final ironic touch to the setting up of the Babington plot by
Walsingham and his agents: 'I would be glad to know the names
and qualities of the six gentlemen which are to accomplish the
designment; for that it may be I shall be able, upon knowledge of
the parties, to give you some further advice necessary to be followed
therein. . . . As also from time to time, particularly how you proceed: and as soon as you may, for the same purpose, who be
already, and how far every one, privy hereunto.'

From Mary Queen of Scots *by Antonia Fraser (Weidenfeld & Nicolson, London, 1969).*

*COUNT GONDOMAR's quasi-diplomatic espionage in James I's
England on behalf of the 'Black Kingdom' (Spain) inspires the dramatic talents of Thomas Middleton.*

I have sold the groom of the stool six times . . .
. . . I have taught our friends, too
To convey White House [English], gold to our Black Kingdom [Spain]
In cold baked pastries and so cozen searchers . . .
Letters conveyed in rolls, tobacco-balls . . .
. . . Pray, what use
Put I my summer recreation to,
But more to inform my knowledge in the state
And strength of the White Kingdom? No fortification
Haven, creek, landing place about the White Coast,
But I got draft and platform; learned the depth
Of all their channels, knowledge of all sands,
Shelves, rocks and rivers for invasion properest;
A catalogue of all the navy royal,
The burden of the ships, the brassy murderers,
The number of the men, to what cape bound:

197

Again for the discovery of the islands,
Never a shire but the state better known
To me than to her best inhabitants;
What power of men and horses, gentry's revenues,
Who well affected to our side, who ill,
Who neither well nor ill, all the neutrality:
Thirty-eight thousand souls have been seduced, Pawn,
Since the jails vomited with the pill I gave 'em.

From A Game at Chess *by Thomas Middleton (London, 1624).*

ROBERT HARLEY, first Earl of Oxford, was Secretary of State for the Southern Department in Queen Anne's reign and in this capacity responsible for relations with a range of foreign countries. He was a controversial character with many enemies ready to exploit his embarrassment at the discovery of a traitor in his own private office. He was not the last British Minister to be embarrassed in such a way.

At this period (1707) Mr Secretary Harley's character incurred suspicion, from the treachery of William Gregg, an inferior clerk in his office who was detected in a correspondence with M. Chamillard, the French King's Minister. When his practices were detected, he made an ample confession, and, pleading guilty to indictment at the Old Bailey, was condemned to death for high treason. The Queen granted him a reprieve, in hope of his making some important discovery, but he really knew nothing of consequence to the Nation. He was an indigent Scot, who had been employed as a spy in his own Country, and now offered his services to Chamillard, with a view of being rewarded for his treachery; but he was discovered before he had reaped any fruits from his correspondence. As he had no secrets of importance to impart, he was executed at Tyburn (26th April, 1708), where he delivered a paper to the Sheriff, in which he declared Mr Harley entirely ignorant of all his treasonable connections, notwithstanding some endeavours that were made to engage him in an accusation of that Minister.

From History of England *by Tobias Smollett (London, 1757).*

SIR HORACE MANN, as British Minister to Florence in the mid-eighteenth century, was charged to report on the activities of the Stuart pretenders to the British throne; he must therefore have been amused to receive the following piece of gossip.

I heard a still better *bon mot* yesterday apropos to the eldest brother [Prince Charles Edward Stuart]. The Dowager Duchess of Aiguillon wore his picture in a bracelet, with Jesus Christ for the reverse. People could not find a reason for the connection. Madame de Rochfort said, 'Why, the same motto will suit both, "Mon royaume n'est pas de ce monde".'

From The Letters of Horace Walpole, 4th Earl of Orford, 1764–1766
(The Clarendon Press, Oxford, 1904).

MAURICE PALÉOLOGUE, the celebrated French diplomat and Academician, reveals in his diaries how sloppy office practices in Foreign Ministries result in the leaking of secret documents to the enemy (a lesson which is drummed into all new recruits to the profession).

OCTOBER 12th, 1894. When Nisard [the Director of Political Affairs at the Quai D'Orsay] had come to the end of his confidences, he asked me if I knew how the intelligence service procured papers from the German Embassy. General Mercier [the French Minister of War] had said that the letter had reached the General Staff by 'the ordinary route'. What was this 'ordinary route'? Hanotaux [the French Foreign Minister] attached great importance to being informed on this point.

I explained to him how the 'ordinary route' worked.

'The intelligence service', I said, 'has succeeded in suborning a servant at the German Embassy. She is a woman of about forty. Her name is Marie Bastian. She is vulgar, stupid, and completely illiterate, but she has been clever enough to gain the confidence of her employers. She is the charwoman; she washes down the stairs, cleans the windows, lights the fires, and sweeps out the offices, and she has the run of the house all day long. It is thus very easy for her to pick up papers which Embassy secretaries or military

199

attachés tear up and put in the waste-paper basket. She periodically hands them over to another counter-espionage agent, Brücker, or sometimes to an officer of the intelligence service. The hand-over generally takes place in the evening, in a chapel of St Clotilda.'

'But how is it possible for anyone to be so foolish as to put papers of any value in the waste-paper basket, even after tearing them up?' Nisard exclaimed, raising his arms. 'How is it that they are not burnt?'

'How are you to deal with negligence? Do you suppose that in our offices . . . ?'

'Don't go on!'

From My secret Diary of the Dreyfus Case *by Maurice Paléologue*
(Secker & Warburg, London, 1957).

ADMIRAL SIR WILLIAM JAMES explains how Guy Locock –
'a Foreign Office official who could assume that manner which is
considered by foreigners to be peculiar to the British diplomatic
service' – managed to plant a bogus Admiralty code book on the
Germans in the First World War. The ruse worked, and misleading
messages were regularly sent in the false code so that they could be
deciphered by the enemy.

And so it happened that on the afternoon of Saturday, May 22nd . . . there arrived in Rotterdam a British official, armed with a special passport and carrying 'important' papers for the Consulate in an obviously official dispatch-case which also contained a copy of the 'new Naval cipher-book'. He had deliberately chosen to arrive that particular afternoon, for the Consulate would be closed at any rate until Monday morning and possibly even until Tuesday, for Whit Monday would be intervening, and a British holiday is (or should be) a British holiday wherever you happen to be. There would therefore be nothing for him to do but 'hang about' for at least a day and a half, and that was exactly what he desired to do.

He engaged his room at the hotel, and strolled out into the garden. A well-built hotel, he saw: and the third window from the left on the second floor must surely belong to the room they had given him. The quay, too, was quite close: he might as well have a look at it. And the quay proved interesting, in particular a little piece of it which was crowded with barrels. There was nothing unusual about the barrels themselves, but he walked about amongst them until he had discovered a position from which, while completely hidden himself, he could keep in view the third window from the left on the second floor of his hotel. After which discovery he returned to his room and very carelessly unlocked his dispatch-case before 'hiding' it beneath a suit of clothes.

Nothing unusual happened that evening, but on the Sunday afternoon a lady arrived and asked for a room. She was a blonde lady who seemed to be by herself. She took no notice of the Englishman who was quietly reading in the foyer, and he did not seem to be particularly interested in her. After dinner, too, he continued to read, and the hall-porter taking pity on a foreigner without friends good-humouredly entered into conversation with him. It must be very dull, he was afraid, for the visitor.

The visitor agreed, but – what was a man to do on a Sunday?

The hall-porter smiled, and edged nearer. Perhaps the gentleman would like a little fun?

The gentleman thought that he would. Unfortunately, he said, he was a stranger to Rotterdam.

The hall-porter became confidential. There was an exceedingly amusing place to go to in the town. Any gentleman from the hotel would be cordially welcomed. If he cared to be given the address and instructions how to get there . . .

Five minutes later a very grateful gentleman was hurrying from the hotel. He was so eager, it seemed, for the promised entertainment that he forgot to lock up his dispatch-case. Yet in spite of the careful instructions he never discovered that 'amusing place'. Once out of sight of the hotel, indeed, he doubled down a side turning, came out on to the quay and hid himself amongst the barrels – with the prospect of a very long wait.

(Incidentally, it is interesting to note that although the Germans went to some little pains to get L. out of the hotel for some hours, they made no attempt to discover whether he had actually gone downtown. But often enough we would find a blind spot of this kind in their Intelligence work.)

201

The blonde lady and her friends wasted little time. Less than half an hour after he had left the hotel, the watcher among the barrels saw the lights switched on in his room. Shadows moved across the blind. Good: they were paying him a visit, and it ought not to take them very long to find the cipher-book. Ah! they must have found it. The light was out. An excellent piece of work. An enemy cipher-book well and truly stolen, almost under its guardian's nose!

But – what would they do with it? There were some agents who, no doubt, would be content to get away with the spoil; but would the blonde lady be so dreadfully clumsy? No, surely she would favour a subtler plan. She would calculate that the 'amusing place' would keep the silly Englishman entertained for at least three hours – more than sufficient time in which to photograph the book page by page and restore it to its hiding-place beneath the clothes. And in that case he would have to remain where he was until the lights in his room had been switched on, and off, again.

So he waited, and at about 1 a.m. his patience was rewarded. The lights went on for a minute or two. Splendid! The cipher-book had been restored. In a little while it would be safe to return.

And at half-past one a very 'drunken' Englishman reeled into the hotel. He tried to explain to the hall-porter what a good time he had had, but found some difficulty with his words. He also found some difficulty in walking upstairs. The kindly porter put him to bed, and everybody was satisfied.

From The Eyes of the Navy by Admiral Sir William James (Methuen, London, 1955).

H.J. BRUCE, the attaché at the British Embassy in St Petersburg described by Robert Bruce Lockhart in an earlier extract, explains the embarrassments that can follow from intercepting the correspondence of other diplomatic missions.

Throughout the 1914 war we were only seven in the Petersburg Chancery with no extraneous secretarial help of any kind, and that in spite of the streams of people to be interviewed, of despatches to be typed, of telegrams to be cyphered and decyphered. These telegrams arrived in piles every morning. They all had of course to be decyphered, many of them to be paraphrased and put into French. The object of the translation was to facilitate discussion when the Ambassador went every morning with his French col-league, Monsieur Paléologue, to see Monsieur Sazonoff, the Imperial Minister for Foreign Affairs. The object of the para-phrasing was not to give away the cyphers. This last labour we might well have spared ourselves, given the highly developed talent of the Russian *cabinet noir* for finding out cyphers. At one of these meetings, Sazonoff opened the proceedings by commenting at length on a telegram the French Ambassador had just received from his Government. Neither Ambassador seemed to notice anything unusual. After the meeting, however, Sazonoff beckoned to my Ambassador to stay behind and asked him whether he had noticed the dreadful *gaffe* which he, Sazonoff, had just made. The Ambassador said No, he hadn't noticed anything, whereupon Sazonoff said, 'I quite forgot, when I commented on Paléologue's telegram, that I oughtn't to have known anything about it till he read it to me, though as a matter of fact I saw it long before he did.' On a later occasion, after the Bolshevik Revolution, an ex-member of the Russian Ministry for Foreign Affairs in the Kerensky Government asked me to meet him at the flat of a mutual friend and, now that he was free to speak, begged me to impress on our Foreign Office the necessity of changing our cyphers as they knew them all 'except the one you got by bag last week'.

From Silken Dalliance *by H.J. Bruce (Constable, London, 1946).*

ROBERT BRUCE LOCKHART recounts how British intelligence agents burn their incriminating papers when the Cheka security police raid the consulate in Moscow during Allied intervention to back the White Russians against the Bolsheviks during the civil war that followed the Russian revolution.

On August 4th Moscow went wild with excitement. The Allies had landed at Archangel. For several days the city was a prey to rumour. The Allies had landed in strong force. Some stories put the figure at 100,000. No estimate was lower than two divisions. The Japanese were to send seven divisions through Siberia to help the Czechs. Even the Bolsheviks lost their heads and, in despair, began to pack their archives. In the middle of this crisis I saw Karachan. He spoke of the Bolsheviks as lost. They would, however, never surrender. They would go underground and continue the struggle to the last.

The confusion was indescribable. On the day after the landing I went to see Wardrop, our Consul-General, who had established his office in the Yusupoff Palace close to the Red Gates. While I was talking to him, the Consulate-General was surrounded by an armed band. It was composed of agents of the Cheka. They sealed up everything, and everyone in the building was put under arrest except Hicks and myself. The special pass I had received from Trotsky still held good. This raid had an amusing aspect. While the Cheka agents were cross-examining our Consular officials downstairs, our intelligence officers were busily engaged in burning their ciphers and other compromising documents upstairs. Clouds of smoke belched from the chimneys and penetrated even downstairs, but, although it was summer, the Cheka gentlemen noticed nothing untoward in this holocaust. As we were to learn later, the Cheka was terrifying but far from clever.

From Memoirs of a British Agent *by R.H. Bruce Lockhart (Putnam, London, 1932).*

L.C. MOYZISCH, a member of the German Embassy at Istanbul during the Second World War, describes the initial approach of the spy 'Cicero' who – as the British Ambassador's valet – subsequently purloined the key to the ambassador's despatch box (while the latter was in his bath) and in this way obtained for the Germans the advance plans of the Allies' D-Day landings. Ironically, the German High Command thought they were being fed false information and disregarded it.

'Who on earth can he be?' I thought. 'He's certainly not a member of the Diplomatic Corps.'

I sat down and motioned him to do the same. Instead he tiptoed to the door, jerked it open, shut it silently again, and came back to resume his seat in the armchair with evident relief. At that moment he really did seem a strange sort of character.

Then, haltingly at first, and in his poor French, he began to speak:

'I have an offer to make you, a proposition or whatever you call it, a proposition for the Germans. But before I tell you what it is I ask your word that whether you accept it or not you won't ever mention it to anyone except your chief. Any indiscretion on your part would make your life as worthless as mine. I'd see to that if it was the last thing I did.'

As he said this he made an unpleasant but unmistakable gesture, passing his hand across his throat.

'Do you give me your word?'

'Of course I do. If I didn't know how to keep a secret I wouldn't be here now. Please be so good as to tell me what it is you want.'

I made a show of looking at my wrist watch with some ostentation. He reacted at once.

'You'll have plenty of time for me once you know why I'm here. My proposition is of the utmost importance to your Government. I am . . .' He hesitated, and I wondered if it was due to his difficulty in expressing himself in French or whether he wished to test my reaction. '. . . I can give you extremely secret papers, the most secret that exist.'

He paused again for a moment, and then added:

'They come straight from the British Embassy. Well? That would interest you, wouldn't it?'

I did my best to keep a poker face. My first thought was that he was a petty crook out for some easy money. I would have to be careful. He seemed to have guessed what I was thinking, for he said:

'But I'll want money for them, a lot of money. My work, you know, is dangerous, and if I were caught . . .'

He repeated the unpleasant gesture with his hand across his throat, though this time, at any rate, it was not meant for me.

'You've got funds for that sort of thing, haven't you? Or your Ambassador has? Your Government would provide it. I want twenty thousand pounds, English pounds sterling.'

I offered him a cigarette which he accepted gratefully, taking a few deep pulls and then stubbing it out. He rose and went to the door once more to make sure that there was no one listening. Then he turned back and planted himself squarely in front of me. I got up too.

'You'd like to know who I am, wouldn't you? My name is quite unimportant and has no bearing. Perhaps I'll tell you what I do, but first listen to me. I'll give you three days to consider my proposition. You'll have to see your chief, and he'll probably have to get in touch with Berlin. On the 30th of October, at three in the afternoon, I'll telephone you at your office and ask you if you've received a letter for me. I'll call myself Pierre. If you say no, you'll never see me again. If you say yes, it'll mean that you've accepted my offer. In that case I'll come to see you again at ten o'clock on the evening of the same day. Not here though. We'll have to arrange some other meeting place. You'll then receive from me two rolls of film, containing photographs of British secret documents. I'll receive from you the sum of twenty thousand pounds in banknotes. You'll be risking twenty thousand pounds, but I'll have risked my life. Should you approve of my first delivery you can have more. For each subsequent roll of film I'll want fifteen thousand pounds. Well?'

I was inclined to think that the offer might be genuine, but I was convinced that, in view of the exorbitant price he was asking, nothing could come of it, particularly since he seemed to expect us to buy the papers sight unseen. I made a mental note to stress the inordinate risk in the memo that I would have to write about all this. I was certain the offer would be turned down.

Nevertheless we agreed that he should telephone me at my office on the 30th day of October at three o'clock. We also agreed that in the event of his offer being accepted we would meet near the toolshed at the end of the Embassy garden.

After these details had been arranged he asked me to switch out all the lights in the hall and on the stairs. He wished to leave the house under cover of complete darkness.

I complied with his request. When I came back to the drawing-room he had put on his overcoat and his hat, which was pulled down low over his eyes. It was past midnight by now.

I stood at the door to let him pass. He suddenly gripped my arm, and hissed in my ear:

'You'd like to know who I am? I'm the British Ambassador's valet.'

Without awaiting my reaction to this he stepped out into the darkness.

Thus ended my first meeting with the man who, a few days later, was given the code name of Cicero.

From Operation Cicero *by L. C. Moyzisch (Allan Wingate, London, 1950).*

KIM PHILBY, the British M.I.6 officer who was a secret Soviet agent, is nearly exposed by a Vice-Consul in the Soviet Consulate-General at Istanbul in 1945.

Having schemed successfully to get himself appointed as head of the anti-Communist section of the British intelligence service M.I.6, Kim Philby was summoned by his Chief in August 1945 and shown a report from the British Consulate-General in Istanbul. A Russian Vice-Consul – Volkov – had applied for political asylum in Britain, offering as an inducement to taking him the fact that he had detailed knowledge of Soviet networks and agents operating abroad – notably of two British diplomats and one British secret service officer who were working for the Russians.

Philby was deeply alarmed. The two diplomats seemed likely to be Burgess and Maclean, who were not yet under any suspicion, and the intelligence officer likely to be himself. He dared not pooh-pooh the report for fear of casting subsequent suspicion on himself, but he did manage both to slow down the speed of the reaction taken to the report, and – even more of a feat – to get himself appointed as the investigating officer.

Before making a rather leisurely journey to Istanbul, ostensibly to interview the Soviet Vice-Consul and assess the value of his information, he contacted his own controller in the Soviet Embassy in London. Urgent messages were sent by the KGB in London to Moscow, and from Moscow to the Soviet Consulate-General in Istanbul. By the time Philby arrived on the scene, the unfortunate Volkov had disappeared – withdrawn on some pretext to Moscow for interrogation, and worse. He was never heard of again. The case was closed.

But not for ever. Although Philby thought he had got clean away with a narrow squeak, when some years later he fell under suspicion as a traitor, Volkov's message was remembered, as was the fact that Philby had been one of the first to know about it. Researches were put in hand. It was revealed that the quantity of cipher messages passing between the KGB station in London and their headquarters in Moscow had increased dramatically in the hours after Philby had been briefed about the case; and shortly thereafter the volume of cipher traffic between Moscow and Istanbul had also stepped up enormously. Late in the day as it was, two and two were eventually put together and the net began to close round Philby.

From an account pieced together by the editor from various published sources.

GUY BURGESS, one of the two British diplomats who defected to the Soviet Union in 1951, finds a novel way of being sent home from the British Embassy in Washington so that he can warn his fellow spy in the Foreign Office in London – Donald Maclean – that the Security Services are about to arrest him.

Although the British authorities had no idea that Guy Burgess had been recruited as a Communist agent even before he joined the Foreign Office, they recognized that he was a heavy-drinking homosexual who was – despite a brilliant mind – a considerable liability. After getting into a series of scrapes in London, he was despatched to the embassy in Washington in 1950 to be given a last chance to redeem his reputation. He was staying with Kim Philby (who was also passing information to the Russians) when the latter received secret intelligence indicating that the net was closing in on Donald Maclean (the other Soviet spy in the FO). Clearly it was necessary to warn Maclean that he would have to make a run for it if he were to avoid exposure and arrest.

The problem for the spies was how to get the message to Maclean, then head of the American Department of the FO in London. Telegrams, telephone calls or letters would all have been intercepted by British intelligence, who had Maclean under close scrutiny. The answer seemed to be for Burgess to go back and warn him personally. But to avoid bringing suspicion on himself, Burgess had to have a reason for going to London: he had to be sent home.

Burgess knew that one more unfortunate incident would be his last as far as the British Embassy in Washington was concerned. The ambassador – Sir Oliver Franks – was already fed up with him. So he set about manufacturing one such unfortunate incident. He already had a reputation as a fast and even reckless driver; now he drove his Lincoln car 'like Mr Toad' (according to Lord Greenhill, who was also in the embassy at the time) across the state of Virginia; when he was stopped by the police, he pleaded diplomatic immunity in the most provocative way. Predictably, the police reported him to the Governor of Virginia and the Governor reported him to his ambassador. This was the last straw for Sir Oliver Franks; he called in Burgess and sent him packing home on the next ship.

Once in London, Burgess had no difficulty in contacting Maclean, but slightly more in persuading him that he had no time to lose in making his escape. In the event, Burgess drove him to the English Channel and the two men slipped away to France, thence to Prague and eventually to Moscow. The case of 'the Missing Diplomats' soon hit the world's headlines; Burgess's speeding offences had served their purpose.

From an account given to the editor by a member of the British Embassy in Washington at the time, and published elsewhere.

AMBASSADOR GEORGE F. KENNAN OF THE UNITED STATES discovers a Soviet microphone in an unlikely place in the American Embassy in Moscow at the height of the Cold War in the 1950s.

In the first months after my arrival in Moscow, nothing untoward was noted. The ordinary, standard devices for the detection of electronic eavesdropping revealed nothing at all. The air of innocence presented by the walls of the old building was so bland and bright as to suggest either that there had been a complete change of

209

practice on the part of our Soviet hosts (of which in other respects there was decidedly no evidence) or that our methods of detection were out of date.

In recognition of this last possibility there arrived from Washington, just before my scheduled departure for London in September, two technicians detailed by our government to give Spaso House a more searching and technically competent going-over. After one or two days of fruitless effort, these gentlemen suggested to me that their efforts might be more successful if I would arrange, on a given evening, to go through the motions of performing some sort of official work in the premises of the residence, instead of at the office. I saw no reason not to do this; and on the evening in question I summoned a secretary to the residence (it was the loyal and devoted Dorothy Hessman, who had already been with me in Washington and was destined to remain with me off and on, in government or outside it, for more than a decade into the future) and proceeded to dictate to her, in the large upstairs living room–study, a body of prose which was intended to sound like a diplomatic dispatch in the making, and must indeed have sounded that way for all but a historically schooled ear, because it was drawn word for word from just such a dispatch sent from Moscow in earlier years and now included in one of the published volumes of American diplomatic correspondence.

This worked. And what followed was an eerie experience. The family, for some reason, was away that evening – my wife was, in any case. I have the impression that the great building was again substantially empty, except for the technicians, Miss Hessman, and myself. I droned on with the dictation, the technicians circulated around through other parts of the building. Suddenly, one of them appeared in the doorway of the study and implored me, by signs and whispers, to 'keep on, keep on'. He then disappeared again, but soon returned, accompanied by his colleague, and began to move about the room in which we were working. Centering his attention finally on a corner of the room where there was a radio set on a table, just below a round wooden Great Seal of the United States that hung on the wall, he removed the seal, took up a mason's hammer, and began, to my bewilderment and consternation, to hack to pieces the brick wall where the seal had been. When this failed to satisfy him, he turned these destructive attentions on the seal itself.

I, continuing to mumble my dispatch, remained a fascinated but passive spectator of this extraordinary procedure. In a few moments, however, all was over. Quivering with excitement, the technician extracted from the shattered depths of the seal a small device, not much larger than a pencil, which, he assured me, housed both a receiving and a sending set, capable of being activated by some sort of electronic ray from outside the building. When not activated, it was almost impossible to detect. When activated, as it was on that evening, it picked up any sounds in the room and relayed them to an outside monitor, who presumably had his stance in one of the surrounding buildings.

It is difficult to make plausible the weirdness of the atmosphere in that room, while this strange scene was in progress. The air of Russia is psychically impregnated, anyway, as ours is not. At this particular moment, one was acutely conscious of the unseen presence in the room of a third person: our attentive monitor. It seemed that one could almost hear his breathing. All were aware that a strange and sinister drama was in progress.

The device in question was of course packed off to Washington a day or so later. . . . I have the impression that with its discovery the whole art of intergovernmental eavesdropping was raised to a new technological level.

The following morning the atmosphere of Spaso House was heavy with tension. I had thought it best to close and lock, temporarily, the room where the device had been found. The Soviet servants, their highly trained antennae positively humming with vibrations, sensed serious trouble, and cast terrified glances in the direction of the locked door, as they passed along the corridor, as though they suspected the place to contain a murdered corpse. The faces of the guards at the gate were frozen into a new grimness. So dense was the atmosphere of anger and hostility that one could have cut it with a knife.

Had I been right, I wondered, to lend my person to this deception? Was it proper for an ambassador to involve himself in this sort of comedy? Or would I have been remiss, in the eyes of my own government, if I had refused to do so?

I am not sure, even today, of the answers to these questions.

From Memoirs 1950–1963 by George F. Kennan
(Little, Brown and Company, Boston and Toronto, 1972).

PRESIDENT CARTER was deeply embarrassed by the prolonged retention of the American Embassy staff in Tehran as the Ayotollah Khomeini's hostages in 1980. He here explains how – with the help of secret agents – he managed to smuggle a few of them out of Iran.

We had been successful in keeping secret the presence of six American diplomats who had found refuge in the Canadian Embassy at the time our embassy was taken. (Some news organizations knew about these diplomats, but at my request did not reveal the information.) Now, with minimum news coverage and the resulting quiet on the streets of Tehran, it was time for our attempt to bring them back to the United States. This was a real cloak-and-dagger story, with American secret agents being sent into Iran to rehearse with the Canadians and Americans the plans for their safe departure. The agents and those being rescued would have to be furnished with disguises and false documents that appeared authentic, and they needed enough instruction and training to convince the Iranian officials that they were normal travelers and business visitors from other countries, including Canada. There were several delays and many adventures as our plans were put into effect.

One agent was sent in as a German – with a forged passport, of course. He adopted a false name, with the middle initial 'H.' When he reached the customs desk, the officials stopped him to comment that it was very strange for a German passport to use an initial rather than the entire name; he had never seen one like this before. He began to interrogate our man more closely, and the quick-witted messenger said, 'Well, my parents named me "Hitler" as a baby. Ever since the War, I've been permitted to conceal my full

212

name.' The customs official winked and nodded knowingly, and waved him on through the gates.

On January 25, everything was in place. Three days later I received word that the six Americans were free. This was not the only occasion when we used secret agents to help us.

From Keeping Faith *by Jimmy Carter (Collins, London, 1982).*

11

Diplomats and War

IT IS OFTEN said that war is the continuation of diplomacy by other means. In fact, war generally represents the failure of diplomacy. There have been exceptional – and usually unscrupulous – diplomats who have worked to bring about wars: Cavour felt that only a European war could consolidate the Risorgimento in Italy, and Bismarck rightly thought that the Franco-Prussian war of 1870 would consolidate the unity of his new Germany. In the great majority of cases, however, a declaration of war not only terminates a diplomatic mission, but terminates it in obvious failure: Sir Neville Henderson – the British Ambassador in Berlin until September 1939 – understandably entitled his memoirs *Failure of a Mission*.

War also makes diplomats redundant. Ambassadors and their diplomatic staff in enemy countries are sent home; those in neutral countries often find they are running espionage agencies rather than normal embassies. It is at least in part for this reason that many diplomats struggle to leave the diplomatic service in wartime to join up in the armed forces; though few find it necessary to go to the lengths of Sir Fitzroy Maclean, who stood for Parliament as a means of getting out of the Diplomatic Service and making himself free to enlist in the army, thus (in Churchill's memorable phrase) 'using the Mother of Parliaments as a Public Convenience'. Many, however, feel the call to serve with the colours, so memorably expressed by Sir Cecil Spring

Rice when ambassador in Sweden just before the First World War:

> I heard my country calling, away across the sea,
> Across the waste of waters she calls and calls for me.

Sometimes, however, as in the United States in the early years of both the First and Second World Wars, there is a delicate and vital diplomatic job to be done in securing the tacit or active support of a neutral country; and it was in fact this task that fell to Spring Rice in 1914–1917.

Public opinion, which at the best of times is seldom enthusiastic about the merits of diplomats, becomes distinctly disillusioned about the profession in times of war. The diplomatic virtues of moderation, fair-mindedness and ability to see the other person's point of view, are at a discount; anything short of unquestioning and often strident patriotism appears luke-warm, wobbly or downright disloyal. Winston Churchill had little time for Harold Nicolson's ultra-civilized approach to information work in the Second World War, and Mrs Thatcher had even less time for feverish and legalistic peace-making intermediaries during the Falklands War. The mood of war is still as it was at Agincourt:

> In peace there's nothing so becomes a man
> As modest stillness and humility:
> But when the blast of war blows in our ears,
> Imitate the actions of the tiger . . .
> Disguise fair nature with hard-favour'd rage:

And if warriors have little time for diplomats in war, it is equally true that diplomats often have little time for warriors in peace. Even in the Napoleonic wars, Lord Granville Leveson Gower was not alone in deploring what he considered the imbecility of military commanders. 'War is too serious a matter to entrust to soldiers' is an aphorism much heard over the centuries in the chancelleries of Europe.

BERNARDINO DE MENDOZA, as ambassador of His Most Catholic Majesty of Spain to His Most Christian Majesty of France in 1590, found himself in the thick of the religious civil wars, championing the Catholic League in Paris against the advance of Henry of Navarre who was still the leader of the Huguenot faction. A former cavalry officer who had boasted that he was born 'not to disturb kingdoms but to conquer them', Mendoza turned his embassy into a citadel.

In those days when Huguenot guns could be heard at the Louvre, when, the last of his plate melted up, the last of his horses killed for food, the courtyard of his embassy a public soup-kitchen, and all his able-bodied servants mustered on the walls, the blind old ambassador limped from gate to gate, leaning on the shoulder of a turnspit, gathering the latest reports and telling the captains how towns were held or lost when he had served with Alva, one cannot help feeling that he was better pleased with the part he was playing than he had ever been when he exchanged smooth lies with princes. One cannot help feeling, too, that the veteran ambassador turned partisan leader in the bitterest phase of a civil war was an apt symbol of what the religious wars had done to the Spanish diplomatic service and, indeed, to the diplomatic corps of Europe.

From Renaissance Diplomacy *by Garrett Mattingly (Jonathan Cape, London, 1955).*

LORD GRANVILLE LEVESON GOWER, as Ambassador to Tsar Alexander I in 1805, deplores the imbecility of military commanders.

There seems to be a certain fatality attending the Plans of this Austrian Court. They left a General at Vienna whose sole business was to break down the Bridge over the Danube before the French entered the Town. Murat persuaded him that Peace was about to be made, and that it wd. be a pity to break down the Bridge when in a few days the Emperor wd. have to rebuild it. It is but a slight consolation that this General is sent in Irons to the fortress of Koeniggratz. This story is a good Pendant to that of Mack, who was made to believe by the French that a revolution had taken place at Paris, and that Bonaparte was marching his Troops into France to restore his Govt., but it is melancholy to reflect upon the alarming consequences of such folly and credulity. The existence of the Austrian Monarchy depends upon Russia and Prussia; if the latter acts with the same Energy as the former, all may yet be well, and I am sometimes even sanguine enough to think that the whole French army might be cut off. But is it not to me personally provoking that what I have been labouring to bring about for this twelve-month should be marred by the imbecility of the military commanders.

From The Private Correspondence of Lord Granville Leveson Gower 1781–1821
(John Murray, London, 1916).

GEORGE CANNING, as Foreign Secretary, disagreed with his cabinet colleague Lord Castlereagh over the conduct of the war with Napoleon, and was thought by the latter to be privately scheming for his dismissal. The quarrel reached such a pitch that a duel was fought between the two men, and Canning was wounded in both his person and his reputation.

Canning had, long ago, made up his mind that Castlereagh was over-weighted at the War Office; and on April 2, 1809, he wrote to the Duke of Portland [the Prime Minister] intimating that unless Castlereagh were removed he must himself resign. Portland consulted the King, and the King seems to have suggested that if Canning would hold his hand Castlereagh might be transferred to another department at the close of the Session. To Castlereagh himself Portland said not a word, and thus, by his timidity, laid Canning open to charges of duplicity, intrigue and bad faith, which, certainly for the moment, and perhaps permanently, damaged his reputation. The Session ended in June; Canning again pressed his point, but nothing was done, and not until September – and then by accident – did Castlereagh hear a word about the matter. His very natural indignation knew no bounds. He demanded satisfaction from Canning; a duel was fought, and Canning was slightly wounded. Meanwhile, both statesmen had retired from the Ministry.

The whole business was unfortunate to the last degree. Damaging to the Government and to the country, to Canning it was disastrous. The country, at a critical moment, lost its two ablest administrators; Canning lost a position in English politics which it took him twelve years laboriously to regain.

From George Canning and His Time *by J.A.R. Marriott*
(John Murray, London, 1903).

SIR CECIL SPRING RICE, as British Ambassador to Sweden shortly before the First World War, expresses his patriotism and Christian devotion in a well-known hymn; the third verse he later suppressed, possibly because he thought it sounded jingoistic.

I vow to thee, my country – all earthly things above –
Entire and whole and perfect, the service of my love,
The love that asks no question: the love that stands the test,
That lays upon the altar the dearest and the best:
The love that never falters, the love that pays the price,
The love that makes undaunted the final sacrifice.

And there's another country, I've heard of long ago –
Most dear to them that love her, most great to them that know –
We may not count her armies; we may not see her King,
Her fortress is a faithful heart, her pride is suffering –
And soul by soul and silently her shining bounds increase,
And her ways are ways of gentleness and all her paths are peace.

I heard my country calling, away across the sea,
Across the waste of waters she calls and calls to me.
Her sword is girded at her side, her helmet on her head,
And round her feet are lying the dying and the dead.
I hear the noise of battle, the thunder of her guns,
I haste to thee my mother, a son among thy sons.

From the papers of Sir Cecil Spring Rice.

SIR HORACE RUMBOLD, as Counsellor at the British Embassy in Berlin in 1914, describes the outbreak of war as seen from the Chancery.

On getting back to the Embassy at 3.15, a telegram came in from the Foreign Office saying that the King of the Belgians had appealed to our King to uphold the neutrality of Belgium, which was being violated by the Germans. The Ambassador was instructed to ask the German Government to immediately cancel any steps they had taken to infringe Belgian neutrality. At that moment the Chancellor was making his great speech in the Reichstag, where all the Ministers were, so my chief went to the Reichstag to carry out his instructions. The Foreign Secretary said that he regretted they could not go back, the German troops had actually entered Belgium that morning and it was a matter of life and death to the Germans to advance on France through Belgium. The Ambassador came back and we sent a telegram off to the Foreign Office in that sense . . .

At 6 o'clock a second telegram came from the Foreign Office, saying that since the despatch of their first telegram our Foreign Office had heard that the Germans had violated the Belgian frontier at Gemmenich. In these circumstances, and in view of the fact that Germany declined to give the same assurance respecting Belgium as France gave last week, our Government must repeat the request to the German Government to respect Belgian neutrality and ask for a satisfactory reply to that request and to the previous telegram to be received in London by midnight that night; if not, the Ambassador was instructed to ask for his passports. This was the ultimatum to Germany.

The Ambassador went off to see the Foreign Secretary, who said that he was not surprised, but that he could give no other answer than that which he had given a couple of hours previously. The Ambassador then went on to say goodbye to the Chancellor; he found the latter in a fury of rage and under the influence of the speech he had delivered in the Reichstag. He made a set speech in English to the Ambassador and said that he considered that England was responsible for the war; for the sake of 'a piece of paper' she had gone in against Germany. Our chief in vain tried to point out to him that we were bound in honour to observe the guarantee which we had given in common with Germany, but it was no good. He came back to the Embassy and sent his final telegram at about half past seven. This telegram was not allowed to go through, as we subsequently found out.

We then knew that we should have to leave within 24 hours. We had gradually made preparations as regards handing over the archives, etc., and we telegraphed to the Consuls to say there was war between England and Germany and that they were to ask for their passports.

That night we were all dining with the Ambassador as usual, pretty well tired out after this most exciting and critical day, when at 9 o'clock the butler brought an Extra just issued by one of the papers, containing in enormous letters the news that England had declared war on Germany and that the Ambassador had asked for his passports. No reasons were given. We heard afterwards that this Extra had been struck off in thousands of copies, packed into motor cars and sent all over Berlin, the sheets being thrown out on to the pavement wherever there were many people about. Simultaneously with the appearance of this Extra, a large crowd formed up opposite the Embassy and we could hear their yells from where we were dining. At about half past nine we went into one of the front drawing-rooms to smoke, when suddenly we heard the smash of glass and realised that we were being attacked. I went to the telephone and telephoned to the Foreign Office to send mounted and foot police at once, as the three men on duty in front of the Embassy were quite unable to cope with the crowd. Meanwhile, stones the size of one's fist came through all the double windows of the front rooms and people climbed up on to the window sills and smashed the windows in with sticks. One umbrella fell inside and we eventually handed it over to the *Times* correspondent as a trophy for the *Times* Office in London.

The attack lasted fully half an hour, until strong bodies of police came along and put a stop to it. Meanwhile the yells from the crowd were not isolated, it was one continuous roar and howl of rage and had we gone out at that moment we might have been killed. At about half past eleven the police had dispersed most of the crowd so we sallied out in two bodies; three of us jumped into a motor car and went to our houses as fast as we could. We were recognised and insulted, but no violence was attempted. The others, who were more numerous, were escorted by police to another motor car, a policeman with drawn revolver got on the box seat and accompanied them. The crowd tried to get at the occupants of the car, but luckily did them no injury.

I spent most of the rest of that night putting my important valuables and papers together and winding up my affairs as best I could. Next morning I found that my wife's maid had returned from Austria, having been five days on the journey. I gave her a few final instructions and then left our apartment for good, hoping that I should see my things again but not at all certain that they would not all be smashed and looted. I then went to the Embassy for the night, picking up our Naval Attaché and one of the Secretaries.

At about 10 that morning the Emperor sent an ADC to my chief to express his regret for what had occurred at the Embassy the night before. This man delivered his message in the stiffest manner possible and, after conveying the expression of regret, he added, on instructions from the Emperor, that the incident would show the Ambassador how deeply the people felt the action of England in ranging herself against Germany and forgetting how we had fought shoulder to shoulder at Waterloo. The ADC also added that the Emperor had been proud of being a British Field-Marshal and an Admiral of the Fleet, but that now he would divest himself of these honours. This strange message only served to show what we had long thought, namely, that the Emperor was not a gentleman.

From the Rumbold Papers.

MR LLOYD GEORGE describes how the news of the outbreak of the First World War reached the Cabinet in London after the Germans had suppressed the British Ambassador's report from Berlin.

It was a day full of rumours and reports, throbbing with anxiety. Hour after hour passed, and no sign came from Germany. There were only disturbing rumours of further German movements towards the Belgian line. The evening came. Still no answer.

Shortly after nine o'clock I was summoned to the Cabinet Room for an important consultation. There I found Mr Asquith, Sir Edward Grey, and Mr Haldane all looking very grave. Mr M'Kenna arrived soon afterwards. A message from the German Foreign Office to the German Embassy in London had been intercepted. It was not in cipher. It informed the German Ambassador that the British Ambassador in Berlin had asked for his passports at 7 p.m. and declared war. A copy of this message was passed on to me, and I have it still in my possession:

> Time: 9.5 p.m.
> Date: Aug. 4th, 1914.
> The following message has been intercepted by W.O. Censor:-
> To German Ambassador from Berlin.
> English Ambassador has just demanded his passport shortly after seven o'clock declaring war.
> (Signed) Jagow.

No news had been received from Sir Edward Goschen [British Ambassador in Berlin].

We were therefore at a loss to know what it meant. It looked like an attempt on the part of the Germans to anticipate the hour of the declaration of war in order to effect some *coup* either against British ships or British coasts. Should this intercept be treated as the commencement of hostilities, or should we wait until we either heard officially from Germany that our conditions had been rejected, or until the hour of the ultimatum had expired? We sat at the green table in the famous room where so many historic decisions had been taken in the past. It was not then a very well-lighted room, and my recollection is that the lights had not all been turned on, and in the dimness you might imagine the shades of the great British statesmen of the past taking part in a conference which meant so much to the Empire, to the building up of which they had devoted their lives – Chatham, Pitt, Fox, Castlereagh, Canning, Peel, Palmerston, Disraeli, Gladstone. In that simple, unadorned, almost dingy room they also had pondered over the problems which had perplexed their day. But never had they been confronted with

222

so tremendous a decision as that with which British Ministers were faced in these early days of August, 1914.

And now came the terrible decision: should we unleash the savage dogs of war at once, or wait until the time limit of the ultimatum had expired, and give peace the benefit of even such a doubt as existed for at least another two hours? We had no difficulty in deciding that the Admiralty was to prepare the fleet against any sudden attack from the German flotillas and to warn our coasts against any possible designs from the same quarter. But should we declare war now, or at midnight? The ultimatum expired at midnight in Berlin. That was midnight according to Central Europe time: it meant eleven o'clock according to Greenwich time. We resolved to wait until eleven. Would any message arrive from Berlin before eleven informing us of the intention of Germany to respect Belgian neutrality? If it came there was still a faint hope that something might be arranged before the marching armies crashed into each other.

As the hour approached a deep and tense solemnity fell on the room. No one spoke. It was like awaiting the signal for the pulling of a lever which would hurl millions to their doom – with just a chance that a reprieve might arrive in time. Our eyes wandered anxiously from the clock to the door, and from the door to the clock, and little was said.

'Boom!' The deep notes of Big Ben rang out into the night the first strokes in Britain's most fateful hour since she arose out of the deep. A shuddering silence fell upon the room. Every face was suddenly contracted in a painful intensity. 'Doom!' 'Doom!' 'Doom!' to the last stroke. The big clock echoed in our ears like the hammer of destiny. What destiny? Who could tell? We had challenged the most powerful military empire the world has yet brought forth. France was too weak alone to challenge its might and Russia was ill-organised, ill-equipped, corrupt. We knew what brunt Britain would have to bear. Could she stand it? There was no doubt or hesitation in any breast. But let it be admitted without shame that a thrill of horror quickened every pulse. Did we know that before peace would be restored to Europe we should have to wade through four years of the most concentrated slaughter, mutilation, suffering, devastation, and savagery which mankind has ever witnessed? That twelve millions of the gallant youth of the nations would be slain, that another twenty millions would be mutilated? That Europe would be crushed under the weight of a colossal war debt? That only one empire would stand the shock? That the three other glittering empires of the world would have been flung to the dust, and shattered beyond repair? That revolution, famine, and anarchy would sweep over half Europe, and that their menace would scorch the rest of this hapless continent?

From War Memoirs of David Lloyd George, *Vol. 1 (Odhams, London, 1934).*

HERR VON RIBBENTROP, by the time he left London in 1938, was already recognized by many as a pernicious instrument of Nazi aggression. Here Winston Churchill recounts the dubious behaviour of Ribbentrop and his wife at a farewell luncheon in their honour given by Neville Chamberlain.

Herr von Ribbentrop was at this time about to leave London to take up his duties as Foreign Secretary in Germany. Mr Chamberlain gave a farewell luncheon in his honour at No. 10 Downing Street. My wife and I accepted the Prime Minister's invitation to attend. There were perhaps sixteen people present. My wife sat next to Sir Alexander Cadogan near one end of the table. About half-way through the meal a Foreign Office messenger brought him an envelope. He opened it and was absorbed in the contents. Then he got up, walked round to where the Prime Minister was sitting, and gave him the message. Although Cadogan's demeanour would not have indicated that anything had happened, I could not help noticing the Prime Minister's evident preoccupation. Presently Cadogan came back with the paper and resumed his seat. Later I was told its contents. It said that Hitler had invaded Austria and that the German mechanised forces were advancing fast upon Vienna. The meal proceeded without the slightest interruption, but quite soon Mrs Chamberlain, who had received some signal from her husband, got up saying, 'Let us *all* have coffee in the drawing-room'. We trooped in there, and it was evident to me and perhaps to some others that Mr and Mrs Chamberlain wished to bring the proceedings to an end. A kind of general restlessness pervaded the company, and everyone stood about ready to say good-bye to the guests of honour.

However, Herr von Ribbentrop and his wife did not seem at all conscious of this atmosphere. On the contrary, they tarried for nearly half-an-hour engaging their host and hostess in voluble conversation. At one moment I came in contact with Frau von Ribbentrop, and in a valedictory vein I said, 'I hope England and Germany will preserve their friendship'. 'Be careful you don't spoil it,' was her graceful rejoinder. I am sure they both knew perfectly well what had happened, but thought it was a good manoeuvre to keep the Prime Minister away from his work and the telephone. At length Mr Chamberlain said to the Ambassador, 'I am sorry I have to go now to attend to urgent business', and without more ado he left the room. The Ribbentrops lingered on, so that most of us made our excuses and our way home. Eventually I suppose they left. This was the last time I saw Herr von Ribbentrop before he was hanged.

From The Gathering Storm *by Winston S. Churchill (Cassels, London, 1948).*

SIR FITZROY MACLEAN, finding it difficult to get out of the Diplomatic Service in order to join the army at the outbreak of the Second World War, resorts to the device of becoming a Member of Parliament and thus disqualifying himself from further employment in the Diplomatic Service.

War, it has been said, is diplomacy continued by other means. Certainly, to me, as I sat at my desk in the Foreign Office, my own occupation, once hostilities had begun, seemed suddenly to have lost its point. I decided to resign my commission in the Diplomatic Service and to enlist.

But this was easier said than done. No sooner had I mentioned my intention of resigning than it was pointed out to me, in no uncertain terms, that my behaviour was extremely unpatriotic. For six years, they said, I had been learning my job. Now, just as I was beginning to be of some slight use, I wanted, in order to satisfy my personal vanity, to go off and play at soldiers; I must lack all sense of responsibility. But, in any case, my resignation would not be accepted. The new Defence Regulations gave the Secretary of State full powers in this respect.

'And what if I simply go off and enlist?' I asked.

'If you do that,' they said, 'the War Office will be asked to send you back at once. In irons, if necessary.'

They had me there. I decided to go away and think again.

I allowed some time to elapse before making my next approach. Then I asked for an interview with the Permanent Under-Secretary for Foreign Affairs, Sir Alexander Cadogan. In the meanwhile I had made a careful study of the Foreign Office Regulations. Paragraph 22 gave me what I needed.

'And what do you want?' said Sir Alexander, who was a busy man, looking up from his desk.

'I want to go into politics,' I said.

'In that case,' he replied, without enthusiasm, for the idea of Party politics is repugnant to the permanent official, 'In that case, you will have to leave the Service.'

I replied that I was prepared for that. In fact, if he liked I could let him have my resignation at once. And, laying a neatly written letter of resignation on his desk, I escaped from the room. A few minutes later I was in a taxi and on my way to the nearest Recruiting Office. It had been simpler than I had expected.

From Eastern Approaches *by Fitzroy Maclean (Jonathan Cape, London, 1949).*

WINSTON CHURCHILL deprecates the diplomatic pressure to define 'war aims' in 1940 and 1941.

In August 1940 he considered the clamour for a Statement of War Aims ill-conceived. We had, he said, only one aim: to destroy Hitler. Let those who did not know what we were fighting for stop and see for themselves. France was now discovering why she had been fighting, and we, since we must win in order to survive, could only take the short view. In January 1941 he made the same point to Harry Hopkins and added that when the war was over we should be content to establish a few basic principles: justice; respect for human rights and for the property of other nations; respect also for private property in general so long as its owners were honest and its scope was moderate. We could find nothing better on which to build than the Sermon on the Mount, and the closer we were able to follow it the more likely we were to succeed in our endeavours. What more, he asked, had a Statement of War Aims to offer than this? He reminded Hopkins of Clemenceau's comment on President Wilson's Fourteen Points: '*Même le bon Dieu n'avait que dix.*'

From Action this day: Working with Churchill, *John Colville's contribution to the memoirs edited by Sir John Wheeler-Bennett (Macmillan, London, 1968).*

AMBASSADOR GEORGE KENNAN, as a junior American diplomat, was interned in Berlin immediately after the Japanese attack on Pearl Harbour and the US entry into the Second World War. The conditions in which he and his colleagues were held under Gestapo supervision for five months were mentally and physically arduous, but unappreciated by the State Department at home. Here he laments the US government's lack of consideration for the plight of their own diplomatic staff.

Although the experience of this internment had not been pleasant, although it had in fact been considerably less pleasant than the bare facts . . . would suggest, the Department of State took little notice of it. When the department did finally take cognizance of our plight and consent to communicate with us by telegram for the first time, which was shortly before our departure and exchange, it did so only for the purpose of informing us that by decision of the comptroller general (which, we were allowed to infer, it was disinclined to challenge) none of us were to be paid for the months we had been in confinement: we had not, you see, been working. A second telegram (the only other word we ever received from Washington during our confinement) was to inform us that, contrary to the original intention to remove us all, half of us were to be left behind, in German custody, in order to free space on the exchange vessel for Jewish refugees. Why? Because individual Congressmen, anxious to please individual constituents, were interested in bringing these refugees to the United States, and this – although the

227

refugees were not citizens – was more important than what happened to us. The department was obviously more concerned to relieve itself of congressional pressures than to worry about a group of its own employees, many with long and creditable records, whose fidelity to duty, and to duty in peculiarly difficult circumstances, had caused them to fall into enemy hands.

From Memoirs: 1925–1950 *by George F. Kennan (Hutchinson, London, 1967).*

A US CONSULAR OFFICER demonstates the advantages of a gradual approach to the problem of helping an imprisoned British colleague.

It is an old rule of diplomacy to approach one's goal gradually and step by step. To unfold one's grand design all at once, Callières warns, may frighten or overwhelm lesser and more timid minds.

At the outbreak of World War II my chief gave me a lesson in the tiny-steps-for-tiny-tots approach, though the design was far less grand. After the British declaration of war, a British vice-consul in Hamburg where I was stationed had been thrown into jail while awaiting repatriation, in retaliation for the arrest of a German consul in Glasgow. The American consul general, Wilbur Keblinger, had taken charge of British interests. He was an old Foreign Service officer, strongly pro-British and not particularly fond of the Germans. Collecting a few of the vice-consul's belongings and adding a few items from his own supplies, he turned them over to me with precise instructions about their delivery.

The director of the Hamburg prison was a polite, old retired officer who welcomed me graciously, no doubt haunted, as so many Germans then were, by the fear that if the Americans were offended they might join the British against them. He had the British vice-consul brought from his cell and one by one I handed over the items: pajamas, shirts, socks, and a toilet kit. When I brought out a phial of sleeping pills the prison director objected that they were forbidden lest the prisoners kill themselves deliberately with an overdose. The peppery little vice-consul retorted angrily that it took more than a stinking German prison to get an Englishman down. Taken aback by this outburst the director handed him the pills.

I then produced a bottle of sherry, explaining that the vice-consul should have it served before his luncheon. The director said nothing but took the bottle submissively. Next I produced a bottle of champagne which, I said, should be brought in properly iced with the vice-consul's dinner. The director shifted uneasily but remained silent. Next came a bottle of gin, another of vermouth, and a cocktail shaker. This, I explained, was for the vice-consul's evening Martini. 'Now, you take one part of vermouth,' I began, turning to the director, 'and four parts of gin, add plenty of ice –' But I had reached the end of my tiny steps.

'*Verdammt!*' the director exploded, 'I am willing to serve sherry and champagne and even gin to this prisoner, but he can damn well mix his own Martinis.'

When I reported back to the consul general he agreed that his grand design had been substantially accomplished.

From Diplomat *by Charles W. Thayer (Harper and Brothers, New York, 1959).*

Qualities and Characteristics
of a Diplomat

DEFINING THE QUALITIES required of an ambassador has been a popular pastime since the inception of resident embassies. Ottaviano Maggi published in 1596 a thesis called *De Legato*, in which he explained that a successful envoy must be a trained theologian and familiar with the Greek philosophers; he must be expert in the mathematical sciences, including architecture and physics; he should be competent in law, music and poetry; an expert in military science; proficient in Greek, Latin, French, German, Spanish and Turkish; and he should be of aristocratic birth, rich and handsome. Not surprisingly, even in the age of the 'Renaissance man' it proved difficult to find candidates who measured up to all these requirements.

Harold Nicolson, in his book *Diplomacy*, lists truthfulness, precision, calm and modesty as his essential requirements. The first of these has been a controversial quality ever since Sir Henry Wotton's frequently quoted remark about an ambassador being 'an honest man sent to lie abroad for the good of his country'; but it is often forgotten that the remark was made in jest and – even so – much resented by King James I, who was Wotton's employer; and, despite the aphorism, the general consensus over the centuries has been that honesty is the best diplomatic policy. M. de Callières, for instance, who published a treatise on diplomacy in 1716 (a century after Wotton) argues that a lie always leaves a drop of poison in its wake, and that it is essential for an ambassador to establish a reputation for honest dealing so that men may trust him. Certainly Sir Edward Grey (the longest consecutively-serving British Foreign Secretary) owed much of his influence to his self-evident probity. Indeed, the theme of probity recurs among those who write about diplomatic attributes. Not many Foreign Ministers would expect to be addressed, as was the Egyptian Minister – it is alleged – on one occasion by Mr George Brown, with the words 'You crafty old bugger, you!'

Nicolson's second quality is precision – an uncharismatic quality which tends to conjure up visions of accountants rather than dashing plenipotentiary envoys. This is the quality most valued in those professional diplomats chosen to serve as number two to a 'political' ambassador (who may have been appointed as a reward for financing his President's election campaign, or because the President wants to get him out of the country). Such 'one-off' ambassadors tend to believe in broad brush-strokes and flamboyant gestures which may need under-pinning by precise professional drafting. Lord Carrington (himself a 'political' High Commissioner to Australia before he become Foreign Secretary) frequently enquired of his Foreign Office officials whether one particular foreign 'political' ambassador in London had been accompanied by his number two when any important representations had been made; when reassured that this was so, he would comment, 'Good, then they'll get it straight.' A tribute to the need for precision.

Calmness, Nicolson's third quality, also sounds unglamorous but is essential. Nicholson had in mind patience, but calmness under fire is now also a quality much in demand. Sir Andrew Gilchrist, when ambassador in Reykjavik at the start of the so-called 'cod war', found his embassy under attack by a stone-throwing mob led by a large and angry Icelandic fisherman; as the stones hit the embassy windows with unerring accuracy, Gilchrist turned to his First Secretary and said, 'Try to remember that chap's face: if he throws a cricket ball as well as he does a rock, we ought to try to get him for the Embassy cricket XI!' On a later occasion Gilchrist was in trouble with another hostile and noisy crowd, this time in Dublin; he decided that noise should be answered by noise, and instructed his Highlander Military Attaché to get out his bagpipes and drown the sound of the opposition. (The incident may have contributed to the decision to appoint Gilchrist director of the Highlands and Islands Development Corporation on his retirement.) If Sir Andrew Gilchrist was not calm, he was certainly cool.

Modesty is Nicolson's final quality for an ideal diplomat. Certainly its opposite – vanity – is fatal, not least because vanity is the mother of indiscretion. Those who always wish to shine in society are frequently tempted to say rather more than they should, and this – for those in possession of Top Secret information – is a dangerous state of affairs. Vanity can also tempt a head of mission to ignore people or facts that have not impinged on his own personal experience. It has long been the practice of British and numerous other embassies to send back to their Foreign Offices 'leading personality reports' on key people in the countries to which they are accredited, so that if someone suddenly comes to prominence or turns up in London, the basic facts about his career and characterisics are already known; one chief I had crossed out a number of important entries in the draft of 'Who's Who in Ruritania' – as it were – on the grounds that 'that man's never been to my house, so he can't rate an entry': vanity hindering efficiency.

I have mentioned earlier that democracies are often less flexible than dictatorships in foreign policy, for the simple reason that more people have to be consulted about decisions. But in one important respect democracies have a diplomatic advantage over dictatorships: their representatives abroad are less likely to be frightened into reporting only what the government at home wants to hear. Communist regimes have suffered badly from being fed versions of events compatible with Marxist philosophy; Hitler was told that the Oxford Union motion that 'this House declines to fight for King and Country' was typical of the spirit of youth in 1930s Britain; the Argentine Junta was assured that Britain would not fight for the Falklands.

One of the most insidious traps into which a diplomat may fall is the habit of speaking to foreign governments, when carrying out unpalatable instructions, in – so to speak – inverted commas. The envoy implies, 'This is what I have been told to tell you, but of course you'll realize that *personally* I regret having to say anything so disagreeable.' If ambassadors are not prepared to put their full weight –

232

including personality, charm and persuasiveness – behind their instructions, then they should resign, or at least request an immediate posting to another place where the problem does not arise.

But diplomats and Foreign Ministers, even the best, come with a great variety of temperaments. Some are so sophisticated and ingenious in their own thought processes that they imagine everyone else is the same. It is recounted that Prince Metternich remarked, on hearing that a foreign diplomat of unusual deviousness had died, 'Now, I wonder what he meant by that?' Equally, other Foreign Ministers manage to anaesthetize problems so that not only confrontation but even decisions are avoided. When Rab Butler – having failed to achieve the premiership – arrived as Foreign Secretary, he was somewhat disillusioned with life and might have been described as excessively 'laid back'. When a problem of some urgency arose, his private secretary wrote on the papers relating to it in his red box: 'This requires a decision.' When the secretary retrieved the box the next day, he found that Rab had added beneath his comment the words: 'Yes, it does.'

In conclusion, one could say that even if diplomats can never aspire to all the virtues outlined by Ottaviano Maggi, and seldom to all those required by Harold Nicolson, they are still shown by most of the examples quoted in this book to be generally upright and often shrewd, which is perhaps more than can be said for some other professions.

––––––––––––––––

THOMAS CROMWELL, Chief Secretary and later Lord Chancellor to King Henry VIII, instructs Sir Thomas Wyatt in 1537 (three years before Cromwell's own execution for high treason) on how to handle a diplomatic mission to the Holy Roman Emperor Charles V. His advice and turn of phrase have stood the test of time better than his spelling.

. . . Your parte shal be nowe like a good oratour, both to set furthe the princely nature and inclynacion of his highnes with all dexterite, and soo to observe th'emperours answers to the said overture and to the rest of the pointes in the same letteres expressed, as you may therebye fishe the botom of his stomake, and advertise his Majeste how he standeth disposed towardes him, and to the continyuance of th'amytie betwene them . . .

From Diplomacy and the Study of International Relations *by D. P. Heatley (Oxford, 1919)*.

SIR HENRY WOTTON, author of the aphorism about an ambassador lying abroad for the good of his country, here takes a different line.

A Friend of Sir Henry Wotton's, being designed for the employment of an Ambassador, came to Eaton, and requested from him some experimental Rules for his Prudent and Safe Carriage in his negotiations; to whom he smilingly gave this for an infallible Aphorism, That, to be in safety himself, and serviceable to his Countrey, he should always, and upon all occasions speak the truth (it seems a State-Paradox) for, says Sir Henry Wotton, you shall never be believed; and by this means, your truth will secure yourself, if you shall ever be called to any account; and 'twill also put your Adversaries (who will still hunt counter) to a loss in all their disquisitions and undertakings.

From A Life of Sir Henry Wotton *by Izaak Walton (London, 1670)*.

LORD GRANVILLE LEVESON GOWER, as Ambassador in St Petersburg in 1805, confides to Lady Bessborough his disillusionment about the deceits of diplomatic life.

Are you aware that the diplomatic Service is a school for falsehood and dissimulation? I am really sometimes shocked at myself for the degree of deceit which I am under the necessity of practising. It is not sufficient to be silent or to pretend to be ignorant of things of which one is informed, but one must hold a language calculated to inculcate a Belief of what is directly the contrary to the real Truth, and you Cannot conceive the degree of amusement the persons who are in the secret derive from the dupery of those whom they deceive; 'comme il est bon ce pauvre . . .'

How I do long to return home and talk over many many things that I cannot write!

From The Private Correspondence of Lord Granville Leveson Gower 1781 to 1821
(John Murray, London, 1916).

SIR GEORGE STAUNTON, whose own diplomatic career was limited to a single mission to China, manages to convey the essence of English insularity when he deplores the pernicious effects of foreign habits.

I have always been disposed to condemn those who, without necessity or some adequate cause, have domesticated themselves for considerable periods in foreign countries, and have thus placed themselves and their children in a position to acquire an undue taste for foreign habits and usages, which they may find it very difficult afterwards to unlearn, when afterwards settling finally in their native country.

From Memoirs of the Chief Incidents of the Public Life of Sir George Thomas Staunton, Bart. *(L. Booth, London, 1856).*

PALMERSTON and BISMARCK both find that foreign ambassadors often do not believe the truth when they hear it, and thus confirm the verdict of Sir Henry Wotton, quoted earlier, that truth can often be the best way of misleading an interlocutor.

'Fearless truthfulness was one of his (Palmerston's) distinctive characteristics, which, while it made him some enemies, in the long run won him more friends. In his intercourse with foreign Ministers, however, it sometimes served a purpose which he at the time little anticipated. I have heard him say that he occasionally found that they had been deceived by the open manner in which he told them the truth. When he laid before them the exact state of the case, and announced his own intentions, they went away convinced that so skilful and experienced a diplomatist could not possibly be so frank as he appeared, and imagining some deep design in his words, acted on their own ideas of what he really meant, and so misled themselves.' (Evelyn Ashley, ii. 301.)

'Bismarck often acted on Palmerston's dictum: "I tell ambassadors the truth, because I know they won't believe it." ' (*Bismarck*, by C.G. Robertson, 151.)

From A Guide to Diplomatic Practice *by the Rt. Hon. Sir Ernest Satow*
(Longmans Green, London, 1922).

SIR EDWARD GREY, as British Foreign Secretary in 1911, is praised for displaying characteristic straightforwardness.

I think Edward Grey has done well because he has been perfectly straight throughout. Each nation has its own line in which it can do better than other nations, and also a line in which other nations can do better than it. It's a pity when we try the latter. The English line is a sort of stolid honesty, a little bit inclining to the stupid. When we try to be clever it doesn't come off; it's like a dog standing on its hind legs. We go further four-legged, though we shouldn't make such a show. This is the trouble with our German friends; they are naturally honest enough, but they labour with infinite pains to acquire a painfully-won habit of mendacity, and the result is that they are always lying and never deceiving.

From The Letters and Friendships of Sir Cecil Spring Rice
edited by Stephen Gwynn (Constable, London, 1929).

MR LLOYD GEORGE shows awareness of the fact that impartiality in Middle Eastern diplomacy can lead to unpopularity.

The earliest recognition I received in Europe of the realities of the British officer's position in Palestine was from the lips of Mr Lloyd George. I had first met him during the Peace Conference, and he was good enough to invite me to breakfast with him alone at 10 Downing Street. Greeting me sternly, he remarked that complaints of me were reaching him from Jews and Arabs alike. I answered that this was all too probable, imagining for a moment from his tone that he was leading up to my resignation. 'Well,' he said as we sat down, 'if either one side stops complaining, you'll be dismissed.' A principle which should hearten All Ranks in the Palestine Service for some decades to come.

From Orientations *by Sir Ronald Storrs (Nicholson & Watson, London, 1937).*

SIR ERNEST SATOW, the great codifier of diplomatic practice, outlines authoritatively what he considers to be the qualifications for a diplomatic career; though not so all-embracing as the demands of his Renaissance predecessors, they remain exacting.

We should . . . be disposed to say that some, if not all, of the following are necessary qualifications for the diplomatic career.

Good temper, good health and good looks. Rather more than average intelligence, though brilliant genius is not necessary. A straightforward character, devoid of selfish ambition. A mind trained by the study of the best literature, and by that of history. Capacity to judge of evidence. In short, the candidate must be *an educated gentleman*. These points cannot be ascertained by means of written examinations. Those can only afford evidence of knowledge already acquired; they do not reveal the essential ingredients of a character. At some posts it is useful to have had a legal training, particularly where the minister for Foreign Affairs is pretty sure to be a lawyer.

Science is not necessary. Geography, beyond elementary notions, is not of great value. The diplomatist will acquire what geographical knowledge he needs of the country to which he is appointed while residing at his post. Few men can know it in sufficient detail beforehand. The writer has heard of a case where the experts of the Royal Geographical Society, on being applied to for information respecting the navigability of a river, gave a seriously misleading answer, and that, too, in spite of having on their shelves a scientific traveller's narrative from which they could have learnt the facts.

Some private income, even though the Government should give

237

a special foreign service allowance, is very desirable in the lower grades of the diplomatic service, and the higher the grade the more of it the better.

From A Guide to Diplomatic Practice *by the Rt. Hon. Sir Ernest Satow*
(Longmans Green, London, 1922).

SIR HORACE RUMBOLD's qualities are extolled by Sir Harold Nicolson, who worked under him when the former was ambassador in Berlin in the 1930s.

His greatest diplomatic quality (apart from patience) was the gift of discernment. He was never a garrulous man nor did he seek to embody his conclusions in epigrams which might be repeated and do harm. He would listen unimpressed and unresponsive to the paradoxes of others, and there would be times when some brilliant conversationalist would pause in his discourse, wondering whether the Ambassador had really understood. Sir Horace always understood: he understood, not merely what was being said, and why it was being said, but exactly what relation even the most gifted sentence bore to reality . . .

Rumbold's extreme value as an Ambassador and negotiator was based upon his utter reliability. The Government at home knew that in him they possessed an agent who would always accurately interpret instructions, or who, if he disagreed with their policy, would say so with moderation and good sense. The Governments to which he was accredited became aware that here was a man without prejudice or vanity, a man of complete integrity, a man whom they could trust to understand and report their point of view, a man whose every word was riveted in concrete.

From the Harold Nicolson papers.

A PLAYBOY DIPLOMAT is found by Sir Marcus Cheke to be a formidable adversary.

Some foreign diplomatists appear to spend all their leisure hours in a whirl of amusement. The experience of the writer . . . has led him to suspect that such men are sometimes the most able of their profession and, if they are the representatives of countries hostile to British interests, the most dangerous. It is not easy to find logical grounds for this suspicion, but sometimes the passion for amusement merely indicates a fierce quest for relaxation after intensely hard work; or the diplomatist in question acquires that curious personal influence which the world is always ready to give the man of pleasure because he appears to know exactly what he wants to get out of life, and to be getting it; or social amusement is used by him as a mask for other much more serious activities. Certainly no diplomatist ever served the interests of his country more adroitly and successfully than did Alfred Horstmann, German Minister in Brussels, and later in Lisbon, between the two Great Wars. This clever and charming man appeared to have only two passions in life: first, the accumulation of antique furniture and *objets d'art*; second, the enjoyment of the most frivolous social pastimes and the cultivation of the society of the prettiest women. Detested and disparaged by those whom he did not invite, he was a favourite subject of conversation among all. Thus he restored the German Legation to prominence or at least to notoriety, and at the same time dissipated the prejudices against his country which had grown up as a result of the 1914–1918 war. Was it really credible that Germany was a nation of criminal mentality which menaced Europe? Here was their Minister, who appeared to think of nothing except his Nymphenburg porcelain, and who spent all night dancing the rhumba! When Alfred Horstmann was recalled from Lisbon by his Government in 1933, he had succeeded in making for his Legation a hundred influential contacts which were to be richly exploited by his successor during the time of the Spanish Civil War.

From Guidance on foreign usages and ceremony, and other matters, for a Member of His Majesty's Foreign Service on his first appointment to a Post Abroad *by Marcus Cheke, His Majesty's Vice-Marshal of the Diplomatic Corps (Foreign Office, London, 1949).*

CHARLES W. THAYER recalls instances of over-ready wit being the undoing of various American diplomats.

Wit, while often an asset in diplomacy, can, if not properly controlled, raise havoc with a diplomat's career. Between the wars a young career officer serving under Minister John Flournoy Montgomery, who had made his fortune in the dairy business, suggested a little too loudly that his chief's motto should be 'All I have I owe to udders'. The young man was demoted and transferred.

Many years later an ambassador who allegedly coined the phrase 'Dull, duller, Dulles' soon found himself in a secondary post in Asia.

In 1959, when Mrs Clare Boothe Luce implied that Senator Wayne Morse's judgment was affected when he was kicked in the head by a horse, she found it expedient to resign as ambassador to Brazil.

From Diplomat *by Charles W. Thayer (Harper and Brothers, New York, 1959).*

LORD GORE-BOOTH, a former High Commissioner to India and Permanent Under-Secretary of the Foreign Office in London, ruminates on the requirements of a modern diplomat. His own histrionic streak was well known: while head of the Foreign Office he dressed up as Sherlock Holmes and travelled to Switzerland to visit the scene of the famous struggle with Professor Moriarty at the Reichenbach Falls.

Diplomats must be able with equal spontaneity and calm to walk backwards out of the presence of the Emperor of Japan, to sit on the floor of an Indian village school and talk with a saint, or to make a speech at the drop of a hat at an occasion on which the chief speaker, the Megalopolitan Ambassador, has somehow failed to turn up. I have done them all. They must be able to contrive anything, bear anything, eat or drink anything and appear to like it, and to be surprised by nothing. And all this must be done without loss of sensitivity or courage.

From With Great Truth and Respect *by Lord Gore-Booth, GCMG, KCVO (Constable, London, 1974).*

Envoi

*PRINCE TALLEYRAND has been the role model for many diplo-
mats over the past two centuries. His ability to move just ahead of
events, and to be the indispensible man in the right place and at the right
time, made him one of nature's survivors. Before the French Revolution
he was already a bishop; thereafter he served successively the Revolution,
the Directory, the Consulate, Napoleon, Louis XVIII and finally the
Orléans monarchy – claiming that he never betrayed anyone until they
had first betrayed themselves, and that he never conspired except when
he had the people of France as his fellow conspirators.*

*There is a pleasant story of him speaking with an aide while there
were disturbances in the Parisian streets outside: barricades were being
manned. 'Who is winning?' asked the aide. 'We are,' Talleyrand
replied. 'But who are "we"?' the aide persisted. 'Ah,' said Talleyrand, 'that I shall tell you tomorrow.'*

*At the end of his long life, with his health failing and his strength
slipping away, Talleyrand was readmitted to the Catholic church. It
was time to adjust his loyalties once more for his final encounter.*

When these last offices had been performed he sank rapidly. He
retained the sitting posture to the end. His room, as well as the
anteroom, was full of relations, attendants, and friends. He died,
as he had lived, in public. When they told him that the Archbishop
had said that morning that he would gladly give his life for him, he
replied: 'Tell him that he has a much better use for it.' This was

his last civility; these were his final words. Afterwards he still listened to the prayers that were being recited and gave signs of comprehending them, until suddenly his head fell heavily forward on to his chest.

The old diplomatist had set forth upon his last mission. Some doubts he may have felt as to the country whither he was travelling, some uncertainty as to the form of government that there prevailed; but he had made inquiries of those best qualified to advise him; he had obtained the most reliable information available; he had taken, not a moment too soon, all possible precautions, and he departed with his credentials in order, his passport signed.

From Talleyrand *by Duff Cooper (Jonathan Cape, London, 1932).*

Index

243